Praise for Amit Goswami

"Goswami ranges far, wide, and deep."

—RUBERT SHELDRAKE, coauthor of *The Evolutionary Mind*

"Amit Goswami is out ahead of the pack with his grounded and wondrous views, delivering penetrating insights into how the universe works."

—MICHAEL TOMS, cofounder of the *New Dimensions* radio series

"... One of the most brilliant minds in the world of science."

—DEEPAK CHOPRA, MD

Praise for the *Quantum Activist* documentary

"*The Quantum Activist* ultimately dares to connect spiritual and practical worldviews, in a breathtaking revelation that contemplates the delicacy of humankind's continued existence on the planet itself, and ways to counter the economic, social, and spiritual menaces that threaten all people. Highly recommended."

—Midwest Book Review

D1007974

how
Quantum
Activism
Can Save
Civilization

Other books by Amit Goswami

Creative Evolution: A Physicist's Resolution Between Darwinism and Intelligent Design (2008)

God Is Not Dead: What Quantum Physics Tells Us About Our Origins and How We Should Live (2008)

The Visionary Window: A Quantum Physicist's Guide to Enlightenment (2006)

The Quantum Doctor: A Physicist's Guide to Health and Healing (2004)

Quantum Mechanics (2003)

The Physicist's View of Nature, Part 2, The Quantum Revolution (2002)

Physics of the Soul: The Quantum Book of Living, Dying, Reincarnation and Immortality (2001)

The Physicist's View of Nature, Part 1, From Newton to Einstein (2000)

Science and Spirituality, A Quantum Integration (2000)

Quantum Creativity: Waking Up to Our Creative Potential, with Maggie Goswami (1999)

The Self-Aware Universe (1995)

The Cosmic Dancers: Exploring the Physics of Science Fiction, with Maggie Goswami (1983)

The Concepts of Physics (1979)

how
Quantum
Activism
Can Save
Civilization

A Few People Can Change
Human Evolution

Amit Goswami, Ph.D.

HAMPTON ROADS
PUBLISHING COMPANY, INC.

Cover design by Linda Kosarin
Text design by Maureen Forys, Happenstance Type-O-Rama
Cover art by Bluedot

Hampton Roads Publishing Company, Inc.
Charlottesville, VA 22906
www.hrpub.com

Library of Congress Cataloging-in-Publication Data available on request

ISBN : 978–1-57174–637–5

10 9 8 7 6 5 4 3 2 1
TCP
Printed on acid-free paper in Canada

Author photo [page 289] from the film *The Quantum Activist* © 2009 by Bluedot
Productions

M.C.Escher's "Drawing Hands" [page 27] © 2010 The M.C. Escher Company-Holland

To the world's quantum activists:
We can *change the world and change ourselves.*

Contents

Preface

Quantum physics in the form of its famous observer effect (how an observer's looking transforms quantum possibilities into actual experiences in the observer's consciousness) is forcing us to a paradigm shift from a primacy-of-matter paradigm to a primacy-of-consciousness paradigm (for details, read my book *The Self-Aware Universe*). The new paradigm is inclusive; it is a science of spirituality that includes materiality. Quantum activism is the idea of transforming ourselves and our societies in accordance with the transforming messages of quantum physics and the new paradigm.

Materialist science, unchallenged for the past five decades, has done its damage. One can argue that our social institutions—capitalism, democracy, liberal education, institutions of health and healing—are all rooted in idealism, even downright spirituality. But now these institutions can hardly be called humanistic, let alone spiritual. Materialism has changed them so much that their spiritual roots are hardly recognizable. For our livelihood, we depend on these institutions, which cater to the forces of separateness that have become the prevailing wind of the world culture.

We have problems galore in our society and culture—global warming, terrorism, and repeating economic meltdowns are the biggies. But other problems are of no less importance. A huge abyss has opened between the rich and the poor, and the middle class is being squeezed, contrary to the expectations of Adam Smith's capitalism. Our democracy is in trouble due to the ever-increasing influence of media and money. Education does not inspire. Health costs are skyrocketing.

All these problems can be traced to the conflict between spirituality and materiality. The good news is that the worldview conflict between spirituality and materialist science has been resolved in favor of an inclusive worldview based on the primacy of consciousness and quantum physics. To bring this message to our social institutions and to put them back on the path of unity is now the challenge!

In a flash I felt the challenge, and the idea of this book and the movement of which it is a part came to me. It took quantum physics for us to discover spirituality within science. We must use quantum physics' guidance to restore spirituality and unity to our society, to our social institutions.

To make social changes is the job of the activist. We need activism that uses the power of quantum physics. Quantum physics gives us ideas that are transformative, that can lead us and our social institutions from separateness back to unity.

To see this, consider that quantum physics is the physics of possibilities. Quantum thinking gives us back our free will to choose from among these possibilities. These free choices are discontinuous, breaking us from past habits. They come from a cosmic interconnectedness that we call quantum nonlocality—an ability to communicate without signals.

Quantum physics even has the potency to break down hierarchies of classical materialist vintage.

Thus the idea of quantum activism—activism that uses the transformative power of quantum physics to change us and our social institutions. The filmmakers Ri Stewart and Renee Slade have made a documentary film—*The Quantum Activist*—that gives a glimpse of the basic ideas. The present book is the explication of those ideas in a complete, applicable form to lay down a manifesto for personal and social change.

In many ways, this is a book of empowerment, of right thinking and right living that prepare us to dare to act on solutions of the many "impossible" problems that materialism has given us—economic meltdowns, terrorism, global warming, and so on. They are impossible only if we try to solve them while staying within materialism. To be a quantum activist is to be empowered to move from the problem space of materialist science to a solution space of the new quantum science based on the primacy of consciousness.

I discuss these solutions in this book: spiritual economics that is concerned with our holistic well-being rather than only our material consumer needs; democracy that uses power to serve meaning instead of using it to dominate others; education that liberates us from the shackles of the known; religion that integrates and unites; and new inexpensive health practices that restore wholeness to us.

And of course, I discuss the solutions in the context of developing right livelihood for quantum activists and their fellows, which includes everyone.

One of the highlights of the book is the open letters to President Obama, laying out what the government can do to help solve the great problems of today according to the principles of quantum activism.

The book is written in a nontechnical style to suit the nonscientist, but quantum activism is for both scientists and nonscientists, anyone who would like to see social changes that are consonant with the movements of consciousness—evolutionary movements that will eventually enable us to create heaven on earth.

I thank all the scientists, philosophers, and mystics who have contributed to the idea of quantum activism. I thank Ri Stewart and Renee Slade for making the documentary *The Quantum Activist,* which has brought the idea of quantum activism to the forefront of public attention. I thank all the people who have become quantum activists since the documentary was released. I also thank Ri for help with the figures included here. Finally, I thank the editorial and production staff of Hampton Roads for a fine job in bringing out this book.

CHAPTER 1

Scientific Evidence for Spirituality Is Here, So What Are You Doing about It?

Science has discovered spirituality: there is now a logically consistent scientific theory of God and spirituality based on quantum physics and the primacy of consciousness (the idea that consciousness, not matter, is the ground of all being). And there is replicated experimental data in support of the theory. In other words, although still largely unsung in the media, we now have a viable science of spirituality that is threatening a paradigm shift from today's matter-based science that exclusively encourages materiality (Goswami 2008a). You can call the new science a science of God, but you don't have to. In the new science, there is no God that is an almighty emperor doling out judgments on us; instead, there is a pervasive intelligence that is also the creative agent of consciousness that you can call God if you want to. But this God is objective; it is scientific.

So what should we do about all this? What can we do to bring God, our own higher source of causation (really!), and spirituality back into our lives and our society? My answer in this book is quantum activism.

So this book is about a new kind of activism. I call it quantum activism because the purpose of this activism is threefold. First, we employ activism to bring media attention to quantum and primacy-of-consciousness thinking and the new paradigm; this will bring grant support for further research and bring about applications of the new paradigm of such undeniable weight and value that the old paradigm will crash under it. Second, we use the transformative power of quantum physics to renew ourselves individually to become exemplars and harbingers for social change in the appropriate direction. Third, we recognize that the current materialism-dominated structures of our social systems are heavily biased against ordinary people pursuing a meaningful life of creativity and transformation. Accordingly, we use activism to change our social systems in such a way that ordinary people can live transformative meaningful lives and fulfill their human potential, and even pursue the happiness that only creative and spiritual pursuits can bring.

But I am getting ahead of myself; let me begin at the beginning. Several years ago, I was giving a lecture in Brazil about the aborning paradigm of science based on quantum physics that brings God (defined in the new way as the source of our own causal efficacy) and spirituality back into our worldview. One student challenged me, saying, "I have heard a great deal about new paradigms that integrate science and spirituality. But isn't it all theory? When can we expect you guys to get busy and give us some verification, some data?"

I was taken aback for a moment and then the answer popped from my mouth: "Actually, we have done our job. The scientific evidence for spirituality that includes experimental data is already here. My question to you is: what are you doing about it?"

That created a lot of enthusiastic discussion in the audience. Here are some samples from that exchange:

- If science has established spirituality, then we should do what spirituality dictates. My religious upbringing says that spirituality is about being virtuous. I'd like to develop virtues—to be able to love, to appreciate beauty, to be truthful, to pursue justice, to be good to my neighbor. But I have already tried that and I am confused. Do I have free will to change? I need guidance. Can the new science give me guidance?

- I admit when I think of spirituality I think of God and I have doubts about God, a reaction to my simplistic religious upbringing, no doubt. These doubts have made me pursue material goals that I know have not made me any happier. If science can show me convincing proof, then I would like to try the spirituality that traditions say will bring me happiness. What does the new science say?

- If spirituality is real, then does it mean that we give up material pursuits in favor of spirituality? What if I want to explore my creative potential? Spirituality and God can wait awhile. What does the new science say about that? Can it help?

※ I gave up on God because how can a good God allow so many bad things to happen. I can't swallow popular Christianity's good-evil split. Can the new science help me resolve my confusion?

※ I'd like to work on solutions to our social problems. Is that spiritual?

Lots of people today are confused about ethics, about the value of religion and spirituality, even about free will and creativity for the pursuit of human potential because of exorbitant claims from mainstream scientists in favor of scientific materialism—the idea that all things, material objects, thoughts, and even ideas such as that of spirituality and God can be reduced to elementary particles of matter and their interactions. Because of its simplistic ideas, popular Christianity does not help in countering these claims. So the view that God is a delusion we would be better off giving up on is gaining ground. In 2009, there was even an advertisement on London buses: "God probably does not exist. So relax and enjoy life." Implicit in this advice is the encouragement: since there is no God to punish you, why not enjoy the pleasures of a hedonistic life rather than suffer the disciplines (since the chance of missing out on spiritual joy is minuscule) of an ethical, let alone spiritual life?

The mainstream scientists are not entirely wrong because the God they denigrate is the God of simplistic popular belief: a God that sits like an emperor on a throne in heaven (wherever that is!) and doles out judgment on people when they die, sending good people to heaven and bad guys to hell; a God that created the world and all living species in it, all at once, a mere six thousand years ago; a God that allows bad things to happen to good people; a God that is supposed to be perfect, and yet His images, us, are so very imperfect.

On top of this, there is the additional valid criticism of what is called dualism: how does the duo—the material world and a nonmaterial God—interact? For interaction, signals carrying energies must mediate. But the energy of the material world alone is always a constant; this is the sacrosanct law of conservation of energy. How could this be if there were energy-carrying signals mediating the interaction of matter and nonmatter? This is the paradox of dualism.

Face it—say the proponents of scientific materialism—there is no God, there is only matter and its interactions, which are the only source of causation. Like God, our free will, freedom to choose God, is also delusion. Get real!—admonish the behavioral psychologists of our revered academe—the behavior of people, by and large, is predictable behavior conditioned by genes and the environment.

So, in view of all this, we have to be clear. What is the nature of the God that quantum physics and primacy-of-consciousness thinking posit? Is the God of the new science compatible with the God of the great religious traditions? I discussed these issues in my recent book, *God Is Not Dead* (Goswami 2008a). Here is a quick summary of the book's most basic point. In materialist science, there is only one source of causation: material interactions. This is called upward causation since cause rises upward from the base level of the elementary particles to atoms, to molecules, and to bulkier matter that includes the living cells and the brain (Figure 1). This is fine, except that, according to quantum physics, objects are waves of possibility and all that material interactions can do is change possibility into possibility but never into the actuality that we experience. Like the paradox of dualism, this, too, is a paradox.

To change possibility into actuality, a new source of causation is needed; we can call this downward causation. When we realize that consciousness is the ground of all being and material objects are possibilities of consciousness, then we also recognize the nature of downward causation: it consists of choosing one of the facets of the multifaceted object of the possibility wave that then becomes manifest as actuality. Since consciousness is choosing from its own possibilities, not something separate, there is no dualism.

An example will make this clear. If we release an electron in a room, the electron's wave spreads quickly all over the room, in possibility. In possibility, the electron can simultaneously be all over the room, in all those different places. But when we measure, we find the electron in a particular place in a given experiment, the place we have chosen for it in that particular instant (Figure 2). In another instant, for another measurement, we may choose differently. For many measurement events involving identical electrons in identical experiments, the sum total of all the individual measurements conforms to a probabilistic bell curve as predicted by quantum mathematics (Figure 3). In this way, quantum physics is predictive and deterministic for large numbers of events and things. Yet for individual events and/or individual objects, there is room for freedom of choice and creativity.

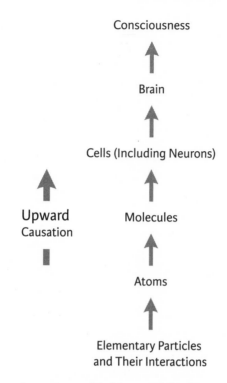

FIGURE 1. The upward causation model of the materialist. Cause rises upward from the elementary particles, to atoms to molecules, and so on to the more complex conglomerates that include the brain. In this view, consciousness is a brain phenomenon whose causal efficacy comes solely from the elementary particles—the base level of matter.

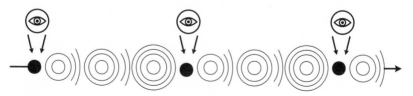

FIGURE 2. Quantum possibility waves and downward causation as conscious choice producing collapse.

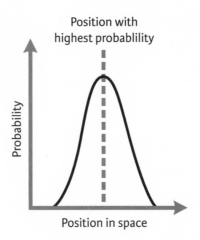

FIGURE 3. A quantum probability distribution.

"Why can't I use my freedom of choice to make my own reality and make good stuff happen all the time?" you might ask. Why aren't you even aware of making choices in the way I suggest? The answer is crucial. The state of consciousness from which we choose is a subtler, nonordinary state of one interconnected consciousness in which we are all one, a "higher" quantum consciousness. Hence the appropriateness of calling causation from it "downward causation" and its source "God."

Mind you, in the interconnected oneness of consciousness, connections happen without signals; the technical name for such signal-less connections is quantum nonlocality. As you may know, in Einstein's theory of relativity, all interactions in space and time must occur via signals. Hence, to use the physicist Henry Stapp's words, nonlocal downward causation must take place from "outside" space and time, yet it can bring about an effect, the actuality, in space and time.

If you see a parallel between this idea and the evocative statement often made in high-level spiritual discussions—God is both transcendent of the world and immanent in the world—that is good. Before the advent of quantum physics, spiritual masters attempted to convey that the relation between God and the world is not one of dualism. When people complained about the vagueness of such statements, they would say, God is ineffable, which would only augment ordinary practical people's difficulty in understanding spiritual wisdom.

In the new science, the relation of God consciousness and ordinary ego consciousness is clear: in the latter, connections and communications must use signals; in the former, signal-less communication is the going thing.

The existence of nonlocal communications among people has been verified and replicated in myriad experiments. Since material interactions can never simulate nonlocality, this kind of experimental proof for the existence of God, looked upon as a higher consciousness, a nonlocal interconnectedness of all being, is definitive.

Do we have free will? To the extent that we can access our higher consciousness and choose from there, you bet there is free will, complete freedom to choose from the quantum possibilities offered in any given situation. Free will to choose the world as well as God and godliness, creativity as well as spiritual transformation.

Quantum physics is the physics of possibilities, and its indisputable message then is that we potentially have the freedom to choose outcomes to live by from among these possibilities. This is certainly helpful empowerment for making personal changes toward spiritual enlightenment or salvation, to which various traditions refer. But there are only a few of us that hear the clarion call of spiritual transformation. How about the rest of us? How about those of us who would like worldly pursuits of meaning to solve worldly problems?

The fact is, humans have been making individual acts of spiritual transformation on a small scale for millennia, but this has not helped our societies much. This was perhaps okay in the past; we were locally disconnected then. But recently, the growth of local connections among us is exponential. Local problems become global very quickly today. The solution of global problems requires no less than global creativity and transformation. How do we bring about transformational change on a global scale? A new kind of spirituality is needed. This is what quantum activism is about.

Additionally, how people earn their livelihood today keeps most people from engaging with questions of meaning and transformation. If you are an assembly-line worker and do nothing that adds meaning to your life during your working hours, after your job is done, all you want is entertainment to keep you functioning in your conditioned, predictable, and controllable lifestyle. We need to change our social systems in order to give people opportunity for transformation.

Social Problems on a Global Scale

Two problems and attempting to solve them put me on the track of writing this book. The first I have already stated: now that we have scientific evidence for spirituality and for an objective and scientific God as the causal source of creativity and spirituality, what can we do to reinstall God in our lives and our world? The second problem, or rather a set of problems, is even more urgent.

There is global warming. There are terrorism, wars, and violence everywhere; quite a few countries possess weapons of mass destruction, and the number is proliferating; nuclear warfare and nuclear terrorism are no longer far-fetched. There are economic meltdowns occurring on a global scale, and their frequency is increasing. These are the three biggies. But there are other problems that are no less important, such as:

- Capitalism was designed to bring capital to everyone, but today the practice of capitalism is recreating the same gap between the rich and the poor that was the case in feudal times. What went wrong in our practice of economics?

- Democracy arose from the idea of government "by the people and for the people." How did our politics become so besieged by media and money that power is once again concentrated in a few hands and is being used for domination?

- Liberal education was designed to encourage everyone to use the mind to process new meaning. Everyone was supposed to share the American dream to bring to fruition the meaning each saw in her or his life. But alas! Today, liberal education prepares us more for jobs that others design for us and less for exploring meaning as we see it.

And this is not all. The skyrocketing cost of health care is another problem for which no cure is in sight. Religions have become less the institutions for investigating and disseminating spirituality and spiritual values that they are supposed to be, and more like other mundane institutions lost in the search for power to dominate others. Why else should religions be so interested in politics? And last but not least, even in the face of an aborning paradigm offering serious theory and replicated data, the scientific establishment seems to be least interested in freshly examining, let alone changing, their worldview based on scientific materialism according to which all is matter; consciousness, God, and, indeed, all our internal experiences are epiphenomena, secondary to matter.

Face it. Individual creativity and the transformation of a few people are unable to make a dent in the global mind-set to initiate changes that will lead to solutions to these problems. A new kind of activism—quantum activism—in which the focus is on both individual and collective change is called for. To give impetus to creativity and transformation on a large scale, we must change the social systems and make them more conducive to people making meaningful changes in their lives.

What is both reassuring and a definitive proof that the current crises are part of a movement of consciousness intended to take us toward global investment in exploring meaning and transformation is this: the changes that our social systems need in order to make room for creativity and transformation of people on a global scale are the same changes that are necessary for the solution of the crisis situation. Finally, the movement of consciousness that we are talking about is the evolutionary movement of consciousness that begins with a paradigm shift.

A New Kind of Activism

It is only fair to acknowledge that just as there are problems galore, so are there activists trying to solve them. We have unjust wars, but we also have peace activists protesting against them with the purpose of stopping the conflicts. We have dangerous ongoing destruction of our environment, but we also have environmental activists protesting against that. We have materialist science and technology threatening religions, so we have religious activists defending antiquated religious lifestyles to save their values. What is the relevance of introducing another kind of activism when activists everywhere seem to go nowhere?

I submit that activism as it is currently practiced has two shortcomings. First, there is a noticeable lack of synchrony in its approach—lack of synchrony between what the activists put in thoughts and words and how they actually live and act. In other words, the activists lack moral authority. In this way, we see peace activists who preach peace but have no access to personal peace. Their protests only polarize, rather than unite people in peace. We have environmental activists themselves lost in materialist consumerist pursuits that destroy the environment. And last but not least, we have religious activists resorting to one of the most antireligious activities—violence in the form of terrorism.

Second, today's activists have no new paradigms to offer, no new paradigm for conflict resolution or for bridging differences or for demonstrating why arts, humanities, and spirituality are important. In the absence of new organizing paradigms, no long-term solution to the problems we face emerges.

And yet who can doubt the importance of activism today? We need social change, and we need activists to bring about social change. In the United States, with change in mind, we even elected a lowly former community organizer as president. The establishment is not going to change of its own initiative; it never has. Instead, it tries to perpetuate its old ways, at best only making trivial changes for show.

Lack of synchrony between what we believe and how we live is due to the incongruence of our belief system. What are we whose blood boils with activist energies missing in our plan of action?

We want to be activists because we believe in some ideal world where justice prevails, peace prevails, love prevails. These are all idealist notions that can be traced back to Platonic thinking in the West and Upanishadic, Taoist, and Kabbalistic thinking in the East. They are part of a philosophy called monistic idealism—consciousness and its ideas come first, consciousness is the holistic ground of all being, and everything else, such as material manifestations, is secondary. In other words, wholeness is primary; the material fragmentation of the manifest world is secondary.

We have forgotten to live this fundamental holistic nature of our being. Today our activists, not unlike the purveyors of good versus evil, perpetuate the separateness that creates the problems we want resolved. We supposedly "battle" the perpetrators of the problems, negativity with negativity. Look at the language we use to describe our struggle. It is separatist; we have already lost the wholeness that we wish to accomplish.

To a large extent, the reason for our collective amnesia is modern (pre-quantum) science, which is based on scientific materialism, the previously stated idea that matter, consisting of independent separate objects, is the ground of all being and all else, including consciousness, is secondary. (Never mind that scientific materialism itself is an idea.) The success of this materialist modern science in explaining natural phenomena and especially the success of this science's offshoot, technology, in improving our lot is so enormous, so widespread, that our entire world culture has been overtly and covertly influenced by its underlying materialist metaphysics. Activists born and brought up in this materialist world culture cannot help but harbor conflicting metaphysical notions that bring about the lack of synchrony between their thought, speech, and action.

While doing a story on Gandhi, a news reporter was quite impressed that the leader spoke at huge gatherings without consulting any notes. When he asked Mrs. Gandhi about this, she said, "Well, us ordinary folks think one thing, say another, and do a third—but for Gandhiji they are all the same." Well, we cannot all be Gandhi overnight, but we can adopt a practice toward that goal. This is what quantum activism is about.

The scientific (re)discovery of God and the elucidation of what God is are part of a paradigm shift going on in science from a science within the primacy of matter to a science within the primacy of consciousness, from a materialist metaphysics to an idealist metaphysics. The new paradigm rests on two metaphysical assumptions. One assumption is that consciousness is the ground of all being. This one is age-old, the basis of already mentioned monistic idealism, or perennial philosophy. But our second assumption— that quantum physics is the law of the dynamic movement of possibilities from which consciousness manifests the worlds of our external and internal experiences—is what makes the new paradigm a scientific one. And it is this assumption that opens us to a new avenue of integral living and can guide us in how to institute both individual and social change. To embrace this new integral way of living, in which the goal is to achieve congruence between thinking, living, and livelihood, is one of the avowed objectives of quantum activism.

The potency of quantum activism comes from its utilization of the transformative aspects of quantum physics for both inner (for the self) and outer (for the society) exploration. But what does this mean? Let's delve into some more details about the quantum.

A Brief History of Quantum Physics and the Earliest Quantum Activists

The word "quantum" literally means "quantity." The physicist Max Planck used the word to denote a discrete quantity of energy. In the year 1900, Planck proposed that the seeming continuity of energy is not the complete story. At its base, energy consists of discrete units that he called quanta. This idea seemed so revolutionary even to Planck himself that he struggled practically his whole life trying to reconcile this idea with his worldview, which was based on the physics that the famous Isaac Newton developed in the 17th century, now called classical physics. Classical physics gave us the great prejudices that these early pioneers of quantum physics struggled to overcome; the same paradigmatic battle continues even today. Among these prejudices are continuity of motion, determinism (the idea that all movements are determined by physical laws), locality (all interactions and communications are mediated by signals passing through space and time), objectivity (objects are independent, separate things), and of course, material monism or materialism (all is matter).

Though Planck never made a notable addition to his quantum idea, others did so. A mere five years later, Einstein followed up Planck's idea and showed that in some experiments light reveals itself as continuous waves; but in other experiments, light behaves like discrete particles, as Planck suggested. Sounds preposterous? It should. How can the same entity, light, exhibit such contrasting behavior as waves that spread out and can literally appear at two or more places at the same time and as particles that are always localized, that move in a trajectory? Soon this was recognized as a paradox that needed to be resolved if quantum physics was ever to be accepted.

The wave-particle duality was not the end of "quantum weirdness." Later, in 1913, physicist Niels Bohr theorized that when an electron jumps from one atomic orbit to a lower one, emitting a discrete quantum of light energy, it does so discontinuously without going through the intermediate space between the orbits. Here it is in the upper orbit, and voila! There it is in the lower, instantly. Bohr called this discontinuous movement a quantum leap. Bohr's theory of the atom was so successful in explaining some of the atomic data that it found acceptance immediately. This idea of a discontinuous quantum leap remains even today, however, an affront to the worldview of most scientists. It is said that Bohr had the idea in a dream and he never had a scintilla of doubt about its truth. But others have to struggle hugely. Erwin Schrödinger, one of the codiscoverers of the mathematical equation of quantum physics once blurted to Niels Bohr in utter frustration, "If I had known that one has to accept this damned quantum jump, I'd never have gotten involved with quantum mechanics."

Some years later, in 1923, the physicist Louis de Broglie introduced the idea that not only light, but also matter is dual, both wave (in some experiments) and particle (in other experiments). New experimental data verified this idea as well. The wave-particle duality was universal.

In 1925–26, physicists Werner Heisenberg and Erwin Schrödinger discovered the mathematical equations of quantum physics in slightly different forms. The classical Newtonian conceptualization of the world has been under threat of a worldview change, a paradigm shift, ever since.

Heisenberg was led to his discovery because he had an intuition that there are certain quantities in physics for which the order in which you measure them makes a difference. I will give you an analogy: you may have noticed that in dating the order in which you utter the words "Do you like me?" and "Do you love me?" makes a great difference in the response from your partner. Anyway, Heisenberg's path to his discovery of the quantum equation of motion led him to another paradigm-shattering discovery: you can never determine everything about the motion of quantum objects! Called Heisenberg's uncertainty principle or the principle of indeterminacy, it is fundamental to quantum physics.

Recall that the old Newtonian paradigm regards objects as independent, determined "things." In accordance with the basic uncertainty, quantum physics regards objects not as determined things but as possibilities. Quantum objects are waves of possibility residing in transcendent potentia (a term coined by Heisenberg), transcending (discontinuously outside) space and time; only when we observe them do they become independently separate particles or things inside space and time. Notice that while clarifying the meaning and resolving the paradox of the wave-particle duality (complementarity, as Niels Bohr called the situation), the new view threatens the classical worldview once again with the idea of transcendent potentia. How many times have you heard scientists complain about the concept of a transcendent God as "supernatural," outside of nature and therefore not scientific? But quantum physics and the new view say: nature includes supernature.

No matter. The early quantum pioneers had their own share of materialists who attempted to get away with interpreting quantum physics in such a manner that objects could be regarded as statistically determined things. Possibilities come with probabilities that quantum physics calculates. That's all we need to make our predictions! So the individual case-by-case determinism of Newtonian physics must be replaced by the notion of statistical determinism; this is all the lesson of quantum physics according to these materialists. Indeed, one can get by with this myopic statistical interpretation when a large number of objects and events in the material domain are involved, as in most applications of physics and chemistry. Even this much, Einstein had difficulty accepting. "God does not play dice," he used to say.

Now we know: the statistical interpretation is useless when we consider single objects and single events, as we must for living beings. Consequently, the materialist science based on the statistical interpretation of quantum physics gives us only a part of the story in the case of biological beings such as we are because for biological beings, single individuals and single events are important.

Wolfgang Pauli was one of the pioneers of quantum physics, famous in his day. One day at an airport baggage claim area, a physicist recognized Pauli and saw that Pauli was distraught. Trying to help, he said to Pauli, "In case you are wondering where the luggage will come, I checked. This is the right carousel and all the luggage will come here." To this, Pauli said, "Young man, I am not interested in all the luggage, just my luggage."

For a discussion of single objects and single events we have to confront the measurement problem, also called the observer effect: how our measurement or observation changes (or "collapses," to use the quantum physicist's favorite jargon) possibility into actuality. As already discussed, the solution of the measurement problem is to think of collapse as the result of choice by a nonlocal consciousness. And God doesn't play dice. We have statistical determinism for many objects and many events to ensure a predictive science of the nonliving. But we also have freedom of choice, free will, for individual acts by biological beings whenever they function from the nonlocal consciousness. Here also, learned memory of previous responses to stimuli brings back predictable, conditioned behavior of the ordinary state of consciousness that we call the ego (Mitchell and Goswami 1992, Goswami 1993), the domain of predictable behavior in psychology. Our challenge is to rise beyond ego to higher nonlocal consciousness and access creativity and transformation.

But to return to these early quantum pioneers, nay, quantum activists, the magnitude of their struggle was truly enormous. In 1935, Einstein introduced the concept of quantum nonlocality in a paper written with two other physicists, Nathan Rosen and Boris Podolsky, but rejected the idea because it seemed to contradict his prejudice that there can be nothing that is outside the space-time universe. Erwin Schrödinger could not handle the concept of the wave of possibility and tried to ridicule it via his paradox of Schrödinger's cat (see chapter 4). And Bohr felt compelled to assert that a measurement by a Geiger counter is enough to collapse the quantum possibility wave and thus missed a tremendous opportunity to overthrow the materialist worldview long before the 1950s, when it became entrenched.

And yet these early pioneers also made progress in pointing out the inadequacy of scientific materialism. As mentioned, Heisenberg stuck to his idea of quantum potentia "outside" space-time, Bohr stuck to his idea of discontinuous quantum leaps, and Einstein never reconciled with statistical determinism. In the process of disturbing the classical worldview of their contemporaries, they themselves were partly transformed. Einstein became humble: I didn't discover relativity by rational thinking alone, he said, when he was older. Bohr accepted complementarity in his lifestyle, so much so that he had the yin-yang symbol stitched into his coat of arms when the King of Denmark knighted him. Schrödinger went on to study the Hindu philosophy of Vedanta and said, after a "superconscious" experience, "I am this whole world." Wolfgang Pauli dreamed the Buddhist archetype of compassion, explored his dream with the psychologist Carl Jung, and endorsed Jung's revolutionary new paradigm idea of synchronicity—coincidences due to a nonlocal common cause. And Heisenberg practiced a basic tenet of the lifestyle of a quantum activist—complementing doing with being. After he initiated students in a problem for their doctoral theses, he told them to relax for two weeks before taking up the problem again.

Including the Whole Human Experience in Our Science

In truth, for biological beings, not even the inclusion of consciousness in our science, which quantum physics forces us to do, is enough. To include the whole human being in our science, we have to validate our internal experiences; calling them epiphenomena of matter does not help. As Carl Jung codified, apart from sensing the external, there are also discernible internal aspects of our conscious experience consisting of thinking, feeling, and intuiting. Of these three, feeling and intuition are not computable, so matter cannot even process them.

What do we feel? We feel energy-like movements that material instruments cannot directly measure. In China, they call these movements *chi*; in India, they are called *prana;* and in the West they are called vital energy. Ancient cultures evolved entire medicinal systems based on the concept of vital energy, such as acupuncture and Ayurveda, that cannot be explained by the theories of conventional allopathic medicine.

What do we intuit? This is the subtlest of our subtle experiences, so opinions vary somewhat. But a long list of traditions and philosophies agree that what we intuit can be thought of as archetypes, contexts of some of the concepts we value most—truth, beauty, justice, love, and goodness, to name the major ones. Of course, we cannot compute intuitive thought.

Even for the mental thoughts, computers can process contents of thought but not their meaning (Searle 1994, Penrose 1991; see also chapter 5). Obviously then, feeling, intuition, and thinking cannot be reduced to secondary phenomena of matter. Right thinking demands that in these experiences of thinking, feeling, and intuition, we are collapsing quantum possibilities of three different nonmaterial worlds, each world corresponding to each of the experiences. Like the physical, all these multiple worlds of possibility are worlds within consciousness. The world of consciousness is a multiverse!

In this way, the classification of the quantum possibilities of consciousness into four compartments, four different worlds—physical (for sensing), vital (for feeling), mental (for thinking), and supramental (for intuiting)—follows from the conceptual structure of quantum physics and our direct experience. How do these different compartments of reality interact without the paradox of dualism? Consciousness mediates their interaction when it simultaneously and nonlocally collapses possibilities from the disparate compartments for its experience (Figure 4). So there is no dualism.

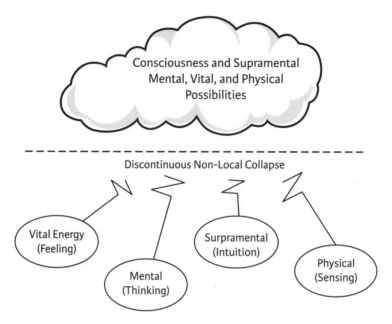

FIGURE 4. Psychophysical parallelism. Consciousness contains four compartments of possibilities. With quantum collapse, the possibilities manifest as the physical object of sensing, the vital object of feeling, the mental object of thinking and the supramental object of intuition.

You look at a lovely person of the opposite sex. There is sensing of a manifest physical object. There is a feeling associated with a point in the region of your body close to your heart that Easterners call the heart chakra. There is thinking in the mind: "Oh, how nice it would be to know this person." There may even be a supramental intuition that is mapped in a thought: I am in love. This is an example of consciousness mediating the interaction of its various compartments so they can manifest at once.

To Recreate a World of Solutions

The beauty of the new paradigm is that upward causation of materialist vintage and downward causation that brings God into the picture are both, together, posited to give us manifest reality. Materiality and spirituality are integrated. This is why I believe an activism founded on the quantum-based new science, quantum activism, will succeed where other activist movements have failed because they are founded on separateness.

You have to recognize the one common aspect of the catastrophic problems I mentioned before—conflict. Current terrorism has its root in the conflict between materialism and religion. It is not only the fundamentalist Muslims of the Middle East who are fighting the materialistic "Great Satan" empire of the United States, but also Christian fundamentalists within this country. Economic and ecological problems are superficially due to the conflict between individual and collective interests, between ego values (such as selfishness and excessive competition) and being values (such as cooperation, win-win philosophy, intuition, creativity, feeling, happiness). Ultimately, these conflicts, too, can be traced to the more fundamental conflict between materialism and spirituality. On close examination, the major reason that health-care costs are rising is our fear of death and the conflict between ignorance (about what constitutes life and health) and wisdom— again, materiality and spirituality. The decline of meaning, ethics, and values in our religions, families, societies, and schools is clearly due to the conflict of outer and inner. Liberal education is torn between material and humanistic/spiritual values. To enter the world of true solutions is to resolve the conflict between materiality and spirituality and outer and inner. And this is the power of the new science. It integrates.

When I first saw things this way, the solutions paraded before my mind's eye: science within consciousness that integrates materiality and spirituality, immanence and transcendence, outer and inner; spiritual economics that deal with both outer material needs and inner subtle needs; deep ecological businesses that are sustainable and cater to both outer and inner modes of production and consumption; democracy in the service of meaning; liberal education that prepares us not only for jobs, but also for exploring the meaning of life; integrative health care that uses both materialist allopathic medicine and subtle alternative medicine; and open-at-the-top religions that teach the universality of values and how to live them in a post-secular spirit.

All these solutions, you will note, have another common feature: they increase ordinary people's access to exploration of meaning and values.

But how to install these solutions in our society! As I pondered this question, an old dream came back to me. I once had a dream in which there were only abstract figures. They were dancing, gamboling, having great fun. A voice in the background said, "They are the angels of doing." Then the scene changed. Some other abstract figures came. And they, too, looked happy, but they were different; they were just sitting quietly. A voice said that they are the angels of being. And then the scene changed again, the angels of doing came back. And so forth. Back and forth, doing angels and being angels, alternating.

When I woke up, I had it—the fundamental mystery of creativity and transformation. It is alternative doing and being. Do-be-do-be-do. Combine the strengths of both doing and being. Bring the lessons of quantum physics to creativity.

Materialists and rationalists look at creativity as a rational, trial-and-error process consisting of only doing. Frame a problem, devise a theory, figure out verifiable consequences of the theory, do an experiment. If it works, bingo, you've got a solution. If the experimental data do not match the theory's prediction, go back to the drawing board and devise another trial theory. All do-do-do.

By contrast, the religions and spiritual traditions of the world all emphasize being, be-be-be. The world of doing is considered illusory, and ignored.

Quantum physics helps us integrate. Quantum physics is the physics of possibilities; possibilities proliferate when we sit quietly in the be-mode, doing nothing. Occasionally, we choose from among the possibilities precipitating an action, a do-mode. We go on alternating between the be-mode and the do-mode until we arrive discontinuously at our insight—the solution. We can process so many possibilities all at once in the be-mode, our chances of finding the solution in this way is much improved over the exploration method of one trial–one error at a time. And creativity researchers tell us that this is really how the creative process works for creative people (Briggs 1990, Goswami 1999).

We have created the problems of our world; we have to recreate the world of solutions. Quantum creativity is our major tool. But that is by no means all of quantum activism. Conventional activism separates, us (those doing right) versus them (the wrongdoers). Quantum physics says that all is movement of consciousness; we are the world. There is no us versus them.

There is only movement toward consciousness or away from consciousness, and it is not always easy to distinguish. The only thing of which we can be certain is that when consciousness is nonlocal, it is inclusive. When we practice inclusivity in resolving conflict, we are aspiring toward nonlocal consciousness.

In conventional activism, we try to change the system, but we want to remain unchanged—we the subjects remain hierarchically superior to an objectified world, a simple hierarchy. Little do we realize that we are part of the system; the system has corrupted our thinking. Can we allow our activism to change us while changing the system? This is a tangled hierarchical relationship with the process of change: we recreate us as we recreate the world.

So quantum activism, the quantum manifesto for personal and social change, uses the transformational aspects of quantum physics—downward causation, quantum creativity, nonlocality, and the tangled hierarchy of relationship between subject and object—to change ourselves and our society.

How Do We Know That the New Science Is Scientific?

But before allowing yourself to be carried away by these arguments, you might be thinking: all I have read so far is still theory; where are the data?

To recap, the new quantum consciousness or God-based paradigm rests on one unverifiable ontological assumption: that consciousness is the ground of being. It is unverifiable because science never enables us to verify its most basic ontological assumption. But our next assumption—that quantum physics is the law that the possibilities of consciousness obey—is fair game for scientific verification. Downward causation and the classification of the possibilities of consciousness into four compartments follow from the conceptual structure of quantum physics and our direct experience. So we center on the two direct, scientifically verifiable consequences of the theory: downward causation and the existence of the fourfold structure of the quantum possibilities.

Bertrand Russell, an avowed atheist, was asked what he would say if, upon dying, he found out there is a God. He replied that he would ask God this: "Why did you not give us the data, Lord?" Well, Bertrand, God has given us the data! We have verified God, downward causation, and the existence of subtle bodies quite adequately.

We have verified downward causation in an enormous variety of data. There are definitive data on distant viewing (one psychic looks at a statue at a marketplace while another psychic, acting as a double blind, draws a picture of the statue from a closet) and transferred potential (transfer of electrical activity from one brain to another at a distance, without electrical connection). The "aha!" insights of creativity, the fossil gaps in the data of biological evolution, and the many cases of spontaneous healing are all examples of downward causation that provide evidence of it. If you try to explain any of these data with material models of reality, you get paradoxes of logic.

The evidence for the subtle bodies abound in such phenomena as psychosomatic illnesses, dreams, mental telepathy, near-death experiences and reincarnation, healing through the use of alternative medicine such as Ayurveda, acupuncture, and homeopathy, and altruism and spirituality (for a comprehensive treatment of all these verifications, see Goswami 2008a).

In short, we have looked for reality, and it is consciousness in both its manifest and unmanifest (which in quantum physics we call potentia and which psychologists label as the unconscious) aspects! Are you excited? So what do you want to do about it?

Materialist science is value free and does not incorporate meaning as a viable entity. Hence in materialism, there is no scope for activism. Things that happen to us and to our worlds are meaningless, valueless epiphenomena of the dance of matter. We can assign pretend meaning and value to things for making our societies livable (as in the philosophy of existentialism), but the lack of authenticity of any assigned meaning and value is bound to create ambiguity in our interpretation of them. We cannot help but become wishy-washy, especially when the meaning and value pertain to somebody else.

But if consciousness is primary, then meaning and values are real, and they must be the focus of our lives. However, the new paradigm has not yet replaced the old one, far from it. So activism is needed to change paradigms, to restore meaning and value to our lives and to our social systems.

It is not going to be easy. In 1999, I was invited along with twenty-nine other scientists and new paradigm thinkers to Dharamsala, India, to talk with the Dalai Lama about the application of the new science to the social arenas in which people earn a livelihood. But who among us would be our spokespeople to explain the paradigmatic subtleties to the Dalai Lama? We broke into a big battle of egos. The filmmaker Khashyar Darvich's documentary *Dalai Lama Renaissance* is about the drama that unfolded at that conference.

Evolution

Thanks to heavy propaganda, today most educated people think that biological evolution is synonymous with Darwinism. The fact is that the fossil data provide overwhelming evidence for evolution but are quite antagonistic to Darwinism in the form of the famous fossil gaps and other anomalies. The undeniable fact is that Darwinian evolution is continuous, but the fossil gaps are proofs of occasional discontinuity in evolution (Eldredge and Gould 1972). The fossil gaps provide evidence for downward causation by consciousness consisting of biological creativity. This is by no means an overstatement. Read my book *Creative Evolution* (Goswami 2008b).

In the new science, evolution is to be seen as the progressive manifestation of the possibilities of consciousness. In this view, the physical world provides computer hardware for consciousness to make representations of the other three subtle worlds. Over time, the representations get better. Evolution is the evolution of these representation-making capacities of matter (Figure 5).

Phase one of biological evolution is now complete. It consists of making better and better representations of more and more of the possibilities of the vital movements of consciousness that represent biological functions in the form of better and better organs.

Phase two begins with the evolution of the highly sophisticated organ of the neocortex of the brain, in which mental meaning can be represented. As you know, the neocortex is much like a computer and its job is to make software representations (memory) of mental meaning in the neuronal hardware. Evolutionarily speaking, right now we are in the middle of the mental age, busily making more and more sophisticated representations of meaning in more and more sophisticated contexts—physical, vital, mental, and supramental. This process is not yet over; we are still in the third of four stages of mental evolution, busily giving meaning to mind itself, the stage of the rational mind. The short-term goal of our evolution is to complete the third and begin the fourth and final stage of mental evolution (Goswami 2008b).

Phase three of evolution consists of developing the capacity for representing the supramental archetypes directly into the physical. This is in our long-term evolutionary future.

What is holding us up is that we have not yet succeeded in integrating rational thinking and feeling. What prevents this is the instinctual brain circuits of negative emotions with which we are born.

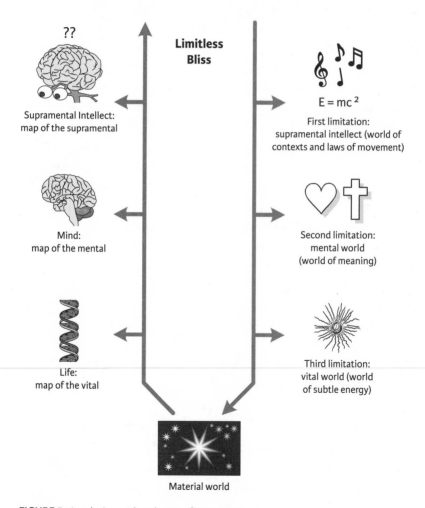

FIGURE 5. Involution and evolution of consciousness.

The archetypes of the supramental provide us with the most profound contexts of mental thinking. Right now, we intuit the supramental archetypes such as love and make mental images (representations) of them. When we live these images, we make new brain circuits that enable us to live the archetype relatively effortlessly. The neuroplasticity of the brain that enables us to make new brain circuits of our learning is one of the most amazing recent discoveries of neuroscience.

You fall in love, making a mental representation of that archetype in association with the feeling of love in your heart chakra, which is subsequently processed in your mind-brain. You then relate to your love-partner in intimate living, making brain circuits of love. But this is one-person-directed love. In subsequent carryings on of that relationship, if you can transform your personal conditional love to impersonal unconditional love, then you are able to love everyone relatively effortlessly. You have made a brain circuit of love. The current short-term goal of our evolution is to make the fruit of such individual achievements of love-circuits in the brain available to all humanity through evolution (see Goswami 2008b). When this happens, all of us will gain the capacity to balance the instinctual negative emotions of hate and competitiveness with the positive emotion of love. Only then can we be free to be fully rational.

Note, however, that representations made through the mediation of thinking and feeling are not the real thing and are always imperfect. So we need phase three for our capacity to love to blossom fully.

Right now, our capacity to love is being put to the test by such catastrophic threats as global warming, terrorism, and nuclear warfare. And love is just one of the archetypes. Social justice is being threatened by the increasing failure of such social institutions as capitalism, democracy, and the media to achieve it. The archetype of good is threatened by the breakdown of ethics. Our wholeness is being threatened by increasing emotion-caused diseases and our inability to heal them due to exponentially rising medical costs.

We need to evolve, and we need it fast. Some of us feel this evolutionary pressure and, wanting to change the world—for the world to come to terms with the evolutionary movement of consciousness—we become activists. But so far, activism has a checkered history. Spiritual teachers tell us the reason: you cannot change the world without changing yourself; evolve yourself first by looking inward, and the outer world will take care of itself.

But this, too, is an incomplete view. We are the world inside and out. Yes, we need to transform the inner, but we also need to pay attention to evolution that involves the outer. In this way, the inner and the outer need to be integrated. This is the job of quantum activism.

Evolution gives us the answer to the puzzle of why a good God sometimes seems to allow bad things to happen to good people. The representations we make initially of God and its possibilities are quite imperfect; they get better with time. In this imperfection is the seed of evil. Evolution is the movement toward the good. The presence of evil only shows that our evolution is not yet finished.

Quantum Activism and Evolution

A quantum activist's work begins with trying to change his or her worldview from a matter-based one to one based on quantum physics and the primacy of consciousness. We have begun right thinking and we ask: now that we know how to think properly about our world, what should we do about it?

Quantum physics, when interpreted through the philosophy of monistic idealism, is transformative. Right thinking—giving up myopic separatist materialist ideas and embracing God and wholeness, downward causation, and the subtle bodies in our lives—is the first step of a transformative journey to wholeness. There is more.

Spiritual traditions look at the journey of transformation as a spiritual journey—a journey toward the spirit, the unmanifest, leaving needs of the manifest world behind. The transformative journey of the modern person, of a quantum activist, is different. Our science within consciousness is telling us that the manifest world is designed to represent the possibilities of the unmanifest better and better as time goes on, through evolution. Transformation is important primarily to serve the evolutionary play of consciousness and only secondarily for personal salvation in spirit. The ultimate objective is to achieve wholeness right smack in the middle of manifest separateness.

Free Will and Access to Real Freedom: The Transformative Aspects of Quantum Physics and Downward Causation

Downward causation, as mentioned earlier, involves choice from quantum possibilities. But there are subtleties.

We make choices all the time. What flavor of ice cream would you like, chocolate or vanilla? We get so attached to our preferences that if we choose vanilla, instead of the chocolate we like, we think we have made a major creative breakthrough. This is the kind of choice through which consumer economists exploit us. Yes, this is an example of downward causation, but the full freedom of quantum movement is not engaged; with either choice, our freedom of choice is compromised by past conditioning.

When we are conditioned, we no longer see possibilities as possibilities. In the movie *The Pursuit of Happyness,* a father (played by Will Smith) explains to his son the difference between the possibility and the probability of going to the baseball game. His son shrugs him away, saying "I get it, I get it, possibly going means we're not going." How do we get over this conditioned mind and access real freedom?

The new science tells us how. Conscious collapse with real freedom of choice is: a) discontinuous, a quantum leap in the style of an electron jumping from one atomic orbit to another without going through the intervening space; b) nonlocal, involving not the individual but the collective or cosmic consciousness; and c) tangled hierarchical, we and what we choose are cocreations.

This last item needs explication. Simple hierarchy you know: when you are the head honcho to some underling, you are the causal level of a simple hierarchy. A Hollywood woman meets a long-lost friend. "Let's have some coffee and catch up." They go to a coffeehouse, and the woman starts talking. After about half an hour, she becomes aware, "Oh, I am talking about myself all this time. Let's talk about you. What do you think of me?" This is the tendency of our ego level of being—being at the causal level of a simple hierarchy.

A relationship is tangled hierarchical when causality fluctuates back and forth between the levels ad infinitum. And what's more, the causal efficacy of the levels of a tangled hierarchy is only an apparent one. The real causal efficacy lies in a domain transcending both.

As an example, look at the Escher picture *Drawing Hands* (Figure 6). Although it appears that the left hand is drawing the right, and the right is drawing the left, in fact, Escher is drawing them both from a transcendent level.

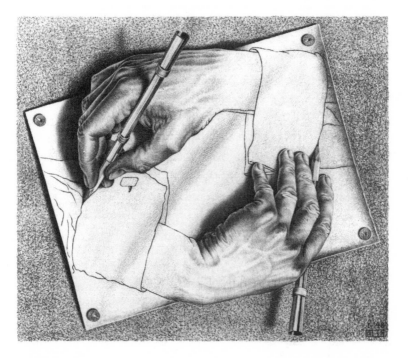

FIGURE 6. *Drawing Hands*, by M. C. Escher. An example of tangled hierarchy.

This is what happens in an event of quantum collapse with real freedom of choice. When we experience ourselves as the chooser, we are choosing from what is known; we are not really free to choose from the unknown. When we choose from the unknown, as in a creative experience, we never feel that we are choosing. I call this nonordinary state of the subject/self the *quantum self* (which traditions call the spirit or a state of superconsciousness), in contrast to the ordinarily experienced conditioned ego. The truth is that the real choice is that of a transcendent consciousness—God, if you will.

We arrive at real freedom when we embrace any of the three quantum aspects of downward causation of choice—discontinuity, nonlocality, and tangled hierarchy. We practice the first in creativity, the second in developing social consciousness, and the third in intimate relationships. All this involves not only what is internal to us, but also the external.

So as quantum activists we do not leave the world; instead, we live the world. We combine right thinking with right living. We walk our talk. We take frequent journeys into the subtle.

Four hundred years ago, the philosopher René Descartes separated mind and matter and gave us the philosophy of modernism. As modern humans, we have used our free will to manifest the human potential quite successfully in the individual dimension in the outer arena, but we have fallen short in the inner as well as the collective and social dimensions. And now the postmodern worldview of scientific materialism has robbed us even of our free will! But never fear, quantum physics is here, giving us back our freedom to choose from quantum possibilities. Now we have to use our freedom to choose to reestablish unity—unity within the separateness of diversity.

Right Livelihood

Right thinking provides the context, and right living—walking our talk— provides the transformative journey of a quantum activist. The question of right livelihood has two aspects. The first has to do with the personal choice of right livelihood. Your livelihood must facilitate your own personal journey of creativity and transformation. It must provide you more time for relaxed being, for example. This is the aspect that conventional spiritual traditions, especially Buddhism, emphasize.

The second aspect of right livelihood is more like conventional activism because we try to change our social institutions so they facilitate our evolutionary journey of better and better exploration of meaning. It is a fact that, through much of our history after the agricultural revolution, we established such strong simple hierarchies that most of humanity has been prevented from exploring meaning and values. In the 18th century, with the advent of capitalism, democracy, and liberal education, things changed quite a bit. These institutions led to the development of a middle class whose prerogative is the exploration of meaning.

Things changed again in the 20th century when scientific materialism began to be established in the 1950s. A postmodern malaise took hold of the collective psyche of humanity, in which deconstruction of our great ideals became fashionable. By the 1980s, the middle class in America was already shrinking, but we have only recently become aware of it. Coincidentally, we have the makings of a paradigm shift in science that is promising to put meaning and values back in our worldview. Now the evolutionary journey of putting people back into exploration of meaning can begin once again. This calls for a revamping of our social institutions.

Materialist pursuits additionally produced crisis conditions, the solutions to which demand similar revamping of our social systems. Revamping our social systems to make them more conducive to the exploration of meaning and values is a major goal of quantum activism. For the quantum activist, taking part in this revamping is an example of what the Bhagavad Gita calls karma yoga—transformation through social action.

So What's in the Rest of the Book?

Thus far, I have analyzed what quantum activism is, and what a quantum activist must aspire to: a burning conviction of scientific and internalized personal living faith strong enough to transform the self and society through living, individually and collectively, the transformative aspects of quantum physics. I also outlined some of the basic principles that guide our choice of livelihood and the principles that must guide the change of some of our most important arenas of livelihood.

In the rest of the book, I elaborate on the know-why and know-how: know-why to do right thinking (part 1); know-how to live with a balance of creativity and conditioning, the gross and the subtle, and thinking and feeling (part 2); know-how to develop social consciousness and act conscientiously toward others (part 2); know-how to live with evolutionary ethics and foster deep ecology in living (part 2); and finally, know-how to change the work arena to bring it into synchrony with the evolutionary movement of consciousness so that we can engage in right livelihood and karma yoga while earning a living (part 3).

In reading this book, you will find that each of its three parts is about a particular path that quantum physics prescribes for illumined living in growing wholeness. Part 1 is a culmination of the search in the West for a wisdom path that is purely Western. As you know, Christianity, the dominant spiritual tradition of the West is fundamentally a devotional path of living (path of love). So ever since Descartes, philosophers in the West have tried to develop a wisdom path to complement the devotional path. It has been difficult because of their insistence on using pure reason. In the East, they bypass this difficulty by using intuition and experience to complement reason. And now we discover that quantum physics and laboratory testing is another way to define a Western wisdom path. However, it is said, correctly, I think, that wisdom without love is incomplete, as is love without wisdom. In this way, right living and walking our talk, the subject of part 2, integrates the two: bringing love into wisdom and wisdom into love.

But all this we have to learn, not away from life, but within everyday life, within the premise of how we earn a livelihood. This is the activistic action-oriented path, which is the subject of part 3.

If any of these paths to wholeness and integrative living appeal to you, you are ready for quantum activism. If you see through the meaning and value vacuity of the pleasure-centered life under scientific materialism, if the philosophy of existentialism and postmodern deconstructionism do not satisfy, you are ripe to engage with quantum activism. If you see the utmost importance of changing our worldview, as all New Agers do, you are ready. If you see through the love traditions of religions so narrow in their love, so lacking in wisdom, you are ready.

Most importantly, if your occupation does not bring you meaning and satisfaction, you are ready for quantum activism. And if your life does not provide you avenues for learning and expressing your values, you are ready to be a quantum activist.

And of course, if you have already found wisdom, love, and purposefulness of life and want to help others in their struggles, then, too, quantum activism is for you.

PART 1

Right Thinking
It's the Worldview, Stupid!

CHAPTER 2

It's the Worldview, Mr. President

An Open Letter to President Obama

Dear President Obama,

In the 1992 election campaign, Clinton's strategists came up with a very effective slogan: "It's the economy, stupid." Your slogan, "Change that you can believe in," was not so bad either. It worked, didn't it? Maybe so, but I think "It's the worldview, stupid" would have been the right one. Please hear me out.

Now that you are at the helm of the country and have started to institute changes, your changes seem more and more to be a mixed bag. Almost everybody (that voted for you and still supports you) feels a little unsure about believing in all of your changes. In some of them, yes; but in others, no.

Specifically, the required changes are about meaning and values, Mr. President. You got that one right when you were campaigning. When you put forward programs in favor of the middle class, universal health care or education, or a green economy, you side unambiguously with meaning and values—no confusion there. But when you side with the programs for bailing out the financial organizations like AIG, are you supporting meaning and values? Hardly. Mr. President, financial organizations typified by AIG have been some of the most unethical organizations in our country. Money has no inherent meaning; it only represents meaning. So people who make money by gambling on money can hardly be said to be involved in a meaningful economic enterprise (any more than ordinary gambling is meaningful).

Your confusion on these questions is not unique, Mr. President. Almost everyone in our society, Democrat or Republican, is confused on these issues. This is where the question of worldview comes in. There is deep confusion there in people's thinking. On one hand, we have the religious worldview, in which meaning and values are clearly and unambiguously important. Science, by and large, is supposed to be value neutral. And most postmodern physicists look at the universe as meaningless. Although some evolutionary philosophers try to bring meaning and values by posing them as the outcome of Darwinian evolution, such work is fundamentally flawed and ineffective, because material interactions cannot even process meaning or value.

Most Democrats have adopted the seemingly more scientific "secular" view. Keep religion away from the affairs of state and politics (even if that means becoming ambiguous about meaning and values). Republicans, on the other hand, find the compromise on values (morality to them) so repulsive that they would rather side with fundamentalist Christians and embrace their rather rigid view of meaning and values than side with secularism.

So is it the old science versus religion or rather science versus Christianity debate? We know who will win that one. In the last few years, quite a few books have appeared suggesting (in an echo of the 19th-century philosopher Friedrich Nietzsche's slogan) that the Christian God sitting on a throne in heaven doling out rewards and punishments for our deeds is dead. Recently, I saw an ad on a London bus: "God probably does not exist, so relax and enjoy life." The hidden message is, if there is no God to punish you, why not equivocate on values and become a hedonist?

Mr. President, some of the people in our financial investment banks took this hedonist message too seriously and developed the schemes that produced the toxic assets that clogged up our banking system. What kind of message are you sending when you bail them out?

I know you are not a hedonist, Mr. President. I also know that you are not a believer in the simplistic God of fundamentalist Christianity. Your God is more sophisticated. During your campaign, when an evangelical Christian preacher asked you about confronting evil, you said, "Evil makes me humble." In other words, you don't separate evil from good. You can see that evil, like the good, exists in us.

But your answer confused the pundits of the media who could not understand you. They preferred your opponent's simple forceful answer, "I will defeat evil." This is the problem. We seem to be caught between the good-versus-evil dualistic view of God and spirituality of the fundamentalist Christian and the meaningless, valueless view of reality held by the average scientist.

And your attendance at church without any cynical political motivation creates further confusion. How can you believe in science (you must, or else why do you support evolution and stem cell research?) and still go to church to pray to God? And if you are a true believer in God à la Christianity, how can you support evolution?

Mr. President, it is a worldview question that deeply divides this country. When you were campaigning, you expressed constantly your ardent desire to integrate—we are not Republicans or Democrats, we are Americans.

Yes, we are Americans, Mr. President, but as long as we identify with the wrong science (hedonistic science has to be wrong as a model of reality if reality upholds meaning and values) or the wrong religion (of a dualist God), how can our differences be resolved? So it is of utmost importance that we resolve the worldview issues.

Now, you may throw up your hands and say, "But those issues are so hard. The greatest of philosophers cannot resolve them." I hope not. One thing we all agree on. You are a fearless person; you are not afraid to tackle difficult questions. And, Mr. President, you have got help. For the past few decades, some scientists, myself one of them, have been trying to develop a new integrative paradigm of science that resolves the divisive issues I mention here. And I am one scientist who thinks we have succeeded.

It's the worldview, stupid. If we are stupid enough not to resolve the worldview issues, integrating us as Americans behind you, solving American problems will forever elude you. But if you are willing to hear me out on the possibilities of the new worldview, what then?

The new integrative science is based not on the primacy of matter, like the divisive science I have been talking about, but on the primacy of consciousness. Can we base science on the metaphysics that consciousness is primary, that it is the ground of all being including matter? Yes, we can, Mr. President. But we have to heed the lessons of quantum physics. Quantum physics describes objects as possibilities, and consciousness serves the causally potent function of changing possibility into actuality through the freedom of choice. This causal potency is nonmaterial. Our research makes it very clear that this causal potency is the same one that the esoteric spiritual traditions (including esoteric Christianity) call "downward causation," which these traditions attribute to God. God is that nonordinary state of our consciousness in which we have total freedom to choose, unencumbered by any personal conditioning.

Ideas do get around, Mr. President. To my surprise, a respected New York Times columnist, David Brooks, chastised you in one of his columns because you are trying to tackle too many problems. Said he, "Why he [Obama] has not also decided to spend his evenings mastering quantum mechanics and discovering the origin of consciousness is beyond me."

There you are, Mr. President. Mr. Brooks must be a clairvoyant. In order to integrate the nation, in order to see your way through the complexity of meaning and value-related issues that are destroying our economy and environment (and breeding terrorism in some parts of the world), you have to discover a new integrative worldview that gives you both God and science. But in order to discover and reconcile that worldview within yourself, you have to spend a few evenings with quantum physics.

If you like what you read and take the new paradigm seriously, then this is what I would like to plead. Under Clinton, the government did one very important thing for health care: it created an office to deliver grants for research in alternative medicine. This helped legitimize alternative medicine in our society. (By the way, if you really want the cost of health care down, look at integrative medicine, which integrates allopathy and alternative medicine under one umbrella.) You can similarly help create an office for research in alternative science devoted to the study of alternative scientific paradigms like the one based on quantum physics and primacy of consciousness. Actually, you can go one better than Clinton.

In 1960, President Kennedy initiated the moon project, and in less than ten years, we went to the moon. Can you not initiate a scientific project to investigate God and downward causation and establish God's existence (or not) to the satisfaction of a scientific consensus? If we can go to the moon, can we not do this? Yes, we can.

Sincerely,
Amit Goswami, Ph.D.

CHAPTER 3

A Brief History of the New Paradigm and More Early Quantum Activism

A paradigm shift in science that is taking us from a divisive, spirituality-denying, matter-based science to one that integrates science and spirituality is now a foregone conclusion. Today, the idea of a new paradigm is based on solid theory and evidence, not mostly on fanciful imagination and wooly ideas as it once was (Ferguson 1980). And like all creative endeavors, the paradigm shift has come with a surprise: science itself has to operate within a spiritual metaphysics.

The fancies decades ago were in favor of a holistic paradigm in which the best accommodation of spirituality possible was pantheism or nature-based spirituality (Capra 1975). According to holism, the whole is greater than the parts. How it is greater is the emergence of novel phenomena that, theorized the proponents, cannot be reduced to the sum of the parts. Life, mind, consciousness, spirituality—all were explained as such holistic emergent phenomena of matter. Hardly anyone at the time questioned the fundamental tenet of materialism: everything is made of matter.

Holism is not the only integrative track. Depth psychologists, starting with Freud and Jung, openly posited the concept of the unconscious that presupposes an irreducible consciousness. However, even Jung (1971), who was perhaps the most revolutionary of all the new paradigm thinkers in psychology, wondered aloud whether his concept of collective unconscious did not, after all, have a genetic basis. Of course, there were transpersonalists such as Abraham Maslow (1971) and Ken Wilber (1977), but they mostly echoed ancient wisdom, not blending enough modern science to be credible. The holistic paradigmers by far dominated the avant-garde new-age thinking: Gregory Bateson, Fritjof Capra, Eric Wantsch, Francisco Varela, Humberto

Maturana, John Lilly, the Nobel-laureate Ilya Prigogine, Karl Pribram, David Bohm, and Roger Sperry, the Nobel biologist who made major contributions to the big hoopla surrounding the left brain–right brain asymmetry as the answer to everything. The list is very distinguished and very long.

Many holists such as Capra depended on systems theory for their analysis. The scope of this kind of analysis is limited, however; only generalities can be discussed. Others—Pribram, Bohm, and Edgar Mitchell, among them—tried the idea of the hologram, both literally and metaphorically. But the hologram is an object, whereas consciousness is also a subject. How does the subject-object awareness come about? This "hard question" cannot be addressed from a materialist point of view (Chalmers 1995).

And spirituality is more than pantheism. An integrative theoretical foundation that could serve as a bridge between holistic thinking within science and psychological thinking within consciousness was still lacking. The work of physicist David Bohm went partway because Bohm (1980) was able to demonstrate downward causation in quantum physics in the form of a "quantum potential" that is nonlocal, and not the result of material interactions. But Bohm stayed within the confines of causal determinism and missed discontinuity and the tangled hierarchy implicit in quantum physics. A complete foundation came about only when quantum physics was properly interpreted in a paradox-free way within the primacy of consciousness (Goswami 1989, 1993; also see the following).

Quantum physicists were not exactly quiet while all the earlier talk of a paradigm shift was going on. John von Neumann (1955) was the first to interject consciousness into physics, and hence all science, by positing that consciousness chooses the actual event of experience from all the quantum possibilities an object represents in quantum physics. His postulate explains the observer effect: observers are always found to have converted quantum possibilities into actual events of their experience. In the 1970s, there was Fred Alan Wolf who popularized von Neumann's idea with the slogan "We create our own reality." Even today, the book *The Secret* and the movie of the same name are recycling Wolf's popularization of von Neumann's idea.

The seriousness of von Neumann's idea can be appreciated only when we engage with the so-called quantum measurement paradox, a most disagreeable thorn in the side of materialist attempts to understand and interpret quantum physics. In the materialist model based on reductionism, elementary particles make atoms, atoms make molecules, molecules make cells, cells make brain, and brain makes consciousness. This is called the upward causation model of causality. However, since all objects are quantum possibilities according to quantum physics, in such a view, possible elementary particles make possible atoms all the way, making a possible brain and possible consciousness (see Figure 1 in chapter 1). How can a possible consciousness coupled to possibilities of an object give us an actual event? Possibility coupled to possibility gives you only bigger possibility. So materialist-reductionist thinking about consciousness cannot explain the observer effect. This is the quantum measurement problem, which is a logical paradox for materialist thinking.

But materialists object to von Neumann's approach to quantum measurement because it smacks of dualism. How does consciousness, if it is an independent nonmaterial dual object, interact with a material object? Such an interaction must require the mediation of signals carrying energy. But energy of the physical universe itself is always constant, precluding any such mediation.

The breakthrough idea is that consciousness is neither a material brain product nor a dual object; instead, it is the ground of all being in which material objects exist as possibilities. In the event of quantum measurement, consciousness (in the form of the observer) chooses from all the offered possibilities the actuality that it experiences, becoming subject-object split awareness in the process (Goswami 1989, 1993). In other words, conscious choice is responsible for manifesting both the proverbial falling tree in the forest and the you that hears the sound of the fall. No observer, no sound, not even a tree.

When we realize that quantum physics demands that we adopt a new metaphysical basis for our science consisting of the primacy of consciousness, the way we look at quantum "weirdness" and paradoxes undergoes a radical change. Now they become our way to investigate the nature of consciousness. As quantum activists, you would be interested in this adventure yourself, which is the subject of the next chapter. But here is a brief introduction.

Crucial to the breakthrough of this primacy-of-consciousness interpretation of quantum physics was the resolution of the paradox of Wigner's friend—in the case of two observers simultaneously choosing among conflicting choices, who gets to choose? The paradox was resolved by three physicists working independently—Ludwig Bass (1971), Amit Goswami (1989), and Casey Blood (1993). They all proposed nonlocality—signal-less interconnectedness of consciousness—as the solution (see chapter 4 for details). We don't choose with total freedom from our individual local ego consciousness, but from a nonlocal, cosmic, nonordinary consciousness.

This is a breakthrough idea on several scores. First, it is now clear that conscious choice for an objective situation (in which large numbers of objects and/or events are involved) is objective because consciousness, being nonlocal, is objective. This validates why quantum physics is able to predict probabilities. Second, for a single event, the scope of creativity remains. The secret behind *The Secret* is that we must choose creatively in synchrony with quantum consciousness to manifest our intentions. In our ego, our so-called free will is seriously compromised, having become a choice between conditioned alternatives: what flavor of ice cream, chocolate or vanilla? That kind of choice. Third, the nonlocality of consciousness is an experimentally verifiable idea.

There was already the work of Einstein, Podolsky, and Rosen (1935) and that of John Bell with his famous theorem (1965) that suggested that nonlocality is involved in interacting quantum objects and how to verify the existence of nonlocality. Alain Aspect and his collaborators actually verified quantum nonlocality in the laboratory in 1982. In the same year, the physician Larry Dossey began making noise about the efficacy of quantum nonlocality in healing, an idea that was verified by Randolph Byrd in 1988, demonstrating nonlocal consciousness and downward causation in prayer healing at a distance. Also the parapsychologist Robert Jahn (1982) published convincing objective data for distant viewing, and Jahn and Dunn (1986) used quantum consciousness, albeit in a slightly vague manner, to interpret their new data.

In 1986, Willis Harman coined the phrase "science within consciousness," anticipating future development of a new science based on the primacy of consciousness. Within three years, I published my papers on quantum creativity (1988) and the idealist interpretation of quantum physics in which God was rediscovered in the form of quantum consciousness (Goswami 1989). Quantum creativity reveals another important aspect of downward causation besides nonlocality: the idea of discontinuity. Creative ideas come to us via discontinuous events of insight, always with an "aha!" surprise. This is anathema to old paradigm thinking. But in the primacy-of-consciousness paradigm, the discontinuity of creativity is explained as quantum leaps similar to the jumps an electron makes from one atomic orbit to another without going through the intervening space (Figure 7).

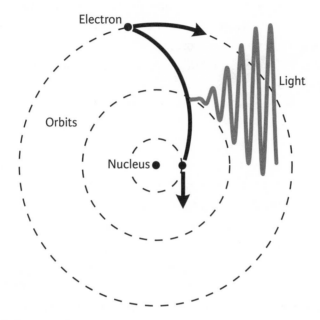

FIGURE 7. A quantum leap.

And last but not least, the physician Deepak Chopra (1990) independently discovered quantum consciousness and downward causation with his revolutionary idea of quantum healing. Science within consciousness was on the way.

Jacobo Grinberg-Zylberbaum (Grinberg-Zylberbaum et al. 1994) discovered the transferred potential (transfer of physical electric potential from one brain to another at a distance without any electromagnetic connection or signals), verifying that quantum consciousness is indeed nonlocal. His data (see chapter 4 for details) were later confirmed by several experiments (Sabel et al. 2001, Wackermann et al. 2003, Standish et al. 2004).

In 1993, I published *The Self-Aware Universe*. In the same year, physicist Henry Stapp published the book *Mind, Matter, and Quantum Mechanics*, making roughly the same conclusions as those in my book, only slightly camouflaged. The parapsychologists Helmuth Schmidt (1993) and Dean Radin (1997) made their major contributions in support of downward causation and the experimenter's intention, as did Stanford engineering professor William Tiller (2001).

We are witnessing no less than science's rediscovery of God and downward causation. But spiritual traditions, besides downward causation, also invoke the idea of subtle nonmaterial bodies, such as mind and a vital energy body, even a supramental body of archetypes from which our values originate. As stated before, as a result of dualism, materialists reject the idea of subtle nonmaterial bodies.

Besides holistic thinking, new psychology, and quantum physics, there were other developments that rapidly took place after the publication of *The Aquarian Conspiracy* (Ferguson 1980), which suggested that something more than materialism may be in the offing. In 1981, biologist Rupert Sheldrake's revolutionary book *A New Science of Life* revitalized the discarded notion of the vital body. Previously, the vital body was viewed as the source of a mysterious life force. Sheldrake correctly theorized that the vital body is the reservoir of nonlocal and nonphysical morphogenetic fields used for biological form building. John Searle (1987, 1994) made his rediscovery of the mind, which Roger Penrose (1991) supported with rigorous mathematics, both researchers showing that matter cannot process meaning, that only mind can and does.

Further data in support of subtle bodies were also accumulating. The near-death researchers made breakthroughs (Sabom 1982, Ring 1984), proving survival after death. Stan Grof (1992) discovered the new technique of holotropic breathing for codifying reincarnational memory, which until then could be verified only by following up on children's recollections (Stevenson 1974, 1977).

Materialists object to subtle bodies because of "dualism"—there is no mediator for the interaction of the subtle and the material. But in quantum thinking, thinking of subtle objects as quantum objects or quantum possibilities within consciousness removes dualism. Consciousness is the mediator (see Figure 4 in chapter 1). When consciousness chooses from material possibilities, it also chooses from one or more subtle body possibilities. In the process of simultaneous choice, consciousness makes a representation of the subtle in matter (Goswami 2000, 2001; Blood 2001).

This gave science within consciousness new power, new horizons to integrate. One is the physics of survival-after-death and reincarnation. What survives? What incarnates? The subtle bodies, of course—in truth, their conditioned quantum mathematics of probabilities (Goswami 2001; also see later). Another application of the new science was to the subject of health and healing.

Acupuncture entered America, chi became a popular word overnight, and soon subtle (vital) energies were being studied by researchers such as the neurophysiologist Elmer Green (Green and Green 1977; see also Page 1992, Eden 1999). Soon bridges were made between the progress in a quantum modeling of consciousness and the empirical and theoretical work of avant-garde medical researchers (Goswami 2004).

In the 1980s, the organismic school of biology (those biologists who ascribe causal efficacy to the entire organism, not merely to the genes) led by Brian Goodwin, Mae Wan Ho, and Peter Saunders kept reminding the scientific community of the incompleteness of neo-Darwinism and several popular books (for example, Goodwin 1994, Ho and Saunders 1984) on the subject were published under their instigation. In the 1990s, the biologist Michael Behe (1996) did his pioneering work in support of intelligent design of living systems by an intelligent designer. The astrophysicist Arne Wyller (1999) suggested that consciousness plays the crucial role in evolution. And finally, in 2008, a bridge was made between Darwinism and the intelligent design theory of evolution using the ideas of downward causation and subtle bodies (Goswami 2008b). The crucial idea here is that the famous fossil gaps of macroevolution (also called punctuation marks; see Eldredge and Gould 1972) are the results of quantum leaps of biological creativity. This way of looking at evolution provided a scientific basis for earlier revolutionary ideas about our evolutionary future by such luminaries as Teilhard de Chardin (1961), Sri Aurobindo (1996), and Ken Wilber (1981).

I am giving you a flavor, not a complete history, of how the new paradigm of science (re)confirming the existence of God, downward causation, and the subtle bodies came to the forefront of scientific thinking and experimentation.

And now the quintessential question: if the data as well as the theory are there (both have been adequately demonstrated in the past decades, as reviewed here) for a consciousness-based paradigm of science, then why aren't the bulk of the scientists (the establishment) accepting the paradigm shift? Why isn't the quantum message getting through to the mainstream scientists? Why aren't even the holists converted to this new quantum physics–based paradigm?

There is no reason for dismay. The situation of the acceptance of science within consciousness among established scientists is quite parallel to the situation of the acceptance of esoteric spirituality among the people of established religions. The acceptance is slow, and there are very good reasons for that.

Modern science was created in an environment of antagonism between science and Christianity. In the West, this battle, through many ups and downs, continues even today. So when Western scientists think of spirituality, they just cannot disassociate spirituality from Christianity (it's an emotional thing, you see), cannot think that there are other religions in the world, and cannot accept that even Christianity has an esoteric tradition in which the concept of God is quite sophisticated and requires much more sophisticated investigation before they reject it outright. So they go on with their narrow-minded squabbles with Christianity just as the world's pop religions go on with their squabbles.

The parallel does not end there. Popular religion has no price tag in terms of responsibility. You are born into it and you are saved anyway (if you think that it is only in Christianity that "Jesus saves," believe me, this simpleminded belief is prevalent in every pop religion). But accepting esoteric spirituality based on the nonduality of you and God makes you responsible for your choices. Responsibility is impossible to take on until you are ready for it. The same is true about science within consciousness. Scientists who accept it cannot shun responsibility. No longer can they do their science in a value-free way. No longer can they remain uncommitted to transformation while pretending scientific objectivity. To be a scientist of consciousness is to research consciousness in your personal life as well as in your professional life. This is a very big change, a very big responsibility.

Remember, materialism is entrenched in the way scientists and technologists today earn their living. As Upton Sinclair once said, "It is difficult to make a man understand something when his salary depends upon his not understanding it."

Finally, scientists today are highly specialized. A quantum physicist does not understand consciousness and is therefore skeptical that what he regards as a psychological phenomenon can solve a problem of physics. A cognitive psychologist or a neuroscientist is unaware that the solution to the paradoxes of perception (why there is a subject in addition to the object(s), subjective quality, etc.) is to be found in the primacy of consciousness and quantum physics. The evolutionary biologist worries about the explanation of the fossil gaps, no doubt, but is not aware of discontinuous quantum leaps. An oncologist knows about the near impossibility of an overnight cure of cancer but is suspicious of the concept of quantum healing, because how can quantum physics have anything to say about healing? It goes on and on.

In any case, the slow progress of the new paradigm thinking is not necessarily bad. Slow acceptance means that scientists are not naive; they see what is at issue here. The philosopher Victor Frankl said, "We must supplement the Statue of Liberty on the East Coast by the Statue of Responsibility on the West Coast." It is possible to argue that there is no hurry for a complete paradigm shift until we have erected such a statue of responsibility, metaphorically, of course.

Meanwhile, the important thing is to gain acceptance for a multicultural approach to all the life and social sciences, following the lead of psychology and medicine. On the other hand, as I have been saying for some time, materialism is a wound on the body of the evolution of consciousness. Isn't it prudent to heal the wound as quickly as possible? Thereby is the importance of quantum activism.

We must heal the wound before it shows signs of malignancy. Previously, I referred to the scientific acceptance of the new paradigm taking its own time. But the popular acceptance does not have to wait. Thanks to the lead time that the coming of Eastern spirituality to the West and a Western revival of esotericism has enjoyed in this holomovement (to use a term created by physicist David Bohm) of consciousness, many more laypeople than scientists are ready to take responsibility. In fact, I fully expect that it will be the popular acceptance of the new paradigm that will drive scientific acceptance.

What does it mean to take responsibility? It means that you commit to transforming yourself according to the need of the evolution of consciousness, using the transformative aspects of quantum physics such as discontinuity and nonlocality. When you do that, you become a quantum activist. An ordinary activist tries to change the world without making any changes in himself or herself; the spiritual activist tries to transform himself or herself, believing that the world will take care of itself. The quantum activist undertakes the journey of personal transformation with the transformation of the whole world also in mind.

So bringing quantum activism to science right now means that if we cannot convince the materialists to give up their old paradigm, let's ourselves be supportive of the development of alternative sciences wherever that is taking place. We do not compete with one another; we cooperate. We don't divide; we integrate. Eventually, the science paradigm that integrates the most will get the nod to be the new paradigm.

It's the Worldview, Stupid!

So what is the lesson of all this for the paradigm shift in science in general? If people support a particular field that entails research, sooner or later that field gains official government recognition that endorses research in the field. The official recognition draws more scientists into the field, which draws more popular support, and on it goes.

Popular support also crucially depends on the perceived practical usefulness of the new paradigm. Government support for physics skyrocketed in this country and Europe as well as in the now defunct Soviet Union because of first, the spectacular role that physics and chemistry-based technology played in World War II, and second, the Cold War competition in weapon making and space exploration. Believe it or not, the major "useful" application of physics that continues to draw government support for physics research is still weapons. Can a paradigm of peace and consciousness become useful in some way in the popular perception to deserve government support, especially financial support for research?

This is crucial. Unless research support becomes available, there is not going to be any significant shift of scientists, no mass exodus, from the materialist paradigm to the consciousness-based paradigm, however spiritually satisfying and however closer to truth the latter may be.

So the immediate agenda of the quantum activist is clear: to consolidate public support enough to generate research support for the new paradigm. Recent data (Ray and Anderson 2000) suggest that there may be a reservoir of some 20 percent of Americans who are closet supporters of the new paradigm. It is the job of quantum activists to bring them out of the closet. The success of the recent movies *What the Bleep Do We Know?* and *The Quantum Activist* also suggests a groundswell in the new paradigm's favor. We may not be that far from the promised land.

There is an untapped source of support for the new science that we must consider. Fundamentalists excepted, most religions would welcome a science that supports God, supports the essence of all religions, and supports religious ethics and values more or less in accordance with religious practices. So one of the priorities of quantum activism is to begin and continue dialogs between existing religions and the scientists of the new paradigm. The majority of religious people in this country and elsewhere are not fundamentalists. We should always remember that.

CHAPTER 4

How to Resolve Quantum Paradoxes and Discover a Scientific God

Quantum physics is paradoxical. It is because of this that the great physicist Richard Feynman said, "Nobody understands quantum mechanics." And the famous Niels Bohr said, "If you are not puzzled when you encounter quantum physics, you could not possibly have understood it."

Why the paradoxes? It is because most scientists today (as in the early days; see chapter 1) try to interpret and understand quantum physics with the metaphysics of scientific materialism—everything is made of matter, the elementary particles of matters. Studying the paradoxes and their solutions gives us amazing unsuspected clues, not only about the incompleteness of scientific materialism, but also about the nature of our consciousness. These paradoxes are your doorway to knowing God, a scientific creator God that is the creative agent of downward causation.

The big new information is that in quantum physics, all objects are depicted as possibility, waves of possibility having many facets. And yet, when we measure them or observe them, we never see possibilities; we see an actual event, a particle, one facet. This is the observer effect. So how does our looking convert the objects from waves of possibility into particles of actuality? What is so special about an observer? Can a material machine do the conversion of possibility into actuality? Is such a conversion even necessary? These are the questions of the paradigm-shifting quantum measurement problem.

But before you tackle the measurement problem, you need to convince yourself that quantum objects are really waves of possibility, you may say. Good. To that end, let us investigate the double slit experiment and the so-called wave-particle paradox.

The Double Slit Experiment and the Resolution of the Wave-Particle Paradox

In the double slit setup, a beam of electrons passes through a two-slitted screen before hitting a second fluorescent screen where the electrons are observed (Figure 8). According to quantum physics, the possibility wave of each electron splits in two as it passes through both slits at once. The result, seen as spots on the fluorescent screen, displays a bunch of alternating bright (where the spots are) and dark fringes (where there are no spots). This, you must admit, is a bit unusual if you are only used to seeing how objects like baseballs behave in a similar situation, in which case there would only be two bright fringes right behind each slit.

The Double Slit Experiement

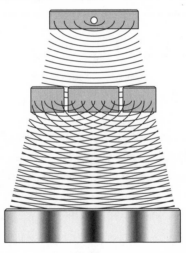

Waveform

FIGURE 8. Each electron passes through both slits simultaneously (in possibility) and interferes with itself producing what is called an interference pattern of alternating bright and dark fringes.

To understand the pattern, we have to invoke wave interference, some-thing that only waves can do. If the crests of the two waves of each electron, upon passing the double slit, arrive on the fluorescent screen together, "in phase," the possibilities increase and reinforce each other (Figure 9), and the probability of the electron being in those places becomes maximum. This is called constructive interference, and this explains the bright fringes. If the crest of one wave arrives "out of phase," that is, with the trough of the other at a place on the screen, it is bad news. The waves destroy each other, with no possibility for the electron to arrive in those places at all: destructive interference. This explains the dark fringes.

Wave Interference

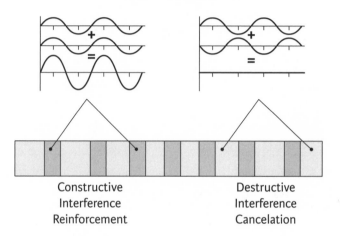

FIGURE 9. Wave interference.

When electrons are collapsed or converted into actualities, they appear as localized spots, just as particles should. But the only way you can rationalize how an electron, a material object, can pass through two slits at once is to accept that the electron does so in possibility, as a wave of possibility. Electrons must be both particles and waves.

If you are still feeling a bit skeptical, suppose we try by a measurement to ascertain through which slit the electron is passing. Metaphorically, we just aim a flashlight at the slits to see the electron. Guess what? As soon as we do that, our attempt to see it collapses the electron wave, the electron behaves as a particle, and indeed what you expect for baseballs is what happens (Figure 10).

Think it over. There simply is no alternative but to accept that an electron is a wave of possibility with the ability to be at two slits at once whenever we don't observe it; and whenever we observe it, it manifests as a localized particle.

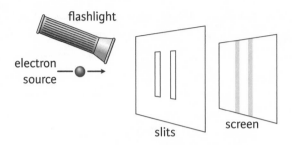

Interference Pattern Disappears

FIGURE 10. When we try to identify which slit the electron passes through by focusing a flashlight on the slits, the electron shows its's particle nature. There are only two fringes—exactly what we would expect if the electrons were miniature baseballs.

To comprehend this fully, it helps to realize that, as possibility waves, electrons reside in transcendent potentia beyond space and time, as Heisenberg noted long ago. They become immanent particles when collapsed. The event of collapse not only manifests the electron as particle, but also manifests space and time with it.

Back to the Quantum Measurement Paradox

In materialist metaphysics, all is matter and we, our consciousness included, are also material phenomena or epiphenomena. So, materialists say, consciousness is an epiphenomenon of the brain. From this vantage point, look once more at the quantum measurement problem. Possible elementary particles make possible atoms, make possible molecules, make possible brain, makes possible consciousness. Now this possible consciousness is looking or interacting with a possible elementary particle. Possibility is coupling with possibility. And what happens? Only a bigger possibility. Think of possible fish in the river. And also possible fishing tackles. But can you ever catch an actual fish with your possible tackle coupling with possible fish? Likewise, thinking of consciousness as a brain epiphenomenon can never explain the observer effect—how our looking converts a quantum wave of possibility into an actuality. We have a paradox.

The great mathematician John von Neumann proved mathematically that material interactions between objects' waves of possibility can only produce other waves of possibility. Even an infinite number of material "measurement apparatuses" such as cameras and Geiger counters—called a von Neumann chain—cannot collapse possibility into actuality. This is called von Neumann's theorem. So von Neumann figured out that a non-material agent is needed to collapse a wave of possibility to a particle of actuality. Since our looking does it routinely, we must have a nonmaterial component—our consciousness. Consciousness chooses out of quantum possibilities the actual events of experience—the particles of actuality.

Unfortunately, the question can be raised: how does a nonmaterial consciousness interact with the material object? Since there is nothing in common between them, they need a mediator, an energy-carrying signal. But the energy of the material universe alone always remains a constant; this is the sacrosanct law of conservation of energy. If signals took energy from consciousness to a material body and vice versa, the energy conservation law would be violated once in a while. But as I said, that never happens. So this is also a paradox, the paradox of dualism, discussed before.

We are not thinking correctly about consciousness—this much is clear. When I started thinking about the quantum measurement problem, I, too, was puzzled by these paradoxes. I even sought a solution from psychology professors, but to no avail. Most academic psychologists think of the brain as a computer and model consciousness as a central processing unit, but that does not help with the quantum measurement paradox. Our observation of a quantum object is still possibility coupled to possibility—a possible CPU looking at a possible electron.

As a desperate step, I turned to mystics. One night, while talking to a mystic, clarity came to me—another way to think about consciousness. This mystic, Joel Morwood, said, "There is nothing but God." And an about-turn from my materialist metaphysics took place in me. I realized that there is nothing but consciousness. Instead of matter being everything, consciousness is the ground of all being and material objects consist of quantum waves of possibilities of consciousness. When consciousness chooses, the choice is from its own possibilities and requires no interaction. So there is no dualism.

You have surely seen a gestalt picture, those wonderful drawings with two meanings found in the same lines. My favorite one has a young woman and an old woman hidden in it (Figure 11). The artist called the picture "My

Wife and My Mother-In-Law." Suppose you see the mother-in-law first. Now try to see the wife. It may lead to a little frustration at first. Do you need to do anything to the picture for this shift of meaning? No, be patient. All you need to do is to shift the perspective of looking.

FIGURE 11. "My Wife and My Mother-In-Law" (based on the original drawing by W. E. Hill).

So it is like this. When consciousness chooses among the material object's possibility facets, it chooses one or another facet just by shifting its perspective of looking. No doing anything, no interaction is needed.

You see how refreshing this is. For millennia, mystics have been telling us that consciousness is the ground of all being, in language such as "Everything is Brahman," or "There is nothing but Allah," or "All is God." When we hear such sentences, we tend to think: How can that be? Aren't those things—Allah, God, Brahman, or Ein Sof—just ideas, abstract stuff? How can solid matter be made of such ethereal stuff?

Suspend your disbelief. Quantum possibility waves can be described by mathematical functions called wave functions. That's all that an object is; in the beginning there is just that, the mathematical entity of a wave function. It is the choice by consciousness that puts substance into the mathematical forms, depending on what we are choosing. If we are choosing a solid body, the structure, hardness, and texture of the solidity all result from our choosing (Blood 1993).

The Paradox of Who Gets to Choose

The next paradox we will discuss, the paradox of Wigner's friend, is important for both the scientist and the quantum activist. For the scientist, it addresses the question of objectivity: the scientist is worried that now that consciousness has entered physics, physics will become subjective and then how can we call it science? For the quantum activist, the ideas of the last section may conjure up the slogan "We create our own reality," with its associated grandeur of making all kinds of personal desires come true, such as a luxury car, a house, and so on. I mentioned the movie *The Secret,* which is centered on the law of attraction: wait and things will come to you. To what extent are these things validated by quantum physics? I have hinted that quantum creativity is the real secret of creating our own reality, but how do we know what the real secret is?

Imagine that Wigner, the Nobel-laureate physicist who thought of the paradox, is approaching a quantum traffic light with two possibilities, red and green; at the same time, his friend is approaching the same light from the perpendicular road (Figure 12). Being busy people, they both choose green. Unfortunately, their choices are contradictory; if both choices materialized at the same time, there would be pandemonium. Obviously, only one of their choices counts, but whose?

In the context of how we ordinarily experience our consciousness, there is only one solution. Wigner knows that he is conscious; for example, he is aware that he is aware. However, he can only ascertain this for himself, never for his friend or any other person. In this way, if he now assumes that he is the only person with consciousness, then only he gets to be the chooser and the paradox is solved. This philosophy is called solipsism, but Wigner could not be happy with it. He found it disturbing that his friend would have to stay in a state of suspended possibility until Wigner looked at him!

Who gets to choose?

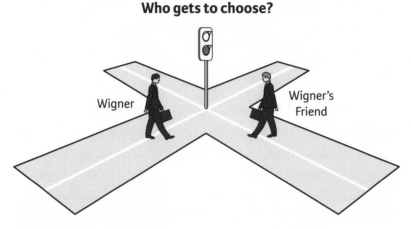

FIGURE 12. Who gets to choose?

As discussed previously, the solution to the paradox is: consciousness is one, nonlocal and cosmic, behind the two people's local individuality (Bass 1971; Goswami 1989, 1993; Blood 1993, 2001). Wigner and his friend both choose but only figuratively speaking; the one consciousness chooses for both of them, avoiding any contradiction. This allows the result dictated by quantum probability calculations that, in many such crossings, Wigner and his friend would each get a green light 50 percent of the time; yet for any individual crossing, a creative opportunity for getting green is left open for each.

Notice that we regain objectivity. Cosmic consciousness, being universal, is objective. You can call it God, but now God is scientific; it is quantum consciousness. And its choice for many people and many events is also objective, being in accordance with quantum probability calculations. So physics and chemistry, indeed any science of nonliving objects, are for all practical purposes safe from any revision.

And yet a window of opportunity has opened for any individual observer for an individual event of collapse where the choice can be creative without violating the overall demand of probabilities. But this freedom of choice is a privilege, not a right. You can earn the privilege if you can access cosmic, nonlocal consciousness where the choice is.

Grinberg-Zylberbaum's Experiment

As mentioned before, the first experiment proving the nonlocality of consciousness unequivocally (that is, with objective machines and not through subjective experiences of people) was performed by the neurophysiologist Jacobo Grinberg-Zylberbaum and his collaborators at the University of Mexico. Let's go into some details.

The principle of locality says that all communication must proceed through local signals that have a speed limit. Einstein established this speed limit as the speed of light (the enormous but finite speed of 300,000 km/sec). So this locality principle, a limitation imposed by Einsteinian thinking, precludes instantaneous communication via signals. And yet, quantum objects are able to influence one another instantly, once they interact and become correlated through quantum nonlocality. Physicist Alain Aspect and his collaborators (1982) demonstrated this with a pair of photons (quanta of light). The data do not have to be seen as a contradiction to Einsteinian thinking once we recognize quantum nonlocality for what it is—a signal-less interconnectedness (discontinuously) outside space and time.

Aspect's experiment is in itself enough to repudiate scientific materialism, but physicists today are a conservative bunch. There is the rumor that at a Physical Society meeting one reputable physicist said to another something to the effect that anyone who does not see the radical importance of Aspect's experiment "must have rocks in his head." But rocks in their heads or not, most physicists choose to ignore the verdict of Aspect's experiment because it speaks of the submicroscopic domain of nature and may not be relevant for the macroworld in which we live.

Fortunately, an experiment in the macroworld soon followed. In 1993, Grinberg-Zylberbaum was trying to demonstrate the quantum nonlocality of two correlated brains. Two people meditate together with the intention of direct (signal-less, nonlocal) communication. After twenty minutes, they are separated (while still continuing their unifying intention), placed in individual Faraday cages (electromagnetically impervious chambers), and each brain is wired up to an electroencephalogram (EEG) machine. Subject A is shown a series of light flashes, which produces in his or her brain an electrical activity that is recorded by the EEG machine, from which an "evoked potential" is extracted upon eliminating the brain noise with the help of a computer. The evoked potential is somehow found to be transferred to the brain of subject B, as indicated by the EEG of subject B, which gives (upon subtraction of brain noise) a transferred potential (similar to the evoked potential in phase and strength). This is shown in Figure 13a.

Control subjects (those who do not meditate together or are unable to hold the intention for signal-less communication for the duration of the experiment) do not show any transferred potential (Figure 13b). What is the explanation of the transferred potential? When I first talked with Jacobo on the telephone, he was clearly puzzled; he wanted me to explain his data. So I flew to Mexico City, checked out his experimental details, and immediately knew the import of his data. The experiment demonstrates the nonlocality of brain responses, as Jacobo suspected, but something even more important—nonlocality of quantum consciousness. How else to explain how the forced choice of the evoked response in one subject's brain can lead to the free choice of an (almost) identical response in the correlated partner's brain? So with great excitement, Jacobo and I (and the two students involved, Leah Attie and J. Delaflor) wrote the paper on transferred potential that was published in the journal *Physics Essays* (Grinberg-Zylberbaum et al. 1994).

Grinberg-Zylberbaum's experiment proved quantum nonlocality by demonstrating that the communication between the subjects could not have taken place electromagnetically. In 1995, I invited him to come to Vivekananda Kendra in India to give a talk at a conference and to begin a collaboration with the scientists there to prove the instantaneous nature of the communication (a more direct demonstration of nonlocality) between the two subjects in the experiment by placing one subject in Mexico and the other in India. Jacobo came and gave the talk, but soon after, before the experiment was put into actuality, he just vanished (rumor is that the CIA may have been involved; I don't know)!

The good news is that not one, but four separate experiments are now showing that quantum consciousness, the author of downward causation, is nonlocal, is unitive, is God. Jacobo's experiment has been replicated several times since 1994, first by the neuropsychiatrist Peter Fenwick and collaborators (Sabel et al. 2001) in London, second by Jiri Wackermann and his colleagues (Wackermann et al. 2003), and again by the Bastyr University researcher Leana Standish and her collaborators (Standish et al. 2004).

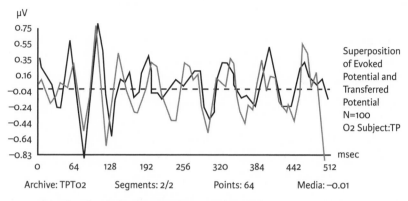

a) Overlap of evoked and tranferred potential (grey line).

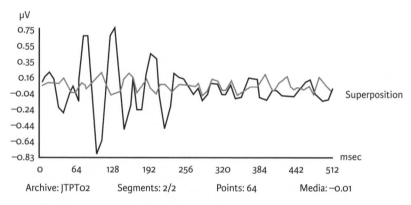

b) Overlap of the 2 potentials for the control group.
Absence of transferred potential (grey line).

FIGURE 13. (a) Overlap of evoked and transferred potiential. (b) Overlap of the 2 potentials for the control group. Absence of transferred potiential.

The conclusion of these experiments is radical. Quantum consciousness, the precipitator of the downward causation of choice from quantum possibilities, is what esoteric spiritual traditions call God. We have rediscovered God within science. And more. These experiments usher in a new paradigm of science based not on the primacy of matter as the old science was, but on the primacy of consciousness. Consciousness is the ground of all being, which we can now recognize as what the spiritual traditions call variously Godhead (Christianity), Brahman (Hinduism), Ein Sof (Judaism), and Shunyata (Buddhism).

Discontinuity Elaborated

Downward causation occurs in a nonordinary state of consciousness that we call God consciousness. Yet we are unaware of it. Why the unawareness? For millennia, mystics have been telling us about the oneness of God consciousness and our consciousness, but we haven't heard for the most part. Why this lack of hearing?

The Upanishads of Hinduism state emphatically that you are That, meaning, you are God! Jesus said, no less emphatically, that we are all children of God. This is a key. We are children of God; we have to grow up to realize our God consciousness. There are mechanisms (conditioning, see later) that obscure our Godness, eventually giving rise to our ordinary I-separateness, which we call ego. This ego creates a barrier against seeing our oneness with God and oneness with one another. Growing in spirituality means growing beyond the ego.

A key point is that the quantum downward causation of choice is discontinuously exerted. If choice were continuous, a mathematical model, at least a computer algorithm, could be constructed for it. Then the outcome of the choice would be predictable, and its author would be redundant and could not be called God, who is causally empowered. Our ordinary waking state of consciousness dominated by the ego smoothes out the discontinuity by compromising our freedom to choose. To be aware that we choose freely is to jump beyond the ego, taking a discontinuous leap, call it a quantum leap.

Whenever you are having difficulty picturing a discontinuous quantum leap, think of Niels Bohr's model of the atom. Electrons go around the atomic nucleus in continuous orbits. But when an electron jumps from one orbit to another, it makes the jump in a very discontinuous manner; it never goes through the intermediate space between the orbits. The jump is a quantum leap.

How does the cosmic, nonlocal quantum consciousness, God, identify with an individual, become individualized? How does continuity obscure the discontinuity? Primarily, via observership and, secondarily, via conditioning. Before observership comes about, God consciousness is one and undivided from its possibilities. Observership implies a subject-object split, a split between the self and the world (see explanation to follow). Before conditioning, however, the world-experiencing subject or self is unitive and cosmic. When God consciousness chooses its response to the stimulus from the quantum possibilities offered to it by the stimulus with total creative freedom (subject only to the constraint of the laws of quantum dynamics of the situation—God is objective and lawful; it is Her laws, after all!), the result is the primary experience of the stimulus (in the superconscious state) in its suchness. As God identifies with the superconscious state, we call it the quantum self (holy spirit, in Christianity). With additional experiences of the same stimulus that lead to learning, the responses get prejudiced in favor of past responses to the stimulus. This is what psychologists call conditioning (Mitchell and Goswami 1992).

Identifying with the conditioned pattern of stimulus responses (habits of character) and the history of the memories of past responses gives the subject/self an apparent local individuality, the ego (for further details, see Goswami 1993). When we operate from the ego, our individual patterns of conditioning, our experiences, being predictable, acquire an apparent causal continuity. We feel separate from our unitive whole quantum self and from God. It is then that our intentions don't usually produce the intended result.

The Question of Free Will

The sum and substance of conditioning is that as consciousness progressively identifies with the ego, there is a corresponding loss of freedom. In the limit of infinite conditioning, the loss of freedom is 100 percent. At that stage, the only choice left to us, metaphorically speaking, is the choice between flavors of ice cream: chocolate or vanilla, a choice between conditioned alternatives. Not that we want to undermine the value of even this much freedom, but obviously, this is not real freedom. It is, in principle, achievable even by machines such as a neural network. Within this conditioned limit, behaviorism holds; it is the so-called correspondence principle limit of the new science: within the limit of infinite conditioning, the new science predicts the same results as the old science.

But never fear. We never go that far down the pike of conditioning; we don't live that long. Even in our ego, we retain some freedom. A most important aspect of the freedom that we retain is the freedom to say no to conditioning, which allows us to be creative every once in a while.

There is experimental data in favor of what I am saying. In the 1960s, neurophysiologists discovered the so-called P300 event-related potential, which suggested our conditioned nature. Suppose as a demonstration of your free will, you declare your freedom to raise your right arm and proceed to do it. Guess what? By looking at machinery attached to your brain, a neurophysiologist can easily predict from the appearance of the P300 wave that you are going to raise your arm. Actions of "free will" that can be predicted are not examples of real freedom.

So is the behaviorist right that there is no free will for the ego? Maybe the mystics who say that the only free will is God's will, to which we must surrender, are right. But then there is the paradox: how do we surrender to God's will if we are not free to surrender?

But again, never fear. The neurophysiologist Benjamin Libet (1985) did an experiment that rescues a modicum of free will even for the ego. Libet asked his subjects to negate raising their arms as soon as they became aware of their willingness to raise their arms. Neurophysiologists could still predict from the P300 the raising of the arm, but more often than not, Libet's subjects were able to resist their will and not raise their arms, demonstrating that they retained their free will to say no to the conditioned action of raising their arms.

Direct Experimental Evidence of Discontinuity: Is Creativity a Quantum Leap?

On the external physical plane, quantum effects tend to be smoothed out at the macro level. We have to look inside at the mental plane, and that's where creativity is and, with it, the evidence for the discontinuity of downward causation.

What is creativity? Creativity consists of a discovery of new mental meaning of value, says researcher Teresa Amabile (1990); it involves a big change in how we process meaning.

Consider Einstein's discovery of the relativity theory. When Einstein was a teenager, he came across a conflict between two theories of physics; one by Isaac Newton, the other by Clerk Maxwell. Both great theories, and both verified in their own right in the domain of their originator's intent. But the domains have overlaps, and conflicts erupt in the domain of the overlap. Einstein worked a long ten years on the problem of resolving the conflict, made some progress even, but a complete solution seemed out of reach. Until one day, he discovered a brilliant new context for his entire thinking. The context of the problem was two conflicting theories of physics; but the context of his solution was how we look at time.

Before Einstein, people thought that time is absolute, that is, everything happens in time while time is unaffected by other movements. Wrong, said Einstein's creative insight. Time is relative to motion. A moving clock, as one carried in a spaceship, runs slower. This new context of looking at time resolved the conflict between Newton's theory and Maxwell's theory and enabled Einstein to discover $E = mc^2$. This is an example of the discontinuity of creativity: the "aha!" surprise proves it. Thus it is that Einstein said, "I did not discover relativity by rational thinking alone."

To their credit, even many materialist scientists today agree with the idea that creative insights are quantum jumps in mental meaning and that they arrive discontinuously. This is partly because there is now a large body of creativity research that, through many case studies, has solidly established that creative insights, be they in the arts or in the sciences, are sudden. It is also partly because many scientists intuit from their own experience the discontinuity of scientific creativity.

And of course, it is not just in science. There is enormous evidence of discontinuous quantum leaps in the arts, music, literature, and mathematics. You can find the evidence in many case histories compiled by creativity researchers (for example, Briggs 1990).

But the best proof for you, dear quantum activist, of the discontinuity of the quantum leaps of creativity is your own childhood experiences of learning new contexts of meaning. The scientist Gregory Bateson classified learning in two ways. Learning I is learning within a given fixed context of meaning, for example, rote learning. But there is also learning II, which involves a shift of the context. This one takes a quantum leap.

I remember my mother teaching me numbers when I was three years old. At first, I was memorizing how to count up to 100. Not much fun, I did it because my mother insisted. She fixed the context. The numbers themselves had no meaning for me. Then she was showing me two pencils, two cats, or sets of three rupees, three shirts. This went on for a while, then one day, unexpectedly, I got it. The difference between two and three (and all other numbers) became clear to me. Implicitly, I had understood numbers within a new context, the set, though not in that language, of course. It was an extremely joyful experience.

In the same vein, you may remember the experience of comprehending connected meaning for the first time in learning to read a story. Or the experience of comprehending what the purpose of algebra is. Or the experience of hearing and comprehending how individual notes properly arranged and composed make music come alive. Our childhood is full of the quantum leaping of such experiences.

Most importantly, there is now objective evidence for discontinuous quantum leaps of creativity. Bateson (1980) found evidence of such quantum leaps in how dolphins are trained to learn totally new tricks. Even more objective, physician Deepak Chopra (1990) saw discontinuous quantum leaps as the explanation of spontaneous healing phenomena, which he called quantum healing (see also Goswami 2004). Last but not least, the fossil gaps of biological evolution are explained as discontinuous quantum leaps of biological creativity (Goswami 2008b).

How Come Experience? The Hard Question

The philosopher David Chalmers created a minor commotion at a conference on consciousness in the 1990s. He asked the assembled gathering of people, many of whom were neurophysiologists, the question: what is the neurophysiological explanation of experience in which there always is a subject and an object? The question is a "hard" question for neurophysiologists because their models of consciousness always seek an explanation in terms of other objects, such as neurons. But, said Chalmers, with quiet drama: objects can only beget objects. Where does the subject of an experience come from?

A paradox from the neurophysiologist G. Ramachandran clarifies further why the question is hard. Suppose, said Ramachandran, you and your friends are looking at a bunch of red roses at a future time when we have the technology of analyzing brain states upon receiving a stimulus (for example, which neurons of which brain area are excited, and so forth). Since neurophysiological description is objective, your brain state does not have any discernible difference from the brain states of your friends. You have no reason to suspect that the measured description of all the other people's brain states is not complete. And yet, you know that as far as your own brain state is concerned, something is left out, namely, your subjective experience of the redness of the roses. So the objective description of your brain state, supertechnology or not, is incomplete. Since your friends' brain states are identical to yours, their objective descriptions must be incomplete as well.

One way out is to give special privilege to the observer, you, which is solipsism; but that is likewise not a desirable philosophy. So the materialist is caught between Scylla and Charybdis: either the objective description is incomplete or solipsism. Hard question, indeed. It is a downright paradox, a breakdown of logic.

The primacy-of-consciousness interpretation of quantum physics can resolve the paradoxical situation of the materialist because, in that interpretation, it is explicitly granted that the quantum physical description of the brain can never include consciousness, the collapser of possibilities, and, in that admission of incompleteness, room is made for a conscious experience.

Even so, the brain and the hard question are not easy problems to handle. The neurosurgeon Wilder Penfield put it well when he said, "Where is the subject and where is the object when you are operating on your own brain?" Mystics express the same sentiment with statements such as "What we are looking for is what is looking." Or consider this one: "[For the brain] the observer is the observed." Even when we begin with a metaphysics of the primacy of consciousness, how the one consciousness becomes two—subject and object—has not been easy to comprehend.

Fortunately, the previously mentioned von Neumann chain gives us a powerful hint. The chain does not terminate with any number of material measuring machines. Such an infinite hierarchy of machines has been correctly recognized (Peres and Zurek 1982) as a "Gödelian knot." The mathematician Kurt Gödel identified such hierarchies as tangled hierarchies, as opposed to simple hierarchies in which the cause-effect relation is one-way between the levels and does terminate (see, for example, Figure 1 in chapter 1). The key point for us to note is that, empirically speaking, the von Neumann chain terminates with the brain, which leads to the conclusion that the brain is not a conventional simple hierarchical machine but has a tangled hierarchy of an infinite von Neumann chain within it. How does the brain manage that?

Circularity, Tangled Hierarchy, and Self-Reference

The artificial intelligence researcher Doug Hofstadter (1980) gave some great examples of tangled hierarchy in systems with causal circularity. For example, consider the liar's paradox, the sentence "I am a liar." If I am telling the truth, then I am lying. If I am lying, then I am telling the truth, ad infinitum. The infinite oscillation of a circular hierarchy is tantamount to a tangled hierarchy. If you think about it, you notice a similar causal circularity in the quantum measurement situation involving the brain as well: there is no collapse without the [observer's] brain, but there is no [actualized] brain state without collapse.

Therefore the solution is: how the brain manages a tangled hierarchy within it is to have a circular hierarchy of two systems within it. One system is connected with perception, a quantum system that presents, in response to an external stimulus, macroscopically distinguishable quantum states to choose from. The other system is near classical, connected with memory making. Perception requires memory, and memory requires perception. How does a tangled hierarchical system like this come about in the brain? If the brain were simple-hierarchical, reductionistic, made in a step-by-step way (as in Darwinian evolution), it would be extremely unlikely (as materialists love to point out) that there could be a macroscopic quantum system in the brain. But as I have pointed out elsewhere (Goswami 2008b), the evolution of a tangled hierarchical system like the brain requires creative downward causation and creative evolution.

In *Print Gallery*, the artist M. C. Escher depicted a young man inside a gallery looking at a picture of a ship that is anchored in the harbor of a town, which has a print gallery in which there is a young man who is looking at a ship. . . . This is a tangled hierarchy because after going through all those buildings of the town, the picture comes back to the original point where it starts, to begin its oscillation again, perpetually holding the attention of whoever is looking at it. If you have seen the picture, you may have wondered why there is big white spot in the middle of the picture. Escher knew that this kind of art has to violate the step-by-step rules of constructing a painting; as a reminder, he put a white spot in the picture to signify discontinuity.

What is most important to notice is that once you enter a tangled hierarchical system such as the liar's sentence or Escher's *Print Gallery,* you can't get out if you keep to the message. The system has isolated itself from the rest of the world of discourse. It is what is called a self-referential system; it is referring to itself.

So similarly, when transcendent consciousness collapses the macroscopic state of the brain, it gets caught in it and identifies with it. In this way, in the brain itself, there is no observer separate from the observed brain state; the observer is the observed! In this way, the brain becomes the observer, the subject that experiences the external stimulus as the object of the experience.

Do you see? God and God's downward causation are essential to resolving the quantum measurement paradox and to understanding the brain.

More on the Paradox of Perception: Idealism or Realism?

Almost every experimental neurophysiologist or cognitivist (in fact, most people) has an underlying model of perception. An object presents our perceptual apparatus—the brain—with a stimulus. The brain processes this stimulus, first with the eye and its retina, and then with the brain's higher centers. Eventually, an integrated representation of the stimulus/object is made defining an image in a field of perception. And it is this image that we see. This is called the representation theory of perception.

But many questions thwart any easy validity to this very reasonable picture. Say, you are looking at a big New York skyscraper. And you see a big skyscraper, no doubt. Obviously, however, your brain does not have enough room for a direct representation/image of this "big" building. So where is this image that you see located?

Furthermore, the representation must be made of neuronal activity of some sort—an electrical image. How do your neuronal activities add up to a big building that you actually see?

In addition, imaging techniques show that the representation requires the involvement of different brain areas that are spatially separated. How does the brain put together all this information if there are only material interactions that are local, taking place via signals that take time to communicate? This is called the binding problem.

Further, how can we tell that the neuronal activities of my brain (the representation) really represent an external object if we can never directly see and compare with the object in its suchness?

Also, are you not assuming that there is somehow a TV screen with a real picture on it (of the external object) in the back of your head and somehow you are looking at it? But if there is a homunculus (a little replica of yourself) doing the looking inside the brain, don't we need another homunculus to retrieve the information gained by the first one? Ad infinitum.

And finally, if all we experience is neuronal sensations in our brain—inside stuff—then why assume outside physical objects at all? Why not say that there is nothing but me and my sensations, why not succumb to solipsism? Or at least why not succumb to the kind of (dualistic) idealism that philosopher Bishop Berkeley posited, which you may have pondered during your college days?

Let's recap this latter philosophy. When Descartes' version of mind-body, internal-external dualism dominated Western thinking and nobody could answer the question of how mind and matter can interact, the philosophy of (dualistic) idealism was Bishop Berkeley's resolution. Berkeley made the point that we receive all the information about the so-called external material world through our sense experiences that are internal. Since there is no way to directly verify the reality of the external world of matter, why postulate it at all? Why not assert that only mind of the mind-matter duo is real? No matter, no problem of interaction.

You may have pondered Berkeley's philosophy in connection with the puzzle, if a tree falls in a forest but there is no one there to hear the sound of the tree falling, is there a sound or not? Newtonian physics says that there must be a sound, whereas Berkeley seems to be saying there is not a sound because there is no "mind" around. So the puzzle was created to discredit Berkeley's idealist philosophy in favor of (material) realism:

There was once a man who said, "God
Must think it exceedingly odd
If He finds that this tree
Continues to be
When there is no one about in the quad.

So Berkeley came up with an answer to the puzzle:
Dear Sir, your astonishment's odd
I am always about in the quad.
And that's why the tree
Will continue to be
Since observed by, Yours faithfully, God.

The problem with this kind of thinking is that it retains the God's Mind–human mind dualism while unifying the mind-matter dualism, and so the usual argument of material monists against dualism can still be raised to refute Berkeley—how does God interact with the human mind?

If all these objections seem valid, why not posit that the brain directly perceives the object? This gives us the philosophy called direct realism: external objects are real and the brain directly perceives them without the intermediary of some internal images of them.

Think. It is a fact that all our knowledge—about brain and about perception—comes from perception itself. How can we use knowledge obtained by perception to refute the direct perception model?

So does the direct perception model make more sense than the representation model and is realism a better philosophy than idealism? Well, the direct perception model, objective realism, has its own shortcomings; it does not explain how the subjective experience inherent in perception can arise from an object (brain) interacting with an external object. There is the old "hard question" again. Also, there are clearly cases in which the properties of the representation-making capacity of the brain enter. For example, in color perception, is the color a property of the object? Most researchers now agree that color is a property of the object as well as that of the brain representation.

Moreover, very importantly, there is Ramachandran's paradox, which we considered previously. Direct perception does not explain the subjective qualia (a technical term philosophers use to connote the specific quality of a subjectively felt experience) of our perception.

So we get into some inescapable conclusions from all this which is why people incessantly debate about how we can perceive at all (Smythies 1994). That the brain makes representations and the representations have an effect on what we see are undoubtedly true. On the other hand, a television screen and a homunculus-in-the-brain viewing pictures on it of an outside object that resembles the outside object is also hard to rationalize. The binding problem is a hard problem for the representation theorist as well. Finally, the philosophical problem of solipsism and dualistic idealism, and, additionally, the problem of comparing with the direct perception model loom large.

Ultimately, the philosophical debate is one between (dualistic) idealism and (direct) realism. Dualistic idealists see the world as ideas and perception happens because of what we see inside of us. Idealists are the pure brand of representation theorists. Realists insist that the objects we see are outside and are the only reality. They want to avoid any reference to objects that are internal like the representations inside the brain.

In the following, I will show that the philosophy of monistic, not dualistic, idealism can incorporate realism in such a way as to offer resolution to all the problems of perception.

Do We Have Two Heads?

To repeat, realism says that only the external object is real; only objects that we find "outside" of us are real because they are public and we can get consensus about them and make them the object of objective scientific scrutiny. (Dualistic) idealism says that we cannot directly see what is "outside" without the help of the intermediaries of our "inside" private representations. So these inside representations must be more real than the objects they represent. Or rather, they better be, because objects in their suchness we will never know.

Two philosophers, Gottfried Leibniz and Bertrand Russell (for a good discussion, see Robinson 1984), have an inclusive solution. Suppose we have a "big" head in addition to the small head that we normally experience, such that so-called outside objects are outside the small head but inside the big head. Then aren't both realism and idealism valid? Realism because the objects are outside (the small head). Idealism because objects are also inside (the big head).

It sounds like sophistry only until you process the solution through quantum thinking. Behold!

Quantum Consciousness and a Model of Perception That Works

We can recognize our "big" head in quantum terminology as our capacity for nonlocal processing, which includes all "small" heads. In other words, when you choose in quantum consciousness or God consciousness, you are operating from the big head, and all objects are "inside" of you. The choice collapses the wave of possibility of an object and also the wave of possibility of your small head, the brain. You identify with the brain state collapsed and do not see it as an object. You see the object/stimulus separate from you, giving you a "spiritual" experience of immediacy in which the object is seen in its "suchness."

If the object/stimulus is one you previously experienced, however, you do not usually recognize this "primary" collapse event. Instead, you see the object upon repeated reflection from the mirror of memory, which is subjective and individual. The memories modulate the secondary collapse events so that your perception of the collapsed object acquires an individual flavor. This is what gives you the subjective qualia of perception.

Experiments show that the processing time of secondary collapse events is 500 milliseconds or thereabouts (Libet 1979). When you finally recognize the object, you are quite identified with your memory, which you have just sifted through unconsciously. You are your ego self conditioned by these memories, the "small" head of individuality. From this perspective, you see the material object to be outside of you because of the fixity of the physical world.

How about that television-image-in-an-inner-theater aspect of the representation theory? We have been forgetting something so far. Along with the external physical object and the observer's brain, there is something else that quantum consciousness collapses routinely—the mind that gives meaning to our observation. The brain representations of the stimulus are literally brain neuronal states. They are not unlike the electronic movement on a TV screen. But we do not see the electronic patterns when we watch TV, do we? Instead, our mind gives meaning to the Rorschach of fluorescent spots on the screen produced by the electronic movement. Similarly, in the case of perception, our mind gives the meaning to the neuronal configurations of the brain representations. Eventually, it is our mind that helps produce the recognizable image of the object of primary perception from the current neuronal representation as modulated by memory.

The model presented also solves the oneness of experience of the binding problem. Because consciousness is fundamentally nonlocal, it can bind together all the different brain areas to produce one unified brain state of collapse.

So the final resolution of all the paradoxical questions of perception based on quantum physics and monistic idealism as presented here combines the best of realism and (dualistic) idealism, direct realism and representation theories. At the same time, it explains the suchness experiences that are denied in the Western philosophical tradition but that have long been recognized as spiritual experiences in all the major traditions. The theory also explains the qualia of normal perception and solves the binding problem. And, most importantly, the problem of the subject-object split nature of conscious awareness and the ego-modality of normal perception are also explained.

Can Quantum Measurement Be Completed by a Material Machine?

Let's summarize:

1. Von Neumann's theorem says that material interactions can only produce possibility, not actuality. This is the mathematical proof of the need for downward causation from a nonmaterial agency.

2. The observer effect makes us, our consciousness, the prime candidate for this nonmaterial agent of downward causation. But then there is the paradox of Wigner's friend—who gets to choose if there are two simultaneous observers? The solution of this paradox reveals the twofold nature of our consciousness: it is individual in

our conditioned and ordinary ego, but nonlocal, cosmic in the non-ordinary consciousness in which free choice is made.

3.   There is also the paradox of circularity: the observer's brain is needed for choice, but without choice, there is no manifest observer or his or her brain in a state of actuality. The resolution is that the subject that chooses is cocreated with the object, the chosen. The brain has a tangled hierarchy in its structure, another name for circularity. Because of the tangled hierarchy, consciousness identifies with the brain and perceives itself separate from the object(s) of perception; tangled hierarchy in the brain produces self-reference. This gives us an answer to what is sometimes called the "hard question": how does the subject arise at all from the interaction of objects that is the brain? It also asserts what mystics say: our separateness from the world of objects is appearance arising from the tangled hierarchy of quantum measurement. East Indian mystics called this causal action that produces separateness *maya*.

In view of all this, it is a bit surprising that many physicists still stubbornly hold on to the notion that material machines are adequate to make quantum measurements, that it is not necessary to invoke consciousness. These physicists cite primarily two ideas that they think solve the quantum measurement problem adequately. One of these ideas is called decoherence; the other goes by the name of "many worlds" interpretation or theory.

Let's take up decoherence. It is a mathematical idea, but be patient; you can grasp it. Quantum objects are possibility waves and can be thought of as packets of possibility with phase relationship (coherence, as in a dancing chorus line) among its components. What does that mean? The phase relationship produces an interference pattern (as in the double slit experiment) that can be measured to tell us the quantum nature of the packet.

For a composite object with a few components, it is easy to do an interference experiment to verify the existence of phase coherence among the components of the possibility packet. What happens for a macro object is that there are so many component micro objects making up the macro that the slightest perturbation will tend to destroy the phase relationships so much so that it would take a very long time, much longer than the life of the universe, to measure the quantum nature of such a packet. So for all practical purposes, such a macro object is not quantum.

You have to see through the falsity of such arguments. The absence of any practical ability to measure the quantum nature in the near future, of course, does not say that the object has become Newtonian, or that a measurement has taken place. In principle, the quantum nature can be measured in a finite time; von Neumann's theorem stands. Decoherence can never substitute for the collapse event.

Much confusion exists because the quantum measurement paradox is often discussed within an intriguing schema called the paradox of Schrödinger's cat. A cat is left in an opaque cage with a door, in the company of a single radioactive atom (with a half-life of one hour, which means that the probability is 50–50 that the atom will decay within the hour) and a diabolical scheme. If the atom decays, then a Geiger counter detects the radiation from the decay. The ticking of the counter triggers a hammer to break a poison bottle, releasing cyanide that kills the cat. If the atom does not decay, none of the sequential things happens, and the cat lives. Since the decay is probabilistic, a quantum process, it follows that at the hour, the cat is a wave of possibility, having two equally weighted facets, dead and alive. The cat is literally half-dead and half-alive!

What the decoherence theorists have been able to show is this (and even this within certain assumptions): there is complete decoherence between the components of such macro description as "Schrödinger's cat is a superposition of a dead cat and a live cat." So if these theorists claim that the cat paradox has been solved, there is a grain of truth in that. But only in the sense that if the cat were a material machine, it probably could not present to an observer a macroscopically discernible dichotomy to choose from.

Many years ago, when I used to teach the Schrödinger's cat paradox to junior level students at the University of Oregon, some students would always ask: why can't the cat collapse its own possibility wave? This is the point! The cat is a living sentient being; there is tangled hierarchy—a discontinuity—in its brain, and that means one very important thing with which the followers of decoherence must engage. A cat's brain, like a human brain, has a tangled hierarchy built into its construction. You cannot reduce the perceptual apparatus of a cat's brain into its microcomponents.

It is an irreducible whole. It is the irreducible whole that can be described as a coherent superposition of macroscopically distinguishable states from which consciousness chooses, precipitating the collapse that gives self-reference. And oh, yes! The cat does not need us to do the collapsing of its quantum state; it can do the job itself as long as it is alive.

As for the many worlds theory, its inadequacy in explaining quantum measurement without paradox is old hash. Think of the double slit situation. According to the many worlds theory, the world bifurcates at the fluorescent plate but not at the slits. How does the universe know when to split—when is a macroscopic material arrangement a measuring apparatus and when is it not? Face it! Material interaction is material interaction; it can never change possibility into actuality, nor can it have a magic by which all of a sudden the universe would bifurcate by the mere interaction of an electron with another material object just because you call it a measuring apparatus.

Theories like the many worlds theory vainly try to show that downward causation is not necessary. But what's the point, in view of the fact that David Bohm has already demonstrated downward causation mathematically, using an approximate average form of the mathematical equation of quantum physics (see chapter 3)?

The fact is that according to the collapse-by-consciousness theory, a quantum measurement event is nonlocal, discontinuous, and tangled hierarchical. And this is experimentally verifiable. Furthermore, material interactions cannot produce or simulate any of these attributes of the measurement event. So the verification of nonlocality, discontinuity, and tangled hierarchy that I have discussed here should convince even the die-hard materialist. And, dear materialist, if you are still not convinced, prove me wrong. Try to construct a conscious computer! You will never be able to do it.

Discovering God for Yourself

I can now tell you the reason for my optimism for planetary transformation. I said before that, even since Descartes, philosophers in the West have been struggling to find a path to God, wholeness, and downward causation using pure reason. They have not succeeded. Even in the East, where there is a wisdom tradition that uses reason combined with meditation, it takes people many years to discover God, wholeness, and downward causation.

Now look at the situation from the point of view of our new Western wisdom path of quantum physics, primacy of consciousness, and experimental data. We have managed to cut down the time it takes for God wisdom to awaken in us from years to days, perhaps even hours.

In the olden days, therefore, people followed the devotional path of transformation rather than the wisdom path. But guess what? The practice of love without wisdom has never worked, explaining why religions of the world have failed for millennia to transform humanity, despite all their efforts. But now that everyone can access wisdom in a short time, we can get to the task of transformation much faster.

Even so, you can argue that not everyone is yet ripe to be a quantum activist. But again, the new science gives us very good reason to believe that even if only a small fraction of us become inspired to change, the change will come for all (see chapter 11).

CHAPTER 5

The Importance of Being Subtle

Jesus, whom I regard as one of the earliest quantum activists, said in the Gospel of Thomas:

> When you make the two one,
> and when you make the inner as the outer
> and the outer as the inner,
> and the above as the below,
> and when you make
> the male and the female into a single one
> so that the male will not be male
> and the female not be female,
> then shall you enter the Kingdom.

In the currently prevalent materialist view, the metaphorical "below," the manifest world is the only one recognized, but this is now history. In the integrative view of quantum physics, the "above" (transcendent consciousness and its possibilities) and the "below" (the world of manifestation) are both validated within the metaphysics of the primacy of consciousness. Understanding this integration opens the door for us to live in such a way as to make the two—transcendent and immanent—as one. In this chapter, we will discuss the remaining tasks that Jesus foresaw for us.

The first is to develop an integrative view for the inner and the outer or, as philosophers put it, the resolution of the mind-body dichotomy. As a political truce between science and religion, Descartes created the dichotomy, but the truce did not last because the dichotomy is not scientifically tenable. Materialists gained ground and the worldview became topsy-turvy in favor of the outer. We need to reestablish the inner on an equal footing with the outer if we ever want to live in integrative balance between the two.

The male-female dichotomy in which the male refers to reason and the female refers to feelings came about in the course of human evolution. The new view of evolution as an evolution of consciousness will show us how the dichotomy arose (see chapter 6) and will also lead the way to integration (see part 2).

Inner and Outer, Gross and Subtle Possibilities

Materialists have bamboozled us into believing that matter is the only thing, although our experience says otherwise. Since our experiences comprise two radically different varieties, one external and public (and therefore gross), the other internal and private (and therefore subtle), traditionally we have distinguished between gross and subtle or matter and mind, if you will.

In the new science, we posit that consciousness carries within it four compartments of quantum possibilities from which it chooses its experiences (see Figure 4 in chapter 1). The four are: the physical, the collapse or manifestation of which we sense; the vital, whose manifestations we feel; the mental, whose manifestations we think; and the supramental, whose manifestations we intuit. Notice once more that there is no dualism in this reckoning because consciousness nonlocally mediates the interaction between these compartments without the exchange of any signals.

Why do we experience the physical as external experiences and the other worlds as internal? The physical is experienced as external and gross because of the micro-macro constitution of matter. At the macro level, matter loses much of its quantum movement and acquires approximate fixity; it becomes gross. Not a bad thing, because that is exactly what we need for a) a reference point and b) consciousness to use matter to make representations of the subtle. The vital-mental-supramental trio does not have any micro-macro division, however. In this way, quantum movement persists in all these worlds. In other words, the possibility waves of the objects of these worlds change too fast to allow you and me to collapse the same thought or the same feeling or the same intuition at the same time. So we each will ordinarily experience thoughts, feelings, and intuitions as private, not publicly shareable, and thus internal and subtle.

What Is the Logical Necessity for the Vital, Mental, and Supramental Bodies?

Materialists claim that neither the vital nor the mental nor the supramental body is needed. The functions of all can be performed by the physical body, which is the only body we have. However, recent research in the field of biological morphogenesis (form-making) has established why we need the vital body. Artificial intelligence research is showing us the value of the mind. As for the supramental, from the days of Plato we have known why the supramental must exist: where would the laws of physics come from otherwise?

Biological morphogenesis has the problem of cell differentiation. All multicellular organisms begin from a single cell embryo, which then divides, making exact replicas of itself, each containing identical DNA. But cells must be differentiated on their way to making organs because cells in different organs perform very different functions. The genes in the cells of different organs are activated differently to make different sets of proteins, thus different functions. But how could this happen if all interactions are local? Cell differentiation works as if the cell knows where in the body it is. In other words, cell differentiation smacks of nonlocality.

It was the biologist Rupert Sheldrake (1981) who first proposed that nonlocal and therefore nonphysical organizing principles, which he called morphogenetic fields, causally affect cell differentiation. If this sounds dualistic, I have further clarified Sheldrake's work (Goswami 2008a) by recognizing the mediating role of consciousness between the morphogenetic fields and biological forms (see the following).

Clearly, Sheldrake's work revives the nonphysical vital body and more. It clarifies its function. The vital body is the reservoir of the morphogenetic fields and is involved with providing consciousness with blueprints for making the biological organs. The physical body cannot do nonlocality because material interactions are always local; material interactions cannot even simulate nonlocality (Feynman 1981).

Now to the logical necessity for positing a nonphysical mind. Artificial intelligence researchers try to construct programmed computers that can think. Indeed, today's computer programs can generate contents of thought versatile enough to fool a human being, once considered to be a sufficient condition for a computer to be called intelligent. But the philosopher John

Searle (1994) first pointed out that, apart from content, thoughts also involve meaning, and a computer, being a symbol-processing machine, can never process meaning. We need a nonphysical mind to do that. Later Roger Penrose (1991) perfected Searle's proof.

As for the supramental, aside from being the source of the physical laws, it also acts as the reservoir for the archetypes of biological functions (of which the morphogenetic fields are blueprints) and the archetypes of mental meaning.

The Biology of Feeling and Emotions

The psychology of the East recognizes feelings as associated with the physiological organs and recognizes emotions as feelings combined with their effects on the mind as it gives meaning to the feelings. According to the Easterners, there are seven major centers in the body—the chakras—in which we feel our feelings. But through the centuries, although the idea of the chakras has found much empirical validation from spiritual disciplines, not much theoretical understanding has come. Now, finally, with the concept of Sheldrake's morphogenetic field, an explanation of the chakras, where feelings originate and why, can be given.

I have treated this subject in some detail elsewhere (Goswami 2004), so I will be succinct. You can discover for yourself what a little quantum thinking enables us to theorize scientifically. First, look at the major chakras (Figure 14) and notice that each of them is located near major organs for our body's biological functioning. Second, make a note of the feeling you experience at each of these chakras; feel free to use your memory of past feelings. Third, realize that feelings are your experiences of the vital energy—the movements of your morphogenetic fields. However, the same morphogenetic fields are correlated with the organ of which they are the blueprint/source. Now arrive at the inevitable conclusion: chakras are those points in our physical body where consciousness simultaneously collapses the movements of important morphogenetic fields along with the organs of our body that represent these morphogenetic fields.

It is the movement of the vital energy at these chakra points that we experience as feeling. Excess movement into (positive movement) the three lower chakras and all movement out (negative movement) are responsible for feelings connected with our instinctual negative emotions: lust, egotism, fear, and so on. Any amount of movement of vital energy into the higher chakras is connected with positive emotions; only movement out of these chakras is experienced as negative.

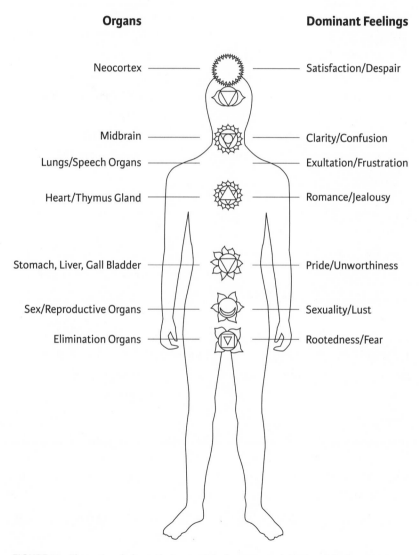

Organs   **Dominant Feelings**

Neocortex ——————— ——————— Satisfaction/Despair

Midbrain ——————— ——————— Clarity/Confusion

Lungs/Speech Organs ——————— ——————— Exultation/Frustration

Heart/Thymus Gland ——————— ——————— Romance/Jealousy

Stomach, Liver, Gall Bladder ——————— ——————— Pride/Unworthiness

Sex/Reproductive Organs ——————— ——————— Sexuality/Lust

Elimination Organs ——————— ——————— Rootedness/Fear

FIGURE 14. The major chakras, their associated organs, and dominant feelings.

The materialists have it all reversed. They think that we feel emotions in the brain, that is, emotions are brain epiphenomena. And then emotion comes to the body through the nervous system and in the so-called molecules of emotion, neuropeptides and such. But actually, it is the other way around. We feel feelings at the chakras and in the midbrain in response to a stimulus. Why the midbrain? Without some central control, we would be torn between seven vital egos, one at each chakra. Only eventually, the neocortex gets into the game, when mind gives meaning to the feelings. In the future, I will refer to the totality of the midbrain circuits and the associated neocortical circuits as the brain circuits of emotions.

Previously, I spoke of the unconscious. The famous Sigmund Freud was the first to discover it, and he talked about unconscious feelings and drives, ego defenses that maintain the status quo, and how these things erupt, signaling our neurosis. He propounded the technique of psychoanalysis to deal with this unconscious stuff.

In 1996, the depth psychologist James Hillman wrote a blistering criticism of psychoanalysis, pointing out how little success the technique has had in its hundred-year history! Psychoanalytic therapy works on the assumption that, in the event of a trauma, we experience a strong negative emotion and suppress it; subsequent recall of the event with the help of psychotherapy should then make the unconscious conscious and relieve the trauma.

In the hundred years since Freud, there have undoubtedly been quite a few cases of miraculous recovery, but I think it is fair to say that Hillman is also right. So why is psychoanalytic therapy ineffective? I suspect that, for most cases, the psychoanalytic picture of a trauma suppression is too idealized. I suspect that, in most traumas, the victim does recall the trauma a few times, enough to make reinforced correlated brain circuits in the limbic brain and the neocortex. The influence of such reinforced brain circuits of traumatic memory will be hard to get rid of through reliving and reconditioning. And this is only the personal unconscious. In addition, there are the instinctual brain circuits of negative emotions giving us eruptions of the collective unconscious of Jungian vintage.

Hence my conclusion: the only viable technique available to us right now to deal with the tyranny of negative emotions is to balance them with the production of positive emotional brain circuits. This is what our journey of transformation is largely about.

How Should We Change?

The recognition that our experiences consist of both the gross and the subtle raises fascinating new questions for all of us, for how we and our social systems should change. Consider:

- In materialism, only behavioral change, change in how other people see us, is important. In the new view, how we experience our internal environment is equally important. In other words, happiness matters.

- In the old view, the answer to the question "What is mind?" is a denigrating shrug, "Doesn't matter." In the new view, mind, the meaning giver, is important. If you don't mind, nothing matters. Matter is important because it enables us to make representations of feeling and meaning.

- In the materialist view, only what we can compute is considered valid, for example, rational thinking based on programmed meanings learned from the past. In the new view, feelings, new meanings brought forth by creativity, and intuitions are all valued.

- In the old view, love is an existential maneuver for sex. In the new view, sex is important not only because it allows our species to continue, but also because it can be used to make love.

- In the old view, our lack of mental health or psychopathology (neurosis) is curable by behavior modification or psychoanalytic techniques. In the new view, neurosis is mostly due to negative emotional brain circuits, and the best medicine is to heal by balancing their effects by making positive emotional brain circuits. This is a great recent finding of neurophysiology: brain neurons are highly plastic, allowing for our lifelong ability to make brain circuits of creative learning.

- In the materialist view, the role of the archetypes in our lives is dubious. Perhaps they have survival value, if they truly have evolved, and perhaps not. At best, they may have social convenience. In the new view, we live purposefully to learn the archetypes, to manifest them in our lives.

✢ In the old view, we live only one life. We live because of the survival drive from our genes, without any real purpose. In the new view, there is meaning in our lives, there is purpose. We need to survive, but only so we can explore meaning and learn the archetypes manifesting it in our lives. But anyone who has tried to manifest any of the great archetypes—truth, beauty, justice, love, and goodness—knows how difficult it is. So our designer (quantum consciousness) designed us in such a way that our mental and vital habit patterns along with our patterns of learning are stored nonlocally (Goswami 2001). When individuals in the future use the benefits of our learning, having inherited them nonlocally from a different space and a different time, they are our reincarnations. This is not just theory; there is substantial evidence in favor of such a view (Stevenson 1974, 1977, 1987).

✢ There is also evidence that the memory of a learned propensity is nonlocal. Some time ago, the neurophysiologist Karl Lashley did an experiment in which he was trying to study the location of the learning of a propensity in the brain. So he trained rats to find cheese in a Y-maze and then systematically began to chop off parts of the rat's brain and test if the propensity remained. Strangely, he found that even with 50 percent of its brain chopped off, a trained rat finds its way to the cheese. The only conclusion is that learned memory of a propensity is nonlocal. An alternative—that memory is holographic—was floated for a while by the neurophysiologist Karl Pribram, but that theory ran out of gas.

✢ In the materialist view, only our physical body is real; our physical body has evolved from an animal ancestry but there is no purpose to it. Our evolution is gradual and continuous, driven by blind chance and survival necessity in a struggle for existence in a changing environment (Darwin 1859). In the new view, in addition to continuous evolution, we have creative phases of evolution in which consciousness purposively creates new organ representation of the morphogenetic fields that are the vital blueprints of biological organs. In the new view, our evolution does not end with the representation making of the vital body, but continues with the better and better representation making of mental meaning once the brain evolves with the capacity of making meaning circuits.

:: The word "ecology" originates from the Greek *eikos,* meaning "place," and *logos,* meaning "knowledge." But usually, we say that ecology is about the knowledge of our physical environment. This is the old materialist view. Now that we acknowledge the internal as where we also live some of the time, our shallow ecology must give way to a deep ecology, in which we learn to care for both external and internal environments in accordance with the philosopher Arne Naess (see Devall and Sessions 1985).

:: Likewise our economics (etymologically, "economics" means the management of place) has to be extended to deal with not only the gross well-being, but also the subtle well-being.

:: Our three most important modern social institutions of capitalism, democracy, and liberal education have evolved under a modernist Cartesian worldview in which the goal was to make the processing of meaning available to increasingly large numbers of people. Under the materialist influence, this lofty goal has denigrated largely to trivial pursuits. Under the new view, we have an opportunity to revive these great social institutions in their original goals.

:: In the old materialist view, health care is all about the physical body and only the materialist medicine of allopathy is valid. The materialist view has given us the current crisis of health care because of skyrocketing costs. The new view recognizes the power of alternative medicine that cares for the subtle bodies and is promising a cost-contained integrative medicine.

:: Materialism, by taking the nothing-but-matter-is-real attitude, has led to the current conflict of science and religion. Through the clever use of secularism—the separation of state and religion— materialists have made it difficult to teach spiritual values to the masses, whereas their own quite unscientific material beliefs (such as "everything is matter") are taught freely in schools all over the world. Some religions have been so threatened by this that they have turned to terrorism to fight back. The new view will usher in a new age of post-secularism, in which spirituality is scientific, allowing a new dialog and truce.

CHAPTER 6

Do-be-do-be-do:
Think Quantum, Be Creative

Quantum physics says that objects are possibilities for you to choose from. Really, the primary ongoing question of your life is: are you going to choose same-old, same-old, or are you going to explore new possibilities? In other words, are you going to live in the conditioned but comfortable cocoon of your ego, or are you going to take some risk, aspire for the new, and explore your quantum consciousness?

If you lived in a Newtonian world, as materialists claim, the question of choice between creativity and conditioning would be moot. In the Newtonian world, depending on which scientist you are talking to, you are the atom's way of knowing about itself, or your genes' way of preserving and spreading themselves. In the latter view, your genes have managed to evolve a brain from their chance mutations driven by survival necessity. At best you are a by-product of your brain, the software of your computer-brain hardware. You were programmed through your evolutionary history and environmental conditioning as you grew up. Any computer is potentially capable of doing, and perhaps better than you, what you call your creative acts.

Fortunately for you, and for all of us, including the materialist, the real world is quantum, and so the question of choosing creativity over conditioning is real. In the real quantum world, your consciousness is the only reality and your brain is the by-product of the evolution of consciousness to make better and better representations of all the mental meaning available for you to explore in all the different contexts you can discover for your exploration. True, your past explorations produced conditioned way stations for your personality and character, but you don't have to be stuck in any one of them. You can always move on, changing your old order, replacing it with the new.

You can easily intuit that this is an exciting journey. I submit that the meaning of our lives rest in this journey, and that we have been engaged in this journey for many lives, something like the hero of the movie *Groundhog Day*.

Thinking Quantum

No one has to tell you how to think according to the dictates of your conditioned way station that you call your ego. It comes to you quite naturally. You often do it quite helplessly.

Creativity is far from this; creativity is not this ego stuff. This statement does not seem to help much until we put some structure to it. To that end, let's consider the rudiments of quantum thinking about creativity.

Quantum thinking consists of realizing that creativity ultimately consists of choosing the new among the quantum possibilities of meaning, giving us a new thought, discontinuous with all previous thoughts. Quantum physics says that the process is something like this: before you choose, waves of possibilities of meaning are developing in consciousness, in your consciousness, but you are not separate from them. This is called unconscious processing.

The virtue of a theory of conscious experience, which we developed in the last two chapters, is that, with its help, we can now formally distinguish between the unconscious and the conscious. "Unconscious" is when your consciousness is not separate from the possibilities that you are processing; "conscious" refers to awareness of the subject-object split—your consciousness is separate as a subject to the objects you are experiencing. (Slight misnomer here, thanks to Freud. Unconscious really means unaware.)

Ordinary thoughts follow a stream of consciousness. They are continuous, one more or less causally following the other. A creative thought does no such thing; it follows no cause, no other thought before. The passage from all the previous thought to the new creative one is fraught with discontinuity. You become separate from your stream-of-consciousness thinking, suddenly caught in a wonderful feeling of surprise. Aha!, a new thought, a creative insight. But you have no idea where the thought came from or how it arose in your awareness. Do more quantum thinking: a creative insight is a discontinuous event of thought, a quantum leap.

If a creative insight is a quantum leap, from what and to what is it a leap? In other words, where do creative insights come from? Perhaps you've already figured this out from the contents of your own creative ahas. Creative ideas come from the archetypal domain of our consciousness. In creativity, we take a quantum leap from the mind to the supramental.

If you catch yourself in that "aha!" moment of a creative insight, you see that your surprise not only involves the novelty of the object of your insight, but also the novelty of the subject of the insight. The "you" that is having the insight is a cosmic you; it is not the usual you with a personality, but a holistic you.

In the process of quantum leaping, your conscious identity has leaped from your ordinary state of consciousness, the ego, to a nonordinary cosmic unity of superconsciousness, which you may call your quantum self.

Realize that whereas you exist in a seemingly continuous state of arousal in your waking state, the arousal of the quantum self is quite discontinuous from this ordinary state of your consciousness. Realize that whereas you in your ordinary ego are local, quite identified with your local personality and history, your quantum self is nonlocal; its identity is the whole cosmos.

And here is the most subtle aspect of the creative experience, observed by only those few who want to investigate the very nature of this creative cosmic quantum self. The quantum self arises in awareness codependently with the new insight, the object in consciousness in its suchness.

In ordinary thinking, you think your thought; you are the head honcho—seemingly, the causal level. The thoughts seem to be secondary to you; they seem to be the caused level. What you have is a simple hierarchical relationship between you and your thoughts. But this is not so in creative thinking when there is codependency of the thinker and the thought—a codependency in which who causes what is blurred. This is a tangled hierarchical relationship.

So whereas you in your ego exist always in a simple hierarchical relationship with your thoughts, your quantum self is tangled hierarchical in its relationship with objects in consciousness.

Quantum collapse events are ideally discontinuous, nonlocal, and tangled hierarchical. Previous experiences, their memories really, corrupt this ideal situation. Since we have a habit of sifting a previously experienced stimulus through reflections in the mirror of memory, this corruption conditions our response to the present stimulus in favor of past responses. As experience accumulates, this corruption tends to dominate our meaning processing. So what we collapse tends to become conditioned—continuous, local, and simple hierarchical.

In every creative event of insight, creative people (let's call them "creatives") rise beyond their conditioning and collapse what is discontinuous, nonlocal, and tangled hierarchical. The mathematician Carl Friedrich Gauss wrote about one of his creative experiences, "Like a sudden flash of lightning, the riddle happened to be solved. I myself cannot say what was the conducting thread which connected what I previously knew with what made my success possible." The poet Rabindranath Tagore wrote about composing his first poem, "The unmeaning fragments lost their individual isolation and my mind reveled in a unity of vision." You can easily read discontinuity, nonlocality, and tangled hierarchy in such comments.

But there is no need to be vicarious about creativity. Anyone can be creative. Anyone can take a trip to the unconscious supramental and directly process the archetypes, albeit unconsciously. Do more quantum thinking. Who are you when you unconsciously process the supramental in search of the new? You are your quantum consciousness, of course. It is only convention to say that whenever there is the new in your unconscious, God comes to process for you. And when God chooses collapsing the creative insight, there is the experience of the quantum self. But think quantum again. Who is having the quantum self experience? Only you. And then there is the experience of the ego with the memory of the "aha!" and you make a mental garland of the supramental flowers of insight. Do you see what adventures you are missing when you think that only geniuses can be creative?

When we are children, we have creative experiences many times; these experiences give us the conditioned contexts of our ego identity. Learning how to be creative when we are adults is learning how to penetrate the ego conditioning when the situation arises. Learning how is not, however, a regression to childhood, negating the ego entirely. It is reclaiming again and again some of our childhood innocence, in spite of the ego, in fact, using the ego.

In brief, here is an important recurring theme of the creative journey. Our creative ideas are the results of the creative play of consciousness, which is the only real play there is in a quantum universe. However, the shadows (memories) of these creative ideas in our mind-brain complex give rise to conditioning, a tendency for homeostatic repetition. Conditioning sets us in a seductive shadow play, making the world appear to be a play of dichotomies: creativity and conditioning, good and evil, consciousness and matter, activism and non-doing, and so forth. To be creative is also to penetrate this oppositional camouflage and develop the ability to integrate the dichotomies.

The Questions of Creativity

The world responds to our questions. Sometimes the response is creative, other times not. But to make progress is to ask questions. Besides the question of how to be creative (for which the answer is "think quantum"), what are some of the other questions of creativity that crowd your consciousness?

Creativity usually refers to acts of discovery or invention of something new of meaning and value. What are some of the manifestations of creativity? This is an easy question. We can almost answer it just by looking around us. Some of us are creative working at an easel, those of us called creative artists. Some of us write poems in the early light of dawn; we are the visionary poets. The scientists among us feel creative when discovering a theorem of mathematics, a law of science, or developing a new technology. Some of us are creative at the piano or on the dance floor. These are some of the traditional arenas for creative acts—art, poetry, mathematics and the sciences, music and dance. But they do not exhaust the scope of creativity.

More recently, the arena of creativity has been recognized to include business enterprises, a very welcome addition to the tradition (Ray and Myers 1986).

The previous are examples of outer creativity, creativity in the outer arena of human expression in which there is a product that everyone can share. But we also have our inner arena, the state of consciousness in which we live, feel, think, and intuit. Not everyone lives the same inner states, the same degree of inner wholeness. In this way, there is inner creativity (Harman and Rheingold 1984), creativity in the inner landscape of experiences, a crucially important arena for the quantum activist.

In the olden days and even now, a large number of people engage in what is called a spiritual journey, in search of God. When looked at closely, it becomes apparent that this is a journey toward self-realization, the discovery of the true nature of the self and living that true nature using the creative process of inner creativity.

But spiritual search (research?) is not the only arena in which you have to engage inner creativity. Much closer to home and everyday life is the idea of applying inner creativity in relationship. If you learn to love somebody with creativity in practice, the experience is radically different from what you ordinarily call love.

Recent development in our healing sciences is showing that, even in healing, there is a scope for inner creativity (Goswami 2004), for quantum healing. We have come that far.

There is much confusion about the process involved in spiritual seeking. The verdict of the new science is that the process involved in both outer and inner creativity is the same, although the products are very different.

Labels such as "outer" or "inner" refer to a classification of creativity. Is there any other basis for classification of creativity? There is indeed. Even popular jargon distinguishes between creative acts of discovery and those that we call invention. What's the difference? Creativity is the discovery of new meaning, but everybody knows that meaning depends on the context. For example, if I say to a human being, "You are an ass," people will think I am rude. But if I say the same thing to a donkey, nobody will complain. So the word "ass" takes on different meaning in different contexts.

The context does not have to be only physical, as in the example I just gave. Our emotions and feelings can also set the context. Additionally, there are those subtler contexts of meaning that Plato called archetypes, which belong to the supramental: truth, beauty, justice, love, goodness, and so forth. If you think about it, a lot of the time we spend in our search for meaning revolves around one or more of these archetypes. For example, scientists mainly search for meaning in the archetypal context of truth. And often, in evaluating their search for truth, they refer to another archetype: beauty.

We can now formally differentiate between discovery and invention. A discovery consists of creating new meaning along with a new look at the archetypal context connected with the meaning. Invention consists of seeing new meaning in a combination of old meanings discovered in old archetypal contexts. Technically, we refer to discovery as fundamental creativity and invention as situational creativity.

Einstein's discovery of $E = mc^2$ required him to make a quantum leap to take a fresh look at the archetypal truth about the nature of time, that time is relative, that time changes with motion. This was fundamental creativity at its best. In the same way, most of the famous impressionist artists—Van Gogh, Renoir, and company—were exponents of fundamental creativity. But suppose I take bits and pieces of impressionist art and paint a composite; even if you find new meaning in it, it would be, at best, an example of situational creativity.

Moving on, here is another question of creativity. What constitutes the creative process? Research shows, first codified by Graham Wallas (1926), that creativity is a four-stage process—preparation, incubation (waiting quietly as a bird sits on her egg), insight, and manifestation (of the insight into a product). But there are many subtleties.

One subtlety, which I mentioned before, has become one of the slogans of the movement of quantum activism. Preparation (doing) and waiting (being) are not necessarily chronological. What really happens before a creative insight takes place is many alternative episodes of doing and being—do-be-do-be-do, like that Frank Sinatra jingle.

Why does the creative process involve so much agony (imagine Michelangelo agonizing over how to paint the ceiling of the Sistine Chapel) and anxiety (for which comedian Woody Allen's neurotic image is the archetype)? Yet who can doubt that there is ecstasy in the creative moment of insight (I hope the image of Archimedes dashing naked in the street of ancient Syracuse shouting "Eureka!" is appearing in your mind's eye) and great satisfaction in finishing a creative product (think of Picasso after he finished the colossal painting *Guernica*)?

The creative question (for which the creative seeks answer) is sometimes called the burning question because it unsettles and agonizes the ego. The ecstasy and satisfaction come from the achievement of wholeness of the quantum self, temporary as it may be.

What purposes do creative ideas serve? This question is important to you quantum activists, I am sure. If creative ideas have no causal efficacy and serve no purpose, as materialists claim, then why undergo so much agony (albeit ecstasy may be waiting for you at the end)? Is it because all creatives want name and fame? Hardly. Everybody knows that there is no short-term guarantee for name and fame in creative work. During Vincent van Gogh's lifetime, there was hardly any recognition of his art. Does this mean that the value of a creative act depends on what people think of it, that creativity is a popularity contest? Maybe one should find a good publicist even before one takes on an arduous adventure in creativity.

No, kidding aside and materialists notwithstanding, creative ideas "disturb the universe." They help the evolutionary movement of consciousness—that is their purpose.

Many of us engage in creativity, but it is a fact that only a few of us are a painter like Michelangelo, a music virtuoso like Mozart, a creative dancer like Martha Graham, a poet like Rabindranath Tagore, or a scientist of the caliber of Einstein. Accordingly, our foremost question is likely to be direct and personal: How can *I* be more creative? Put in another way: What limits our creativity? Can we overcome these limits? Can we reach all the way to the stars?

We all remember being creative as children. We wonder how most of us seem to lose the sense of wonder that pervades our childhood experiences, settling into an adulthood dominated by the mundane routines of a stale world. At those times, we ask a more pertinent question of development: Is adult creativity reserved for a chosen few, the so-called geniuses like Einstein and Martha Graham? Are geniuses inherently different from the rest of us, or is it possible that, given proper developmental opportunities, anyone can be a genius? A related question has to do with age. The physicist Erwin Schrödinger did his most important creative work (the discovery of the mathematics of quantum physics) at the ripe age of forty, and at the age of fifty-five wrote a definitive influential book on the nature of life, which inspired a whole generation of biologists. Can anyone, or only the geniuses, sail the creative seas at any age?

For inner creatives, especially seekers of spiritual enlightenment, the essential creativity question in this materialist age boils down to this: Does God even exist? Enlightenment is a promise of heaven, but does heaven even exist to make the journey toward it meaningful?

For quantum activists, understanding the new science resolves these doubts.

But questions aside, doubts aside, here is something nobody can deny. We become most alive, most joyful when we are creative; our creative moments are the greatest moments of our lives. We cherish creativity so much that participating in or witnessing the product of other people's creative acts enlivens us.

But even these poignant observations raise other questions. Can we spend all of our time in the pursuit of creative acts? Is there a way of creative living that surpasses in quality all other ways of living? Can we live our lives with creativity as the center?

The quintessential question is: Are there answers to these questions? Or, you guessed it, does thinking quantum resolve all these creativity questions?

The answer to both aspects of this question is a resounding yes. Quantum thinking gives us satisfying answers to all the questions of creativity you ever wanted to ask, and more. Quantum thinking will inspire you to delve into creativity. In part 2 of this book, I elaborate on how we can engage in creativity in our daily lives and also how we can manifest in our lives what we discover.

I will summarize the goal of quantum activism in relation to creativity with these lines from the poet Rabindranath Tagore (I have paraphrased them slightly):

> Where fear does not create barriers impenetrable
> Where the mind is free to take risk
> Where neither reward nor punishment
> But honest curiosity motivates,
> Where we can listen to the cosmos
> Whispering its purposiveness to us,
> Into that land of creative freedom
> Let my world awake.

Creativity, Reincarnation, and Mental Propensities Required to Create

Can anyone be creative? In the foregoing, I said yes, but obviously there must be more subtlety here. For any endeavor, the success depends on our motivation, the strength of our intention. How creative we are must depend on how motivated we are toward creativity, toward finding soul-satisfying answers to our inquiries, to our need to know.

It is a fact that there is a huge spectrum of creative people. Anyone can be creative, but what factors determine our place in the creativity spectrum? And this question is important for both outer and inner creativity.

The materialist answer is based on what is called genetic determinism—who we are depends entirely on our genes. But this way of looking at us is a dead end; there is no evidence for it.

So what determines our place in the creativity spectrum? Sure, environmental conditioning plays a role, even genetic conditioning may play a limited role (such as being a factor for our physical stamina), and even chance may play a role. But is there one factor that plays a pivotal role?

I think there is such a pivotal factor and it is determined by our reincarnational history—the learning we accumulated through many past lives. Additionally, the idea of reincarnation helps us settle the question of motivation as well.

Materialists do not like the idea of reincarnation; for them there is only the material body, and its death is the finale for us. But our creativity is living proof that meaning and its archetypal contexts are real "things," yet they are not material; matter cannot process them. Where do they reside then? Well, mind is the domain of meaning, and the domain of the archetypes is the supramental.

Matter cannot process feeling either; there will never be a computer chip for feeling, the science fiction imagination of *Star Trek,* notwithstanding. Feeling belongs to the domain of the vital body of consciousness. Together, as discussed in the last chapter, these three—the vital body, the mind, and the supramental—constitute our subtle body in contrast to our gross material body. When the material body dies, the propensities of the subtle vital and mental bodies survive and reincarnate in another physical body. Therefore the ideas of survival after death and reincarnation are not popular religious nonsense, as was once thought.

There is more, however. There is now much accumulated empirical evidence in favor of both survival after death and reincarnation, as well as a good detailed theory that explains all the data (Goswami 2001). The theory and data on reincarnation suggest the pivotal factor in determining our place in the creativity spectrum.

The empirical evidence for survival after death consists of the vast data on near-death experiences (Sabom 1982). This does not concern us here. The empirical evidence for reincarnation consists of the data on quite a few geniuses, born into non-talented families, who showed signs of creativity starting at a very early age. Clearly, these geniuses defy any explanation in terms of genetic or environmental conditioning. The East Indian mathematician Srinivasa Ramanujan and the German music virtuoso Wolfgang Mozart are two of the notable examples. Ramanujan was born into an entirely nonmathematical family, yet beginning at an early age, the fellow could perform summations of infinite mathematical series, just like that. And although Mozart's family was somewhat musical, this could hardly explain how a six-year-old Wolfgang could compose original musical scores. Facts such as these must be considered as evidence that these geniuses are born with innate creativity passed on to them from their previous incarnations (Stevenson 1974, 1977, 1987).

Theoretical considerations based on the new science give us further clarity. Previously, I cited two classes of creative acts: those acts of discovery that we call fundamental creativity and the acts of invention that we call situational creativity. Following the terminology of yoga psychology, let's denote the propensity for fundamental creativity by the Sanskrit word *sattva* ("illumination") and that for situational creativity by another Sanskrit word, *rajas* ("passion"). There is also the propensity for no creativity at all, the tendency to exhibit only conditioning in one's actions. Let's denote this propensity by the Sanskrit word *tamas* ("darkness"). Collectively, I will refer to these propensities of the mind by the Sanskrit word *guna*, which means "quality."

Reincarnational theory (Goswami 2001) based on the pivotal idea of nonlocal memory suggests that what we bring from our past reincarnations includes these three mental propensities of sattva, rajas, and tamas. Mind you, conditioning is ever present; it is a price we pay for growing up and cluttering our brain with memories. So tamas dominates when we begin our reincarnational journey, giving way only gradually, through many incarnations, to the creative tendencies of rajas and sattva.

Clearly, our place on the creativity spectrum depends crucially on our bringing with us when we incarnate anew a lot of sattva—the capacity to discover. Discovery is the most highly regarded act of creativity. The more sattva we bring, the more is our tendency to delve into fundamental creativity. In the same way, the reincarnational inheritance of rajas determines how successful we can be in the empire-building type of creativity, situational creativity. And how much sattva or rajas we can bring to bear in this life depends on our reincarnational history.

The purpose of our reincarnational journey is to discover the archetypes and manifest them in our lives, a job that takes us many incarnations (Goswami 2001). This provides us the personal motivation toward creativity; the archetypes motivate us toward creatively discovering them.

In the movie *Groundhog Day*, the hero is driven by the archetype of love from life to life until he learns love's selfless essence. We all are doing that sort of thing, pursuing one archetype or another. Like the hero in the movie, we remain unconscious of what we are doing when we begin our reincarnational journey, catching on to the game only as we mature.

The discovery of the archetypes requires fundamental creativity. Situational creativity then allows us many secondary acts of elaboration based on our discovery. The more sattva we have in a particular life, the more we can engage with the direct discovery of the archetypes. Then we are using creativity "in the search for the soul." If we have sattva mixed with a modicum of rajas, our search for the soul can be complemented by much needed worldly applications of the fruits of our soul journey. Alternatively, creatives of fundamental creativity and those of situational creativity can join hands.

How do we increase our motivation to be creative? One way is by purifying our sattva. Here is the good news, however. In times of social crisis, the survival motive kicks in, motivation for change gains wide popularity, and paradigm shifts follow easily. This is what is happening right now.

You may have heard that the Mayan calendar ends in 2012 and some people are predicting an end of the "world as we know it" at that time. I really think that this is a good metaphor for what is happening because a paradigm shift of the huge scope we are talking about will certainly be the end of the world as we have known it.

It is heartening to note that in the time of crisis and paradigm shifts, problems to be solved require going back to the basics, a new beginning. The solutions do not need to be sophisticated, and anybody, even without much talent, but with creativity and motivation, can handle them.

One more thing. We take rebirth with a clear learning journey in mind. In Sanskrit, this is called *dharma,* which means a learning agenda. Dharma is an agenda that facilitates our search for fulfillment on our creative journey. Our individual dharma tells us the field of our creative endeavor.

Have you noticed that some people do their creative stuff, be it situational or fundamental, with a certain easy-without-effort flow? The mythologist Joseph Campbell lived his life in such a flow; he followed his dharma. In fact, he was so enthused about it that he used to advise others to "follow your bliss."

I have a vision of how the much-needed rapid change will come into our midst. Millions of creatives, quantum activists all, following the lead of the paradigm shift in science, will engage their dharma and bring creative transformation into their chosen field in the arts and humanities, in economics and business, in health and healing, in politics and education, and, last but not least, in religion.

It is a fact that, apart from personal creativity, our societies as a whole also progress, becoming more and more creative, a process that we call the building of civilization. Without civilization, we would still be "reinventing the wheel" over and over. Building civilization also takes place in spurts. We call these spurts renaissance.

This brings us to the subject of evolution. But don't look at evolution with the Darwinian lens; you will be lost in the smoke and mirrors of vain ideas like chance and necessity, which give you no notion of the purpose of evolution or the creativity involved in it.

Creativity and Evolution

One of the most startling aspects of quantum creativity that is emerging is that biological evolution itself involves a progressive series of quantum leaps, creating greater and greater purposeful complexity, so that even more purposive aspects of our existence can be manifested (Goswami 2008b). As noted, the empirical evidence for these quantum leaps is the famous fossil gaps that Darwinism cannot explain. Who makes the quantum leaps? The fossil gaps involve a change of at least the species, so the creativity involved is at least the creativity of the entire species consciousness.

It took many quantum leaps to evolve us from the one-celled prokaryote to the nucleated eukaryote to the multicellular organisms to invertebrates to vertebrates to mammals to primates to humans. Most of this evolutionary journey has been the evolution of better and better representations of the vital blueprints of forms, leading to better and better organs to carry out our biological functions. Eventually, when the neocortex of the brain evolved, mental meaning could be represented.

Human evolution has been the evolution of the meaning processing of the mind. Initially, the mind was giving meaning to the physical world. We call this the evolution of the physical mind. Anthropologists identify this stage as the hunter-gatherer stage of human evolution. A main feature of this stage was male dominance.

With the development of small-scale agriculture, however, a stage came that anthropologists call the horticultural age, when humans settled down and men and women began to work together with more or less equal work and equal rights. The leisure afforded by this age allowed the mind to begin to give meaning to feelings, leading to the vital mind. The vital mind is compatible with the physical mind and integrated that previous stage within its workings.

Some feminist anthropologists call the stage of evolution of the vital mind the golden age, and I have to agree with that assessment. There was no male-female dichotomy then. This did not last, however. With the development of heavy agricultural machinery, men took the upper hand again and began the next stage of meaning processing, the meaning of the mind itself, relegating women to the lesser job of the vital mind.

The mind processing the meaning of mind or the meaning of meaning is, of course, called abstract thinking, in which rationality dominates. Rational thinking is logical and computable, whereas feelings, not being computable, can be considered irrational. In this way, the vital mind was never integrated with the rational mind. Instead, it was denigrated and left to the "lesser" sex (who are the ones who need it anyway for childbearing and rearing, or so it was argued) to process.

We can speculate that at the stage of the evolution of the vital mind, first, the mind must have given meaning to the three lower chakra instinctual feelings, making correlated brain circuits in the neocortex to complement the limbic brain circuits of the pure feelings. The two sets of brain circuits working together in association give us the experience of so-called negative emotions—fear, lust, anger, jealousy, competitiveness, and so on. Mind you, in that era, nonlocality dominated people's consciousness. In this way, the unconscious arousal of these emotions that we continue to suffer even today is akin to the collective unconscious of Jungian vintage.

After the negative emotional brain circuits were complete, the mind must have started to make limbic and neocortical circuits corresponding to the higher chakra feelings such as love. This stage was never finished, being aborted when the age of the rational mind arrived. The effect of this must have been devastating, so much so that it was immortalized in the biblical myth of the "fall" from Eden (Goswami 2008b).

Fortunately, before the fall, women managed to develop the very positive emotional brain circuits corresponding to maternal love, which is unconditional. And men and women both developed the limbic brain circuits of the (positive) feelings of spiritual "awe" and altruism. Neurophysiologists have recently discovered both of these circuits. By the way, the experience of awe is being touted as the reason why "God won't go away." With downward causation scientifically demonstrated, we can now recognize that God is more than a God spot in the brain (I sometimes jokingly refer to it as the new G-spot).

Notwithstanding these exceptions, negative emotions certainly dominate us today because we never completed the job of making positive emotional brain circuits corresponding to the higher chakras. We made some good beginnings, as the efficacy of Jungian psychology amply proves. Every man and woman does have the archetypes of gods and goddesses ready to guide them (Bolen 1984, 1989) in their transformational journey. Completing this job is crucial to our subsequent evolution, which should consist of mind giving meaning to intuitions—the evolution of the intuitive mind.

In the developmental history of our rational mind, we take, typically as children, many creative leaps of discovery (fundamental creativity) into the supramental to discover the contexts of (abstract) thinking. But as an adult ego, a homeostasis sets in, and our mind identity becomes complacent with the learned repertoire of logical structures or what we call a belief system. Normally, we are more capable of situational creativity than fundamental creativity.

Consequently, we in our rational mind display the tendency of simplifying and marginalizing the supramental origins of our learned repertoire of contexts in terms of simple dichotomies—good and evil, beautiful and ugly, true and false, love and hate.

To integrate emotions and reason, we have to reestablish the supramental as the pivot of our adult lives. This is the agenda of the next stage of the intuitive mind.

Creativity as the Preparation for the Next Stage of Our Evolution

In my earlier writing on quantum creativity (Goswami 1999), I wrote a section entitled "Creativity and the Preparation for the Next Century." I was too conservative. Creativity is our preparation not only for the new century or new millennium, but also for the next stage of our evolution, no less. How we get to the next quantum leap of evolution is now a most important question.

The truth is, in the course of our evolution in consciousness, we have gotten stuck. We live in an age when a materialist science still dominates and forces of separateness and a determined-machine mentality reign supreme. This mentality breeds mediocrity and consumerism even in the arena of traditional creativity; we become "soul starved." What most of us don't realize is that what starves the soul is not the lack of money to consume soul food, but the lack of creativity to produce soul food. And when mediocrity and consumerism produce soul starvation en masse, the really creative people in our society, instead of being the heroes of our society whom we follow toward the evolution of consciousness, become "outsiders" whom we mistrust as "too dangerous" to follow as examples. As a creative today, you have to be a conformist or an entertainer in order to be heard.

We cannot respect creative people unless we ourselves appreciate the value of creativity enough to become producers as well as consumers of soul food.

In quantum activism, apart from learning about the nature of creativity, we emphasize how to be creative, how to motivate creativity individually and collectively, and how to build a creative society in preparation for the next stage of human evolution, in preparation for the development of a truly nonlocal species consciousness for the entire human species. I discuss these latter subjects in detail in parts 2 and 3 of this book.

The genie of our creativity is bottled up for most of us; to liberate the genie is to become a genius. We live in an age when we interact with machines more than we do with other human beings. In this age, to give up conditioning and machine-certainty and embrace the uncertainty of a creative life is a challenge.

But never mind. As I envision, the evolutionary movement of consciousness is under way and many of us hear its call (Aurobindo 1996, Teilhard de Chardin 1961). If you are reading this book, you are one of those people, and understanding what creativity entails, how the creative process works, and what role creativity plays in your self-development and evolution are already essential components of your creative journey. Quantum activism is intended to act as your guide to further your journey.

To summarize, quantum activism encourages you to:

1. Understand the quantum nature of creativity and the creative process enough to practice creativity, not blindly but with awareness.

2. Shift from engaging creativity in selected areas of life to all areas of life.

3. Shift from exclusive engagement with outer creativity (creativity in the pursuit of a product that everyone can see and admire) to both outer and inner creativity (creativity in the pursuit of transformation of your being).

4. Shift from an unbalanced "ethereal" life of fundamental creativity to one that is integrated and balanced with worldly situational creativity and even with ordinary conditioned areas of life. In other words, work toward a balance of your propensities of sattva, rajas, and tamas, and eventually toward transcending them altogether.

5. Focus your creativity according to your dharma, your particular learning agenda for this life.

6. Shift your motivation for engaging in creativity from a personal one to one centered on both the personal and the evolutionary movement of planetary consciousness.

When you feel inspired to put creativity in the center of your life and to synchronize your own movement in life with the evolutionary movement of consciousness, then you are ready to make the inner and outer, and the male and the female as one.

> Thinking about creativity?
> Asking questions?
> Your questions are firefly glimpses
> Of the soul calling you.
>
> Do you hear the lapping of possibility waves
> On the shore of your mind?
> Then look through the quantum window.
> Face to face with your original self
> The quantum leap will take you by surprise.
>
> *(Goswami 1999)*

PART 2

Walking Our Talk
The Quantum Journey to Transformation

CHAPTER 7

Kennedy Gave Us the Moon, Can You Give Us God Back, Mr. President?

Dear President Obama,

You ran for president on a platform of change. Real change, you said. Change that we can believe in. Well, how many real changes have you made so far? Change so real that we can believe in it? Change so real and so believable that we ourselves may believe in changes and make a few?

Oh, yes, Mr. President, everybody in a leadership position knows that we Americans need to change. Without us making changes in our cynical, wasteful, and extravagant lifestyle, the problems we face today in America and the world cannot be solved. But you can help by showing your resolve to make changes.

We have become cynical, Mr. President. Today, we have hardly any ideas, philosophy, or principles to believe in, to guide our lives, to make real changes. How did it get this way? Starting in the 1950s, there came the scientific materialists. Materialists have always been there among us with their hedonism and epicurean philosophy: eat, drink, and be merry. Only a few people heeded them. But in the fifties, with the discovery of the DNA's double helix structure, scientists became emboldened to challenge religious faith in unprecedented ways. First came the assertion that we can understand life itself, starting from molecules. We will synthesize life in the laboratory and show that no vital force is necessary, and certainly no God, to make little green apples.

Then came high-energy physics and its extravagant claim. Show us the money for high-energy machines and we will show you the elementary particles that are the building blocks of all things. And knowing that, we will investigate biology and psychology from first principles. Nothing will be out of reach of our mathematical savvy.

Finally, came computer science and the search for artificial intelligence, computers with mind. By producing mindful machines, we will demonstrate that we human beings, too, are the machines we have all along been suspecting we are. Here comes the proof, here comes the proof....

Three strikes, and God seemed to be out, out enough from everybody's belief system for people to be cynical. If God does not make little green apples, why bother about ethics or principles by which to live or do business? Take care of numero uno—you. Get real. There is no meaning; the physicist has said so. "The more the universe seems comprehensible, the more it seems pointless." Pay attention to real things like real estate. So this excessive attention will produce boom and bust in the housing market, so what? Cheap credit is available to Americans, why not? We are worth it! Do, do, do; buy, buy, buy; make money, no matter that you don't care anymore why you are giving up your precious leisure time to make meaningless money.

The philosophers among the cynical gave us existential philosophy. There is no real meaning and value to live by, but we must pretend that there is. But philosophy itself was undermined relentlessly, not that it needed undermining. Who reads philosophy these days? With our economists and political leaders telling us incessantly that we need consumers and their spending to keep our economy going, the littlest hesitation that people had about spending on their credit line gave way.

It is we consumers that demanded big cars and gas-guzzling SUVs from Detroit. We brought down General Motors. We produced the bulk of the greenhouse gases that threaten climatic catastrophe. It is we who indulge in unhealthy habits and refuse to engage in preventive positive health practices to keep disease away and reduce health-care costs. It is we who develop the chemical dependence on drugs (for temporary relief) that supports the pharmaceuticals and raises health-care costs.

It is we who became so fearful after 9/11 that our leaders could manipulate us into unneeded wars. It is we who bought into the materialist scientists' line about love being sex and brain neurochemicals, and lost the potencies of the energies of love when we most needed it, to balance our fear.

And it is we who jumped the gun and bought into the materialists' bold declarations without waiting for delivery. Have the materialists delivered? Biologists have not gone very far in the attempts to produce life in the laboratory. Artificial intelligence researchers have failed to build a computer that can process mental meaning. True, elementary particles of matter have been discovered. But to discover the mysteries of life and mind based on that knowledge? Only in the promissory materialism of true believers!

But a new dawn is coming, and a few of us are already appreciating its early light. There is now mathematical proof that matter cannot produce life in the laboratory, cannot process meaning. There is mathematical proof that we need nonmaterial interaction (call it downward causation) to make quantum possibilities (the outcome of material interaction that is called upward causation) into actual events. This downward causation comes with properties like nonlocality (signal-less communication) and quantum leaps (discontinuous jumps without going through intervening steps) that material interactions can never simulate. But these special properties are what our great spiritual teachers such as Jesus and Buddha have attributed to God and God's interaction with the world. And guess what, Mr. President? There is now plenty of experimental and empirical evidence in favor of downward causation and so, by inference, of God. In fact, the data keep growing.

Alright, alright! I concede that these theories and data are far from being accepted by a scientific consensus. The majority of scientists still believe in scientific materialism, that is, that matter, not consciousness, is the ground of all being. What is worse is that these establishment scientists refuse to engage with our alternate models of reality. Why this benign neglect? The new science says that to be a scientist of consciousness is to be more conscious. We have to practice what we preach; walk our talk. But materialists like being cynical; like the Washington establishment, the scientific establishment is resistant to change.

Please don't underestimate the power of benign neglect, Mr. President. The church sat on Copernicus's paradigm-shifting discovery for 100 years. Here is where you can help. In the 1960s, President Kennedy promised us a trip to the moon, and he delivered—within ten years. In truth, a moon trip was not even needed for any practical reason (other than showing those communist Ruskies that we democratic Americans are superior!). But today we need God. We need God to believe in if we are to believe in ourselves and in our ability to change. To change our bad habits of consumerism, we need new economics, a new worldview, and access to real freedom of choice. All this requires discontinuous changes of quantum leaps—the Grace of downward causation.

So here is my proposal, Mr. President. Give us God. Declare a scientific emergency. Convene all scientists, of the new paradigm and of the old, give them research grants, with one objective in mind. Settle the question of God. Since we already have a good theory of spirituality based on quantum physics, which has already passed the test of scientific rigor, this should not be too hard. We also have some pretty convincing data. If we put even half of the American ingenuity that took us to the moon into this, we can scientifically settle the question of God. Forever.

Our founding fathers wanted to define the "American dream" as having unlimited access to life, liberty, and the pursuit of happiness. All people are created (with) equal (potential), so they should have the opportunity for realizing that potential. Or so our founders thought. Under the aegis of materialism, the American dream became narrow: big house, great car, and unlimited access to consumerism. That is all. But your election changed all that, Mr. President. On that electrifying night of November 4, 2008, the old American dream was revived, if only for a few moments. If the son of an African citizen and a white middle-class woman, a boy who grew up in Hawaii and Indonesia, then spent his young adulthood as a community organizer on the South Side of Chicago, can be president, then any American can fulfill his or her potential.

So help us find God. If God comes back into our belief system, if freedom and creativity with downward causation come back into our belief system, we can forever believe that the American dream is about fulfilling our potential. We may even get on with it, make changes, and actually achieve something. Goodbye, cynicism; hello, change.

Now that is change we can believe in, Mr. President. It heartens me that you seem to be a believer in God and you see the subtleties in the God question that the new science is discovering. On the question of conquering evil, you said that evil makes you humble. That is all the proof I need to make my claim. Also, you showed courage in publicly proclaiming that you will attend church to offer prayer.

A journalist recently asked me about these letters I have been writing to you. "Is your intention to convert Mr. Obama into a quantum activist?" To this I answered, "Mr. Obama may already be a quantum activist."

But you don't have to be a quantum activist to see merit in my proposal. Mr. President, we have made enormous progress; we have a viable science of spirituality. All we need is consensus. Ultimately, truth will stand anyway. But by hastening the process, you can hasten what you want: to bring real change to how people in America and around the world think, live, and earn their livelihood.

If we can go to the moon in ten years, can't we settle the God question in the four years of your presidency? Yes, we can.

Sincerely,
Amit Goswami, Ph.D.

CHAPTER 8

Right Living for a Quantum Activist Is a Balancing Act

A tourist enters an old curiosity shop, looks around, and discovers a barometer. He has never seen one before. Curious, he asks the shopkeeper, "What is this?"

The shopkeeper says, "It is a barometer. It tells you when it is going to rain."

"How does it do that?" The tourist is now very curious.

Unfortunately, the shopkeeper does not know, but rather than admit it, he says, "Oh, very simple. Hold the barometer in your hand. Now put your hand out through an open window, and after a second or two, pull your hand back in. If the barometer is wet, you know it is raining."

"But," objects the tourist, "couldn't I do the same thing with my bare hand? Why do I need a barometer for that?"

The shopkeeper answers gravely, "Yes, you could. But that would not be scientific."

This story illustrates perfectly why popular religions today have lost their appeal. The shopkeeper knows the importance of the barometer in foretelling the weather but cannot tell the buyer how the barometer does so. In the same way, our guides of pop religions emphasize the importance of spiritual rituals and practices but cannot explain how they work, perplexing a lot of people. With the new science to guide us, the explanatory gap no longer exists. And with the idea of quantum activism, we have a viable "guide for the perplexed."

So now I reckon you are ready to explore discontinuous transitions in your thought patterns and the scope of nonlocality and tangled hierarchy in your intersubjective experiences. Now you are ready to undertake the quantum journey of transformation.

Right Living Is a Balancing Act, But What Do We Balance?

In America, we grow up wanting to live to fulfill the American dream, essentially reinterpreted today as a pursuit of happiness in materialist/consumerist terms. Right thinking makes you realize that the pursuit of happiness is much more than wearing designer clothes or owning a big house and/or a Porsche. How can we live in synchrony with, even serve, the evolution of consciousness in manifestation? First, by rising beyond the mere satisfaction and pursuit of our material needs (which separates us further and further from the whole); and second, by paying attention to our subtle needs that have movement toward wholeness built into them. These two steps help us realize that right living is a balancing act.

Materialists negate meaning and values, leaving room only for pretend meaning and values in the existentialist sense. The phrase "right living" appeared in the Buddha's teaching. So perhaps spiritual traditions define the term better. Alas! The conventional people of spirit try to live life weighted so heavily toward the spirit, so much in the pursuit of only the spiritual supramental values, that they tend to ignore even the pursuit of humanistic meaning such as the arts. In today's materialist culture, growing up the way we do, only a few of us can take such a big leap directly from matter to spirit without going through the subtle levels of thinking and feeling. And moreover, that's where our evolution is at. So the path of the quantum activist is the middle path: the material and the supramental are valued, but so are the mind and its pursuit of meaning and even the vital body and the feeling dimension. This is a path everybody can follow; we recognize from the get-go where we are in our evolution.

To the materialist, life is the playing out of genetically, evolutionarily, and environmentally conditioned programs—the brain circuits. Spending life in the service of the brain circuits that include the instincts and the pleasure centers is the goal. To the spirit seeker, the object is to live in the embodied spirit (the quantum self, in our scientific terminology). It is spirit or bust—as unrealistic as it may be at this stage in our evolution. Neither approach works for long. Pleasure ends up in pain—separateness. Unrealistic spiritual aspiration ends up in disappointment—also separateness.

The quantum activist aspires to live in growing balance between the two extremes. If we don't complement the separateness-producing tendencies encoded in our negative emotional brain circuits with attempts to manifest what is good in us, how can we ever explore our potential? So the quantum activist must heed the necessity of making quantum leaps to the supramental; for the quantum activist, living in the ego and living in the spirit have to be balanced. Additionally, the quantum activist recognizes that manifesting the content (thinking and feeling) of a spiritual experience (the insight) is as important as the supramental context. And the manifestation of the content requires sophisticated structures of the mind, many repertoires of representing meaning and feelings—the brain circuits again. So creativity and conditioning have to be balanced.

Religions of old attempted to "kill" the brain circuits (they boost the big bad ego) by not using them. Stay away from stimuli; drop out of family life and society. Give up the ego of pleasure and pain; opt for the perpetual happiness of your higher self. In this way, people of the most idealistic bent were encouraged to escape society. Society and its evolution suffered as a result.

But in truth, you cannot kill the ego this way. Also, there is no need. Without the ego, "how does the Zen master go to the bathroom?" In truth, the ego is important in the creative process, even for most of the spiritual experiences. What we need to do is find a good balance of the pleasure-seeking ego and the happiness of the quantum self.

You may have seen the movie *The Secret,* in which it is propounded that there is a law of attraction via which things that we intend come to us if we simply wait; we do not have to do anything. This is good advice for Westerners with their busy do-do-do lifestyle. But waiting is only part of the law of manifestation. The whole secret of the creative process of manifestation is not only that we learn to wait, but also that we learn to balance doing and being in a dance that alternates between the do-mode and the be-mode. The creative process, as I often say, consists of do-be-do-be-do, a joint effort of our do-mode (which is dominated by the ego) and the be-mode (which has God potential). And why not? Thoughts and feelings are quantum objects—waves of possibility—that spread when you are not thinking—and collapse when you come back to the do-mode and think. When these two modalities touch, as in that immortal portrait by Michelangelo on the ceiling of the Sistine Chapel of God and Adam reaching out to each other, the experience of flow (Csikszentmihalyi 1990) accompanies the discontinuously arrived creative insight (recall that in the new science we recognize insight as the result of a quantum leap from the mind and/or the vital body to the supramental), and a creative act takes place. We write a poem, write a musical score, develop the mathematical equations of a scientific phenomenon, heal ourselves all in basically the same way.

Gross/subtle, outer/inner, conditioning/creativity, ego/quantum self, doing/being, pleasure/happiness, these are examples of dualities that tend to separate us from the whole. "To make the two one," balancing the dualities in our living, is what right living is for the quantum activist.

There is one more duality, male/female or reason/emotion, which I have emphasized before. We aborted working on balancing this one when we prematurely transited from the era of the vital mind to the era of the rational mind. It turns out that to integrate the two, we also have to integrate intuition in our lives.

In general, the inner-outer dichotomy has resulted in an East-West dichotomy, East emphasizing the inner, the West the outer. This, too, needs to be integrated and, to some extent, it is already happening. Now to some more details.

Balancing the Gross and the Subtle

Materialists partake surreptitiously of the subtle (at the least, to avoid boredom), but they frequently admonish themselves to "get real," telling themselves to bring their attention back to the pursuit of the gross. Likewise, the spiritual aficionado avowedly tries to "get real" by embracing the subtlest of the subtle, the beyond the beyond, and ignoring the gross as illusory maya, but succumbs (often secretly) to the pursuit of the gross quite a bit. For the quantum activist, there is no conflict of worldview there. The really real is the unmanifest, agreed, but the quantum activist knows that the play of evolution takes place in the manifest and both gross and subtle are necessary for making manifestation possible; both are important. In this way, the quantum activist pays attention to both gross and subtle and tries to achieve a balance in pursuit of the two.

To achieve balance, the quantum activist pays attention to the nuances of the material dimensions of life such as collecting information and making a living, but does not get lost, does not identify as such with his or her professional persona unless there is personal or social meaning in it. The quantum activist openly explores and enjoys the subtle—feelings, meanings, and values, soul food all—in the growing balance between the gross and subtle.

In the process of rebalancing, we move from information to intelligence (see chapter 9). Remember that intelligence is not just responding to a problem to be solved, but also responding appropriately. Information alone may not be enough. The intelligent person complements information processing with the processing of meaning, feeling, and value, and thus finds the appropriate response.

It is, however, a fact that the waking life is too much dominated by the gross material. So it is a good strategy for the quantum activist to pay attention, at least in the beginning, to dreams, wherein the subtle dominates. Dreams are the realm of feelings and meaning, even the supramental, as occasionally in the Jungian "big" archetypal dream in which an archetype of the collective unconscious shows up.

In the olden days and to some extent even now, spiritual practices were identified as things like meditation, prayer, the reading of good books, selfless service. Love, maybe, but only as devotion to God or only as a useful accompaniment to selfless service—objective love. A specific "time-out" for spirituality is important for the quantum activist, but the quantum activist engages in spirituality in everyday living as well as in isolation, as somebody doing important things that will bring change to society, and as nobody special doing nothing special. Love is not only to be explored in events of charity and service to others (the exploration of quantum nonlocality), but also in intimate relationships, even carnal relationships, to try to surrender simple hierarchy to tangled hierarchy and to achieve a balance of reason and emotion.

Balancing the Various Subtle Domains

Of utmost importance to the quantum activist is the balancing of the various subtle domains at play in our persona—feeling, thinking, and intuition.

To the materialist, thinking is everything, rationality is supreme. Like the gross, rational thinking is computable and predictable, deterministic; only this can materialists value. Even the fact that their pursuit of rationality often gets mired in the pursuit of power to dominate others and in other negative emotions does not bring them to an acknowledgment of the importance of feelings. Even the fact that the progress of scientific research itself depends on unpredictable quantum leaps of creativity does not influence the strict rationalism of the materialist. All this because feeling and intuition, being unpredictable, are not subject to control. To the materialist, control is everything.

Materialists undermine the thinking of the mystics—people who have "enlightening" spiritual experiences—because "mystics are irrational." But materialists misinterpret; mystics are nonrational, not irrational. They transcend the rational not only by frequent exploration of the intuitive domain, but also by being up front about it.

So mystics are one step ahead of materialists; they embrace both the rational and the intuitive planes, but they don't value very much the progress made in the rational plane. Invariably, spiritual traditions tend to denigrate the creativity involved in the processing of meaning in outer manifestation—creativity in the arts, humanities, and sciences. This will not do for advancing evolution. So in contrast to the mystic, the quantum activist must balance both outer creativity, which mainly serves the mental and vital dimensions, and inner creativity, which mainly serves the supramental, in their lives. Both are important for our evolution.

Many mystics also tend to avoid stimuli that arouse base feelings and negative emotions, never bothering to balance and transform them. This has led to much misconception about the behavioral usefulness of mystical "enlightenment." What good is enlightenment if it does not enable a person to behave with equanimity even when faced with stimuli that call for anger, greed, or lust?

Inner creativity with the idea of transforming the mind has been the traditional popular tool of spiritual seekers with the objective of attaining insight or samadhi (or satori or enlightenment or gnosis, or whatever you may call it). Carnal love that requires working with and transforming the (vital) energies of emotions is left out in these (male-oriented) traditions.

In the 1980s, the spiritual women of America rose en masse to protest the male dominance in religious traditions and coined phrases like "feminine spirituality" and "the feminine face of God." We quantum activists have to integrate the dualities of this unproductive male-female dichotomy and practice creativity even with carnal love when it is part of our daily lives.

Attention to carnal love in everyday life is important because it potentially involves the most satisfying intimate relationship. The greatest challenge I envision for evolution is the challenge of transformation of negative emotions into positive ones. Look around you. In all our social organizations, negative emotions—greed, egotism in the pursuit of power, lust, competitiveness—are rampant. If we ourselves don't know how to transform these negative emotions, how can we ask others to show restraint and emotional maturity? And where best to explore negative emotions than in intimate relationships, which offer a safe place and also make hiding difficult.

The transformation of negative emotions involves creativity in the domain of the vital, engagement of the creative process in the domain of vital energies. The practice of unconditional love in intimate relationships falls in this category. Everybody knows instinctually how to use sex to make love. But try making love unconditionally. This we have to explore; our evolutionary future depends on it.

So how do we do our balancing act? Thinking dominates our lives, but it is not even directed thinking. It is undisciplined thinking associated with memories. To discipline it and bring directedness, we slow down our thoughts, and nothing is better than meditation to achieve this. Slowing down increases the gap between thoughts; in those gaps, there is room for change via unconscious processing.

We do the same for our emotional life. In the West, for the sake of efficiency, we try to suppress emotions, only to find that they have become unruly, erupting uncontrollably. We develop "moods" and temper. So to restore balance, we begin expressing emotions. And when we express, we concentrate on the chakras and learn to feel pure feelings as the movement of vital energy at the chakras. When the emotion is negative, you can feel the movement of energy in your three lower chakras. As you learn to attend to this movement, you will notice a remarkable thing. These movements slow down. Now you can meditate on them and gain directedness over them. The more you gain control, the more they become impotent; you find that you don't really have to act them out.

The practice is the same with positive emotions, except for one difference. For positive emotions, when you gain directedness and control, practice acting out the emotions.

Coming back to how to make unconditional love, do this little practice. Whenever you feel warmth or a tingle at the heart chakra, do an act of love, something kind, something compassionate to another, with empathy. This helps you make a brain circuit of that positive emotion. With every opportunity, reinforce that circuit by repetition.

Mothers have enormous opportunities to develop brain circuits of unconditional love because little babies are such wonderful stimuli for the heart chakra. And mothers act on it, too. So most mothers love their children initially quite unconditionally. But then they become stingy and possessive—my child; they lack empathy. Also, they do not want to love others unconditionally; what's the gain in that? These mothers are missing a most wonderful opportunity for transformation.

For balancing intuition, we learn to pay attention to our intuitions, to synchronicities, to big dreams and lucid dreams. We undertake projects that require creativity in order to make changes in our behavior, and we practice do-be-do-be-do with these projects. Progress may be slow, but we never give up. Intuitive life improves, and then one day, insight (see chapter 10).

In the next chapter, I will present these balancing tasks in the more formal language of mental, emotional, and supramental intelligence.

Tuning to the Needs of Social Transformation and Evolution

Downward causation works through individuals. In that context, I previously introduced ideas such as creativity and conditioning; individual evolution via reincarnation, which involves rebirth after death; and dharma, the sense of destiny we bring from our past lives to the present one (see chapter 6). Delving into any of these phenomena will help you personalize God, downward causation, and the subtle bodies.

I have already introduced the idea of the biological evolution of our entire species that is in our future (see chapter 6). Can the force of downward causation, which acts individually, be taken to influence the evolutionary movement of the collective? I believe the answer is yes, and this highlights one of the basic objectives of quantum activism—focusing simultaneously on individual and collective evolution. How do we do that?

How do I make changes, any important changes that matter? By changing my mind-set, my context of thinking. As an individual, I can do this by following the creative process. Then I have an insight. If I am sufficiently moved by my insight, I manifest the insight in my life, I change my lifestyle.

But if I am tuned to my personal evolution through myriad reincarnations, then I may be able to fine-tune my program of personal growth. Through watching my tendencies, and especially through meditative remembering of unusual propensities of my childhood, I may intuit my dharma, the specific personal growth task that I have brought to bear in this life (see chapter 6). I may be inspired to direct my explorations of creativity and love so that first I fulfill my dharma. What next? This is where thinking about the social needs of evolution becomes important.

Like the individual, the society and culture are also entrenched in mind-sets, and there are quite a few of them, some of them oppositional to one another. In America, there are the mind-sets of the Republicans and Democrats, conservatives and liberals, religious fundamentalists and materialists, activists and hedonists, management and labor. There are so many conflicting interests.

To compound the problem, almost everybody believes in computers and information processing as the solution to all ills (the Al Gore syndrome). Teachers and university professors are eager to make lists of information to which every student should have access. Several years ago, Professor Alan Bloom (1988) wrote a best-seller about what a college student should "know" to be worthy of getting a college degree, but all of it was information, the ability to quote other people's thinking.

But mind is about meaning. The mental stage of the evolution of which you are part is about evolving the processing of meaning—yours and everyone else's. The goal is, first, to make meaning processing accessible to all people and then, second, to create opportunities so people can appreciate higher meanings, even discover the supramental contexts of meanings for themselves. But the opposite movement is what is actually taking place right now. You can see it everywhere.

Philosophers used to be passionate about the nature of reality. Now they are keen to deconstruct all metaphysical discourse on the nature of reality. In a previous era, lawyers were interested in the pursuit of justice. Now they are more interested in how to use the (by itself) meaningless letter of law to the advantage of their clients and even for their own personal advantage. Previously, journalists were interested in the pursuit of truth in order to keep a check on people pursuing power. The overall attempt was to elevate people's experience of the meaning of everyday reality. But now journalists are more interested in scandals and other exercises of negative emotions that only degrade people's experience of meaning.

The truth is that the materialist scientists' success in explaining the material world and the conditioned aspects of the subtle worlds has confused everyone about God and downward causation, about the veracity of engaging in the pursuits of the soul (meaning, creativity, and love), and about the necessity of achieving godliness (social justice, etc.).

The philosopher E. F. Schumacher (1977) wrote a book in which he described an experience in the now defunct Soviet Union. He was surprised to see that the magnificent cathedrals of the old regime were preserved entirely as museum pieces in that culture; there was no other use for them. In America, people's belief in God is now so superficial that the ideas of God, soul, and godliness—the three fundamentals of all religions—are fast becoming either museum items or contexts for political polarization, with little help needed from the deconstructionists.

Materialism has become a wound on the body of consciousness, as a result of which the evolution of consciousness is now stalled. Will the wound become malignant? Or can we heal it?

There is pain from this wound, huge pain from which our species consciousness is suffering right now. The psychiatrist Stan Grof's "holotropic breathing" technique enables the participant to reach a more holistic identification beyond the ego. Initially, Grof's clients were going through what seemed to be prenatal and perinatal experiences related to the human birth (Grof 1998). But the philosopher Christopher Bache and others have been able to reach, via Grof's technique, deep experiences of pain and suffering that can be interpreted as a collective pain of the entire human species (Bache 2000). I really think that this collective pain is due to the materialist-caused wound in the body of our collective consciousness. Ordinary pain is due to a disconnection between our vital morphogenetic field and the organ with which it correlates. So there must be a major disconnect between the outer and the inner in our collective experience.

Since it is all a movement of consciousness, I don't ever doubt that the wound is going to be healed, but as quantum activists, we have quite a job to do. We have to do our individual soul work, but supplement it with developing a social consciousness in ourselves and in our social institutions so that we all, once again, come into sync with evolution.

I hope you can see what to do at the personal as well as at the societal level. We have lost our way; we have to find our way back from information processing to meaning processing. We have to attain emotional maturity; we have to give attention to our vital dimension, but give up our preoccupation with negative emotions. Additionally, we must actively pursue positive emotions.

In the West, traditionally, the arts have dominated subtle energy exploration. But recently, the arts have lost the place they previously held in the awareness of most people. We have to bring back the appreciation of the fine arts in our society.

In a previous era, people were interested in exploring the subtle, the meaning that takes us toward ever-more subtle positive vital energies. In those days, we appreciated the fine arts. We would curl up with good literature on a long winter evening and find that relaxing. We would even recite poetry to each other. We learned to enjoy the fine arts from our childhood. Are children today encouraged to do these things? Almost universally, the answer is no. Even when we explore the subtle—meaning and feelings—it is at the shallow level. The aim is materially oriented. We have all become "Shallow Hal," not only in our pursuit of romance, but also in all pursuits of life.

This is part of that materialist wound. To heal it, we have to bring back, individually and collectively, explorations galore in the subtle dimensions, deep explorations that take us deeper into the subtle, not toward the material. We have to develop a keen awareness that ethics are important, even though religions are no longer able to give us guidance in pursuing ethics. We have to develop an evolutionary ethics suited to our evolutionary needs, and practice them. And we have to do all this, not only for America, but en masse, all over the world, involving a large part of humanity, eventually all of humanity.

In the chapters to come, we will explore these social transformation challenges for the quantum activist. In part 3, I will discuss the problems with our social institutions, and why and how our evolution has stalled in each, so that we can see our way toward the solution.

Balancing East and West

In the early 20th century, we defined the conflict between (materialist) science and spirituality as one between West and East. The Western culture ignored the spiritual and the Eastern cultures ignored the material (the historically predominant occupation of science). The poet Rudyard Kipling wrote:

> East is East, and West is West
> And never the twain shall meet.

And this was true then. The West was already a materialist scientific culture, but the Easterners stubbornly held on to their spiritual cultures and it seemed they would never budge. Of course, many people still believe that this is so. Alas! The East is now also rapidly giving way to a materialist culture.

Eastern spirituality fundamentally professes oneness of consciousness and, until recently, spirituality was a way of life for Easterners. But under the aegis of the old Western science, dualism at first reigned while the society remained spiritual. Eventually, however, dualism yielded to material monism, and consciousness was assumed to be brain-based, individual by nature, and conditioned (via biological and sociocultural evolution) to operate on the survival-of-the-fittest competitive individual mode. Eventually, consciousness itself came to be regarded as merely ornamental or operational. What happened in science affected the society at large; religion became cynical and spirituality was marginalized.

Fortunately, rapid change is under way. A brain-based consciousness conflicts in a major unsolvable manner with quantum physics. So science is undergoing a paradigm shift (see part 1). In this new paradigm, the Eastern model of oneness of consciousness is found to be the right way to think about consciousness. Thus this paradigm is paving the way for an integration of science and spirituality, of modern West and the old East (Goswami 2008a).

There is another subtle conflict between the Eastern and the Western approach to life. Easterners, by and large, consider spirituality as the goal of their lives. It is believed that the individual "soul" (looked upon as a deeper level of conscious identity beyond the ego of one life) reincarnates many times. Only when the soul learns the secret of its spiritual being of oneness and incorporates the knowledge in its living is the individual liberated from this birth-death-rebirth cycle. In the West, even outside of science, reincarnation has traditionally not been a popular concept. Most people in the West believe that there is only one life, and this life should be spent in the service of "doing"—accomplishments. You can see that this "accomplishment orientation" contributes to environmental overload, the ever-widening gap between the rich (the accomplishers) and the poor (the nincompoops), and to skyrocketing medical costs via costly technology to prolong life (so that accomplishments can continue).

But here again, quantum physics, by reviving the concept that we are all potentially God the creator, is giving us a new theory of creativity and a new resolution to the conflict. When we understand creativity as a quantum process, we find that both doing and being are important; neither can be ignored. So the integration of the Eastern be-be-be way of living and the Western do-do-do way of living is the do-be-do-be-do way of living that I have been advocating (Goswami 1999). It is also very telling that a 1983 Gallup poll showed that a full 25 percent of Americans believe in reincarnation.

The Rudyard Kipling poem, from which I quoted previously, has other telling lines:

> But there is neither East nor West, Border nor
> Breed nor Birth,
> When two strong men stand face to face,
> Though they come from the ends of the earth.

When the doing people of the West come face to face with the being people of the East and they become one and the same people, then the new age arrives!

CHAPTER 9

From Information to Intelligence

We are in the mental age of evolution. With the biological evolution of the brain, mind could be mapped, and ever since, we have been evolving in the exploration of the mind, in the exploration of meaning. What does this involve?

The exploration of meaning requires both situational and fundamental creativity. Fundamental creativity gifts us with new contexts for meaning exploration; situational creativity is our vehicle to explore further these discovered contexts in accordance with societal and personal needs. Engaging in creativity then is the first evolutionary need of the mental age.

But for further evolution to take place, meaning exploration must spread to as many members of the human species as possible, if not all. So this means that not only must we make sure of our personal creativity in the exploration of meaning, but we must also make sure of everyone's access to meaning processing and mental creativity. This gives a new dimension to ethics, doesn't it?

Ken Wilber (2000) has pointed out another important thing. At every stage of human development, says Wilber, the previous stage must be integrated. As with development, so with evolution. The current mental age of evolution of the rational mind must integrate the evolution of the previous age of the vital mind. This translates into the integration of the processing of feeling and the processing of meaning.

We can see why the integration of emotions is necessary. Without giving up negative emotions in favor of positivity toward others, how do we ever help others to progress toward fulfillment in meaning processing?

In the previous chapter, I spoke of how the prevalent materialist beliefs of our society seem to have stalled evolution. Here I will take one by one the three evolutionary needs elucidated in the preceding paragraphs to sort out what the problems are in order to get an inkling of where the solutions might be.

From Information to Meaning

Some politicians love to say that this is the information age. They believe that processing information on the large scale we are capable of today (and it is getting even better, right?) is the ultimate in achievement and, therefore, the information age is the golden age of our civilization. This is a very narrow view of the human potential.

What is information? If you don't have any information about the answers to a problem, then all possible answers are equally probable, a not-so-desirable situation. With information, the probabilities of particular answers grow, and your chance of getting the appropriate answer improves. So information is certainly useful. But information per se is often not tantamount to solving the problem at hand. Neither does information give you satisfaction or make you happy. Sure, it can be exciting to use email to communicate extensively around the world. And that may help to keep your worrying mind at bay. It is also an occasionally effective medicine against boredom to go surfing on the Internet for information that may be handy later. But is your worry gone because you gained information? Is your boredom gone as a result of your extensive exploration of ever-more information? Are your problems solved? Hardly. The worrying mind gets anxious about the next item of worry. Stop net surfing, and the suffering called boredom is back again with gusto. The busy mind has to be kept busy or else it will be unsatisfied and unhappy.

You can say that the intelligent use of information surfing is not to avoid boredom, but to amass money that can bring you satisfaction, even happiness. But examine the life of people who have amassed money, those very innovative money managers of Wall Street. Satisfaction comes when you have engaged your mind with something meaningful. And happiness is enjoying a relaxed moment, doing nothing. Are these money managers engaged in meaningful enterprises? Hardly. They are just making money, which is a means, not an end. Are the money managers capable of relaxing? No, they are not capable of enjoying life, of being happy. Instead, they try to find solace for their stressful life in pleasure, which is not only a poor substitute for happiness, but also a detriment to happiness, sometimes everybody's happiness, in the long run.

I am not saying that information processing is bad, or pleasure is bad, just that they are quite limited achievements. Like money, information processing is also a means, not an end. That is why it gets boring after a while. Surely, you can intuit that there must be more to being human than accumulating lots and lots of means. It is like gaining access to a lot of mountain lakes, but never having the mind-set to enjoy the water.

Remember the film *Pretty Woman*? A fellow is lost in the game of information and moneymaking. And who saves him from his self-imposed dungeon? A prostitute. But this is no ordinary prostitute. She is a prostitute who sells her body for money, to make a living, but not her mind, a prostitute who knows the importance of meaning processing and teaches it to her beau out of love. (And of course, the pretty woman herself is stuck in a meaningless profession from which she, too, is rescued at the end!)

It's not just about mental suffering or boredom or missing out on satisfaction and happiness. Look around you. There are environmental problems, a by-product of our search for money without paying attention to meaning. We are running out of cheap energy! Violence, terrorism, global warming, overcrowding, the health-care crisis, economic meltdowns—there are problems galore, and surely, you recognize that these problems are not entirely tractable even with the best of information processing.

Take the case of terrorism. After 9/11, it became a preoccupation of our society to analyze the failure of our intelligence machinery, all based on information processing. But if we paid even a little attention to meaning, nothing like this would ever have happened. Terrorism has always existed, and often it is not a bad thing when used against tyranny because the goal is to increase the access of meaning processing for more people. Just remember that the freedom fighters of the American Revolution began as terrorists from the point of view of the British monarchy. Good or bad, the saving grace of olden-day terrorism was that it was contained; it was a small-scale activity, relatively speaking. Modern terrorism, on the contrary, is large scale, capable of affecting many (often innocent) lives at once. Modern terrorism is a direct result of the production of modern weapons capable of large-scale destruction and dissemination of those weapons without thinking out the consequences—which is a reduction of people's access to meaning processing. Weapon sales by the United States and other technologically capable countries continue unbridled even after terrorism has become a worldwide problem. We have created the modern terrorist by neglecting meaning in preference to money.

If information processing cannot give us tangible answers to questions of physical and mental health, environmental pollution, energy shortage, violence, and the deterioration of society, is there another way to proceed that will give us tangible answers? Is the tangible solution to these problems paying attention to meaning processing, so as to make the transition from information to meaning?

Yes, that is the first step. And fortunately, there are already paradigm shifters in some segments of our society who see this and have begun emphasizing meaning. In this way, we have begun to see the creative development of alternatives in our sciences, in medicine and health, and in our businesses. This emphasis has to spread to all our other enterprises: economics, politics, religion, and, most importantly, education.

Mental Intelligence

What is intelligence? It is the capacity to respond *appropriately* to a given situation. Those who developed the IQ (intelligence quotient) test tell us that all our problem-solving capacities are mental in nature; they are logical, rational, algorithmic capacities, and, as such, they are also measurable. So the intelligence quotient that IQ tests measure relates to our mental intelligence. But is that all there is to mental intelligence?

Problem solving for an IQ test is algorithmic, so people who tout rationalism are quite happy with IQs and rational-logical mental intelligence as the only measure of people's intelligence.

You can see that IQs really measure little more than machine intelligence; the test focuses mostly on the capacity we have for using the mind as a machine. We need only process meaning in the contexts etched in our memories. The bigger storage of memory we have giving us access to a vast repertoire of learned contexts (information), the greater our IQ is. The greater our reasoning power or algorithmic processing capacity, the higher IQ we have.

It is like the grandmasters of chess who memorize the successful moves in thousands of contexts of board positions. So whereas we ordinary mortals struggle with figuring out the future effect of a particular move, the grandmaster makes his or her move simply from memory, using only a little reasoning to adapt to the present situation.

But real life is not a chess game played with a fixed board and fixed rules. Nor is life a series of IQ tests. The contexts for our meaning processing change constantly and often unpredictably. They may not be big changes of context, but nevertheless just memory processing and situational reasoning will not be enough to find the appropriate response in meaning. Suppose a Zen master holds up a marker and asks you, "What is it?" And you say, "It is a marker." Now the Zen master says, "I will hit you thirty times." Strange response, but Zen masters are famous for their strangeness. And guess what? If you have never been to a Zen master, it is unlikely that you will even know what the Zen master is trying to say to you! Maybe he is just a sadist.

When I was a beginner in the Zen tradition and encountered this particular behavior, I didn't understand it. I just attributed it to quirkiness—everybody knows that Zen masters are quirky, right? Only ten years later, when I was reading John Searle's article (1987) on mind and meaning, did I understand that the Zen master was trying to draw our attention to the fact that a marker is not only a marker used for writing, although that is its most frequent use. A marker *can* also be used to hit someone (although not very hard). Heck, a marker can even be used as a barometer: if you measure the time it takes a marker to fall from a given height, you can figure out the atmospheric pressure at that elevation.

So mental intelligence is more than IQ intelligence because mind is more than a machine, more than our remembered responses to previous stimuli.

Who hasn't heard the term "street-smart" or the phrase "the school of hard knocks"? These refer to mental intelligence as opposed to formal IQ intelligence. People who are street-smart or have learned from the school of hard knocks don't depend on their memory of formal learning of artificial simplified contexts. They look at real-life contexts just as they are—always a new context that requires a new response. In other words, creativity, albeit outer creativity.

There are other situations in which IQ intelligence, information processing, is useless. Mental information processing always takes place within given contexts of thinking. If the problem you are looking at requires a brand-new context, you are stuck; no amount of information thinking or net surfing will help.

Einstein was not an information fancier. A teacher once asked him in a test situation, "What is the speed of sound?" Einstein said, "I don't clutter my brain with details like that."

What is the lesson from all this? To integrate meaning in our being is to be elevated from machine mental intelligence to real mental intelligence, which is the capacity to take an occasional quantum leap of meaning.

But I submit this is only a first step. Creativity directed to a product in the outer arena of the world is outer creativity; it is important but not enough. Evolution demands more.

There is another step. Loosely speaking, it is the step of paying attention to our inner lives, to direct our exploration in such a way as to establish meaning in the center of our being.

We pay attention to the interface of the outer and the inner. We pay attention to events of synchronicity (outer events that reverberate with inner meaning); they then assume more importance and become signposts of where life should take us. When we engage in creativity while paying attention to the play of synchronicity in our lives, the unfolding of meaning becomes more obvious, clearly amplified.

We begin paying attention to dreams—the ongoing unfolding of our life in the realm of meaning. Everyone knows that what is intense in our waking life affects our dream life. Similarly, we allow the intensity in our dream life to affect our waking life.

The thought comes sooner or later: can we direct our creativity to change the director of our inner processing? Instead of the mental ego directing our inner life, can we let the higher power of God/quantum consciousness direct our inner theater? Not just during the episodes of some outer creativity projects, but on a more regular basis. Thus begins the journey of inner creativity—taking quantum leaps to change our inner life.

But very soon we become aware of a difficulty. Our emotions create problems with changing our inner life to make meaning its center point. So we begin to pay attention to our feelings, our emotional life.

And this is good; this is an essential part of our evolutionary need. Don't forget that evolution requires that inner creativity not only becomes a going thing for me, but also for all humanity. To ensure that, I need to open my heart to everyone in my local interaction sphere and give each a helping hand toward creativity if I can. This requires giving up competition in favor of cooperation, giving up negative feelings in favor of positive feelings toward others. But how to do that!

Emotional Intelligence

Is there intelligence aside from IQ intelligence and true mental intelligence? In the West, some people have long recognized in the culture the fashionableness of suppressing emotions. We, men especially, are taught to suppress emotions because when emotions cloud our psyche, mind and mental logic cannot function very well, and even the best IQ is not of much help. Only by suppressing emotions can we retain control and use our high IQ to its fullest extent to succeed in life, or so we are told. The problem with this approach is that if we become emotion suppressors, we suppress all emotions. We suppress not only the negative emotions such as anger, which are detrimental to appropriate action that demands reason, but also positive emotions (such as love), which we covet and intuit add to the quality of life. What kind of intelligence is it that reduces the quality of life instead of enhancing it?

If you like science fiction, you can see the ongoing theme of the famous *Star Trek* shows here: reason versus emotion. Reason is efficient, reason enables you to function better in a crunch, but without emotion, isn't the reason for living compromised?

So in recent years, there has been much talk about emotional intelligence—intelligence that enables you to appropriately respond to emotions. But emotional intelligence is a funny beast. Suppose there is anger in your environment and you are caught up in it. You are not suppressing it, but if you express your anger along with everybody else in the environment, doesn't the situation only get worse?

Okay, so you neither express nor suppress, what happens? Have you done this? If you have, you have discovered that it takes tremendous effort and a disciplined practice. So people with a limited commitment to exerting effort and discipline succumb to either suppression (in the West) or expression (in the East).

The idea of disciplined practices for achieving emotional intelligence has made it into the psychology literature. Let's look at these practices as espoused in a popular book by psychologist Daniel Goleman, *Emotional Intelligence* (Goleman 1995): 1) awareness of one's own emotional nature; 2) emotion management; 3) controlling emotions in the service of goal-oriented motivation; 4) empathy (the ability to share other people's emotions without losing one's objectivity); and 5) handling emotionally intimate relationships.

Awareness training makes you aware of what your emotional habits are, whether you express or suppress, how you emotionally interact with others, and so on. Awareness practice also enables you to react to emotion without suppressing or expressing but, rather, just meditate on it, at least to a limited extent. Emotion management is prioritizing when to express and when to suppress, and when it is best to do neither, that is, meditate. Controlling emotions (namely, suppressing them) when your job calls for it is the civilized compromise into which every professional is forced. The practice is to suppress as consciously as you can.

Empathy is something every psychotherapist attempts to have, but, as they very well know, it can be an arduous practice. And you know what? Practice helps, but it never makes it to perfection. This is why therapists burn out.

I have been researching this subject for a long time, ever since I had a discussion with the yoga psychologist Uma Krishnamurthy on this subject at a conference in Bangalore, India. I had brought a group from the United States to the conference, at which both Uma and I were speakers. We both attended a small meeting in which some people of our group were sharing their feelings and it got a little out of hand. In other words, I didn't do very well as a group leader in keeping emotions under control. So Uma taught me about the difference between sympathy and empathy. I had become sympathetic with the group members, she said. Like them, I, too, had wallowed in negative emotions. Instead, I realized, I have to learn to relate with empathy—the capacity to feel other's emotions without losing one's objectivity.

Long practice on developing empathy has taught me one thing. Practice just cannot make you transform into an empathic being; in difficult situations, sympathy always breaks through and you pick up suffering from the person you are trying to help. In those situations, you have to stay with the problem until you have taken a quantum leap to objectivity. But please note that even the quantum leap does not permanently transform you into an empathic! It just enables you to see through a particular situation.

The last item on the list of emotional intelligence practices is handling intimate relationships. Participating in an intimate emotional relationship is the ultimate practice to take you beyond ordinary emotional intelligence. This subject is an important aspect of the transformational practice of a quantum activist, so I devote part of the next chapter to it.

If you have tried it, then you know one thing. You cannot resolve an emotional conflict at an intimate level without paying attention to the present context. No previous learning will do. In other words, you need to take quantum leaps on a regular basis to maintain an emotional intimate relationship.

People who look at emotions in a brain-based way, that is, assume that emotions are brain phenomena, also assume (wrongly) that the brain can be trained to learn all the five aspects of emotional intelligence mentioned. Fortunately, in a consciousness-based science, emotions are only secondarily brain-based (the brain circuits); primarily, they are psychological effects of feelings that arise in the vital body connections at the chakras. These psychological effects of feelings have two sources. First, mind gives meaning to feelings and in the process "mentalizes" them (Goswami 2004). Second, feelings have correlated physiological effects that, by affecting the representation maker, the brain, also affect the mind, that which is represented in the brain. Physiology affects psychology.

The mentalization of feelings is unfortunately tricky, and we often interpret feelings wrongly. In those cases, the solution is to invite the supramental to see the problem correctly, hence the need for quantum leaps.

So emotional intelligence practiced with the inclusion of occasional quantum leaps is what is required to satisfy the evolutionary need of integrating meaning and feeling.

The New Evolutionary Ethics

Traditionally, in the East, social ethics are largely ignored; ethics are practiced rigorously only as a preparation for spiritual enlightenment. In the West, the advantage of social ethics was recognized early on, but materialism has eroded the practice considerably. Most of us suffer from severely ambiguous feelings as far as ethics are concerned because, according to materialist science, the scope of ethics is very limited.

Biologists, the neo-Darwinists, have invented a form of scientific ethics based on biology, a principle called genetic determinism (Dawkins 1976). The idea is that our behavior is entirely determined by our genes; we are gene machines. Our mind, consciousness, and macro behavior, all have one ultimate purpose: to perpetuate our genes and guarantee their survival. It follows from this perspective that we should have some interest beyond selfishness, some natural tendencies of selfless altruistic behavior. For example, if I have some genes in common with another person, my genes would naturally gain propagation and survival by taking care of this other. Hence I behave altruistically toward another depending on how much genetic commonality I have with that person.

This is a good theory because if the theory were correct, this kind of bioethics would have been compulsory—our genes would have made sure of that. Unfortunately, the empirical data on altruism just do not conform to this theory.

In the olden days, fear of hell or desire for heaven was an incentive to follow ethics. But who do you know that takes heaven and hell so seriously anymore as to sacrifice selfishness, especially when there is ambiguity?

And yet, ethics and values are important to enough people today to have made a difference in the 2006 American midterm elections, which became a referendum on the war in Iraq. I submit that the reason so many of us, even today, have a conscience to think ethically in the face of so much growing unethical behavior in our societies is embedded in evolution. There is an evolutionary pressure that we experience as a calling, and we respond.

Of course, religions have universally supported ethics in various forms (do good, be good; do unto others that which you would want others to do unto you; if I am not for myself, who am I? if I am only for myself, what am I?). For dualistic and simplistic religions, the rationale is clear: fear of God.

In scientific terms, we can give a better rationale for ethics and the good-evil distinction. Good is that which takes you toward wholeness, and evil is that which takes you away from wholeness. But this may prove too ambiguous for situations where you most need clarity. Also, as religious ethics, these may not be proactive enough.

We need a new set of ethics to live by, no less. Can quantum physics give us more directed incentive toward ethical action? It can. It does.

Quantum physics is the physics of possibilities and hints that we, the observer/participant, choose from these possibilities the actual event of our experience. When Fred Alan Wolf coined the phrase "we choose our own reality" based on this hint, his dictum spread like wildfire among New Agers. The same thing happened when *The Secret* (both the book and the movie) suggested that we manifest what we intend for ourselves by choosing it and waiting. The idea became very popular among New Agers but also became the butt of jokes in comic strips because, obviously, the idea is too simplistic.

Previously, I mentioned one subtlety of the choice among quantum possibilities. The consciousness we choose from is not the ego, but a nonordinary cosmic state of consciousness, which traditionalists call God. Only when "my" ego intention resonates with the intention of God's "will" does my intention become manifest. But what is the criterion for "God's will"? In other words, on what basis do we choose when we are in that cosmic God consciousness? The answer emerges when you consider evolution.

There is an evolutionary movement of consciousness that is shifting toward manifesting the supramental archetypes in us. God's will is always driving us toward that goal. When we have a creative encounter with God and a creative insight comes, we have the ultimate ethical choice: shall I use this insight for selfish means or shall I use it for the greater good, for the evolutionary goal of the movement of consciousness? The clearer we are about our ethics, the more appropriate is our action that follows the creative insight. Let's call this evolutionary ethics.

Suppose we solidly base our actions on evolutionary ethics, on the very scientific notion of the evolution of consciousness and the demand of evolutionary movement of consciousness on us that meaning processing must be a privilege for everyone. In this way, the active principle of evolutionary ethics is: *our actions are ethical when they maximize the evolutionary potential of every human being.* Imagine a society where such an ethic is in place, what this will do to our politics, to the practice of law and journalism, the practice of businesses, to the practice of health and healing, to how we educate our children.

Previously, I spoke of mental and emotional intelligence. Evolutionary ethics demand that the pursuits of mental and emotional intelligence must be undertaken and achieved by the bulk of the entire human species; future evolution demands it. How do I not only achieve true mental intelligence supplemented by emotional intelligence for myself, but also help all my fellow humans achieve the same goal? The new science has some answers (see chapter 11).

If it bothers you that some people are able to get away with ethical violations (for example, the investment bankers who helped cause the 2008 economic meltdown and still drew huge bonuses), don't worry. They can get away now, but Captain Karma eventually gets everyone. You have to learn to be ethical, or else you get forever caught in the birth-death-rebirth cycle and karmuppance.

Right Relationship with the Environment: Deep Ecology

Hopi Indians are famous for their emphasis on right relationship, not only with people and things, but also with the environment, including that of the whole planet.

In the inward journey of conventional spirituality, right relationship with the environment is much ignored. No doubt this has led to the modern movement of deep ecology—our ethical responsibility must extend to the whole biota of the earth, Gaia.

As I've noted previously, "eco" comes from the Greek *eikos,* meaning place, and "logy" comes from the Greek *logos,* meaning knowledge. Ordinary ecology is about the knowledge of our physical environment. But we live not only in a physical world, but also in the three subtle worlds—vital, mental, and supramental. Deep ecology, then, refers to the knowledge of both our external and internal worlds, and it asks us to have ethical responsibility for all of these environments in which we live.

But deep ecology is meaningless if you hold to scientific materialism because you will be asking too much of yourself, asking a machine (you) to have relationships with other less sophisticated machines and to have relationships based on unjustified rules of ethics.

Only when we have established an evolutionarily ethical relationship with all our fellow human beings is it time to ponder our ethical responsibility to all creatures, great and small, including the responsibility to our nonliving environment. Only then does it make sense to ask what our responsibility is to the planet earth, to Gaia, and act each according to the answer we get. Why not engage in all this at once? It behooves us to remember the words of the poet T. S. Eliot (1943):

> Go, Go, Go, said the bird
> Humankind cannot bear too much reality.

It is just more practical to engage with deep ecology step-by-step.

Deep ecology requires not only abiding by a few rules for preserving our ecosystem or passing a few governmental laws preventing environmental pollution, but also taking actions in ambiguous situations that demand a creative quantum leap.

When you take such a quantum leap, you realize one astounding thing: *I choose, therefore I am, and my world is.* The world is not separate from you.

When we do this en masse, we will leap into a truly Gaia consciousness, which has already arisen in human vision from a different context. (I am referring to the Gaia theory of the chemist James Lovelock; see Lovelock 1982.)

Supramental Intelligence

You notice that all of the exploration agenda of the quantum activist—true mental intelligence, emotional intelligence, evolutionary ethics, and deep ecology—require occasional forays to the domain of the supramental. In some sense, these are examples of supramental intelligence. In earlier times, spiritual traditions guided people toward personal liberation, to shift the identity from the ego to the quantum self. The ultimate goal was total transformation to where supramental intelligence is used whenever appropriate, easily, and without effort. Unfortunately, an honest appraisal of the spiritual history of our planet suggests that very few people have ever arrived at easy-without-effort supramental intelligence by achieving total transformation.

It should be obvious that much of humanity will be routinely capable of growing supramental intelligence when the next step of our evolution from rational to intuitive mind gains momentum. So instead of personal liberation, we make evolution our priority.

This is a very profound change. When liberation is our goal, when it is liberation or bust, we become exclusively centered on personally arriving at the quantum self identity, which remains elusive. The achievement orientation itself becomes a barrier to the goal. When we center on evolution, it is no longer all or nothing, and we value the insights gained on the path. We engage in evolutionary ethics to gain insight into the archetype of goodness; we engage in creativity in science to develop insight into the archetype of truth; we engage in aesthetics and the arts and architecture to gain insight into the archetype of beauty; we engage in emotional intelligence practice in intimate relationship to gain insight into the archetype of love; we engage in law, news media, even politics to gain insight into the archetype of justice; and so forth.

When we stabilize the insights gained by those supramental journeys we make in how we live our lives, we are acquiring characteristics of supramental intelligence. To some, this may seem quite imperfect; our mental representations of the supramental will never match the real thing, they might (correctly) point out. But this is the best we can do. We are preparing the entire human race for the eventual next step in its evolution: the omega point, the capacity to make physical representations of the supramental. We don't entirely give up our journey toward liberation, but we put it on the back burner for now.

Walk Your Talk

Creative insights in the outer arena require a lot of hard work to manifest into a product. It is a fact that many people enjoy the creative process, have the insights, but cannot master the effort needed to finish the product. Only because of all the goodies (the carrots of behavioral psychology) that may come our way, this laziness in manifesting never reaches epidemic proportions.

In inner creativity, however, the manifestation stage is, if anything, even harder than outer creativity. And the behavioral rewards, the goodies, are not public but private. Because of this double whammy, many more people stop their creative process at the level of the insight; they don't try much to live their insight.

What is worse is that in a subtle way the prevalent materialist culture invades the mind-set of the inner creative. The inner creative falls for what Chögyam Trungpa Rinpoche called spiritual materialism and starts teaching what he or she knows from quantum leaps but has not manifested in being, with the expectations of the same rewards that drive outer creativity: name, fame, power, money, sex, outer accomplishments, and so on. (Alas, Trungpa Rinpoche himself was not entirely exempt from this mind-set.)

Some transpersonal thinkers (for example, Wilber 2006) complicate the situation further by introducing a certain glamour and mystique about the superconscious states one achieves with the quantum leaps by classifying such experiences. The classification may be useful, but the bottom line does not change. Without carrying through the manifestation stage, no permanent transformation takes place from any quantum leap, however exalted the classification you give it.

This overemphasis on the mere superconscious experience will not do for a quantum activist. We must break this tendency to be lazy at the most crucial point of our personal development and manifest in our being every supramental insight we have.

The New Age spirituality movement eventually got so tired of the dalliances in the typical New Age guru's behavior that they coined the phrase "walk your talk." Unless we see your insights reflected in your behavior, we won't listen.

This is good. For the quantum activist, this "walk your talk" is a must, along with the obvious rejoinder, "Don't become a guru."

One more thing. However many forays to the supramental you take, the mental representation of it that you make and live will always be context bound, and so your "transformation," learned behavior based on these mental representations, will never meet with the demands of every situation. In other words, there will always be occasions in which your behavior will not be appropriate, given the fact that your transformation is not yet perfected. You remain a practitioner of transformation, just preparing humanity for the next great evolutionary adventure. No big deal.

In short, quantum activists must never take their transformations seriously, or take themselves seriously; they must develop a sense of humor about themselves.

Remember that you have very likely been practicing supramental intelligence for quite a few lifetimes. Why not identify with your character, with what you learn and transfer from one lifetime to another in the form of non-local memory, rather than with local memory?

As your identity shifts in this way, you will notice that you are kind to others who have not yet made such a shift and are more accepting of their fallibilities. A tolerant quantum activist is a mature quantum activist.

The Overmind

Sri Aurobindo, one of the people who started all this new evolutionary thinking, also coined the word "overmind," which describes our situation perfectly. When we develop many positive emotional brain circuits, manifesting many vital and mental representations of many supramental insights in many contexts, we have done the next best thing to total transformation: we are approaching the developmental stage of the overmind. Carl Jung called this stage individuation. From an evolutionary point of view, this is our best strategy for a goal (hard as it may be to arrive at) at this stage of our evolution.

CHAPTER 10
Exploring the Quantum Tools for Right Living

Quantum physics was discovered through the study of the motion of elementary particles at the atomic and subatomic level. Many people still cannot get over the prejudice that quantum thinking must be engaged only when we deal with the submicroscopic world of matter. The same people also think that the world is fundamentally made of matter and the real world is objective, local, rational, and deterministic. These people cannot rise beyond the concept of IQ brain-based mental intelligence in their belief system, although many of them take regular forays into the supramental when they creatively discover the solutions to their scientific problems. Their relationship with the world outside their profession may be seriously handicapped because of their faulty belief system. They more often than not live a loveless life (that is, they live in their head, not their heart), they cannot discriminate between good and evil consequences of either their professional or their social work (they are not bothered by developing the atomic bomb or such things), and happiness and emotional equanimity elude them, but they don't know why.

The problem with a worldview that is strictly objective, deterministic, and materialist (scientific materialism–oriented) is that it gives us a highly skewed view of us and our consciousness, emotions, meanings, conscience, and values. In materialism, everything is made of matter; thus consciousness and all subjective phenomena related to it, such as conscience, are relegated to mere epiphenomena of matter (as a gold ornament is an epiphenomenon of gold) without causal efficacy. If consciousness has no causal efficacy, how can we transform? How can we apply the dictates of our conscience? How can we love?

But science is changing, and people who are following this change are realizing that they have to take a transformative path in order to develop a 21st-century science and a code of living that can deal with transformation. Such people are consciously using supramental intelligence (limited though it may be). It is as a result of their work that a scientific treatment of transformation removing all confusion on the subject can today be given.

Once we understand the quantum principles, it greatly facilitates our attempts to develop supramental intelligence. The truth is, everybody has access to the supramental world; many of us just don't explore it for one reason or another. The materialist people do not use it optimally because of faulty ideology in which they have vested interest. What is your reason?

It doesn't matter. With help from quantum principles, as explained later, I am convinced that your reasons for avoiding the supramental will dissipate and you will be able to move onto the transformative path (unending as it may seem), leaving behind the information superhighway to nowhere. The world and its 21st-century problems need you and your capacity for processing supramental intelligence.

You probably like to dance occasionally. Dancing has a unique spontaneity that sometimes surprises the dancer; it seems to happen by itself, effortlessly. When even a limited amount of supramental intelligence manifests in us, it is like dancing in the world much of the time. Resonating with Lewis Carroll, "Will you, won't you, will you, won't you, won't you join the dance?"

The Quantum Tools Toward Supramental Intelligence and Transformation

Why is transformation a relatively rare commodity? The psychologist Abraham Maslow, who did a definitive study of (partially) transformed people (Maslow's term for these people was people of positive mental health), estimated that maybe 5 percent of all people belong to this category. What is the explanation of this rarity?

Let's put it in a different way, in keeping with the mystic philosopher Jiddu Krishnamurti. He used to chide people, and I paraphrase: Why can't you change? Why can't you embrace nonviolence? Great teachers have given you the message of nonviolence for millennia, and good recipes, too. You all have tried to follow them. But why do you fail? Why does a vast majority of people fail? Because you try to be nonviolent in a continuous way. You think, today I will be a little less violent, and tomorrow even less. It doesn't work like that!

So how does transformation work, if not through continuous effort, if not by applying rational intelligence? Can any movement, any change be discontinuous?

There are two reasons that people tend to be skeptical about discontinuous change. One is that as adults they seldom experience a discontinuous movement of consciousness. Generally, our experiences are continuous. We look outside, close our eyes, or go to sleep; when we open our eyes or wake up from sleep, the same outside world is there. Continuity seems to prevail. If we look inside, we find thoughts and feelings that seem to make up a continuous stream of consciousness. The second reason for skepticism is the brainwashing that goes on today under the guise of scientific education in favor of rationality, in favor of a continuous algorithmic answer to every problem.

From its very inception, quantum physics has told us of the validity of the concept of discontinuous movement. Consider once again Niels Bohr's picture of the discontinuous movement of the electron in the atom. In the atom, the electrons go around the nucleus, the core of the atom, in orbits; this part of the electron's movement is continuous, one little bit at a time. But when the electron jumps from one orbit to another, something it does whenever there is emission of light from the atom, the electron never goes through the intervening space. One moment it is here; and then it is there, instantly. This quantum leap, Bohr style, remains a good model of discontinuous movement in nature.

Can we describe the movement of quantum leap via continuous algorithms, via mathematics, via causal logic, via mechanical modeling? No. So where does the doctrine of continuity (which underlies determinism—if motion can be determined even in principle, continuity must prevail so we can calculate, at least in principle) stand now? The doctrine of continuity has to be given up!

The materialist can still hope that maybe quantum physics is not the final theory of physics, or maybe quantum physics can be reformulated in such a way that continuity prevails. But the success of quantum physics seems to indicate the futility of this kind of hope.

Alternatively, the materialist can hope that, although discontinuity undeniably prevails in the submicroscopic world, maybe it does not make it to the macroworld of our experience. Maybe when the movement of jillions of submicroscopic objects is involved, all discontinuity gets wiped out and continuity prevails once more. But this hope also does not hold up (see chapter 4).

And as for your lack of personal experience of the discontinuous movement of consciousness, relax. It is not as foreign to you as you think. Have you seen the cartoon "The Physics Teacher," by Sidney Harris? Einstein stands before a blackboard trying to discover his law $E = mc^2$. He writes $E = ma^2$ and crosses it out. Next he tries $E = mb^2$ and crosses it out. The caption says, "The creative moment." So why do you laugh when you see the cartoon? Because you know intuitively that creative discoveries do not involve step-by-step continuity; instead, they are the products of discontinuous insight.

The truth is, when you were a child, you used to take such discontinuous quantum leaps of thought quite regularly. That's how we learn things that require new contexts of thinking, such as a new mathematical concept, reading meaning in a story, and abstract thinking for the first time.

And if childhood is too remote, think of those moments when you intuit something. What happens? What is intuition? Why do you call certain thoughts intuition? Because there is no rational continuous explanation for such thoughts; there is no contextual precedent for such thoughts. An intuition is your glimpse at a future quantum leap.

In this day and age you may also take a different track. You may go see the movie *The Secret* and get inspired by its message that you can manifest anything. When you fail a few times, you may remember the lesson of quantum physics: the intention for manifestation must resonate with nonlocal consciousness. Then is the time to do the following exercise.

Exercise: Creative and Transformative Intention

Sit comfortably and quietly. An intention must start with the ego, that's where you are. So at the first stage, intend for yourself; be forceful; try to manifest your intention.

At the second stage, recognize that you can have what you want in two ways, having it all by yourself, or having it because everybody (which includes you) gets it. So now intend for everyone, for the greater good. Begin by expanding your consciousness to include all people in your vicinity; then include in your consciousness everyone in your city, in your state, in your country, and finally in the whole world.

At the third stage, your intention must become a prayer: if my intention resonates with the intended movement of the whole, then let it come to fruition.

At the fourth stage, the prayer must pass into silence; it must become a meditation. Stay in meditation for a few minutes.

Of course, initially with this exercise, you will probably try to manifest physical things: a helicopter would be nice! You want to fly. If you keep at it, there may be a phase when you see a lot of flying dreams and the experience is frustrating. In the dream you fly so well, but you wake to find that you are grounded, you can't fly; your helicopter has not manifested. Then one day, when you wake up, a different idea occurs to you. Suppose the dream is trying to draw your attention to the fact that you *can* fly in your dreams, although you can't in physical reality. In other words, you can be creative in the subtle, and that is where you work on your powers of creativity and manifestation.

Transformation involves the same kind of discontinuous quantum leap in the movement of consciousness as acts of creativity in science, math, art, and music. I call the latter acts outer creativity and the former inner creativity.

So the first exploratory quantum tool for developing supramental intelligence is discontinuous quantum leaps. The following are a few practices for quantum leaping.

First Practice: Exploring Gaps in Stream-of-Consciousness Thinking

Sit quietly and comfortably with your back straight. Close your eyes and watch your thoughts as they come into awareness and fade away from awareness. Try not to be partial to any particular thought; regard all of them as the same passing show. The analogy of watching clouds in the mind's sky may help.

When you start this meditation, you will notice how one thought quickly replaces another. Your mind is racing. After a while, especially with practice, your mind will slow down and successive thoughts will seem to appear with distinct gaps between them. Don't get too excited. You have not discovered "no thought" or emptiness of mind because even in the gap your subject-object split of awareness remains. This is a good place to be, however, because quantum leaping is much facilitated from such a place.

Second Practice: Exploring Sudden Involuntary Phenomena

When you are in the midst of seemingly sudden involuntary phenomena such as a sneeze or an orgasm, be intensely aware. Practice to see if you can stop yourself right before sneezing or right before an orgasm. Again, a sneeze or even a sexual orgasm is not a quantum leap or a true discontinuity. But being aware in such moments is a proven recipe for the facilitation of a quantum leap.

Third Practice: Exploring the Gap Between Sleep and Wakefulness

Watch carefully if you can remain aware right up to the junction of wakefulness and sleep. From this awareness, quantum leaping is a distinct possibility. You may have heard how many creative people get their ideas while in a reverie; this is precisely your objective.

If you want more practices like these with the same objective of quantum leaping, read the appendix of Paul Reps' book on Zen (Reps 1957); they are called the 112 meditation techniques of Siva.

Quantum Nonlocality

Consider now another important principle of the materialist's worldview: locality. Locality is the idea that all influences that cause movement or change travel through space and time continuously, a little bit at a time. So influences that are in the local vicinity have more effect; the influences farther away are far less effective. An example derives from how a wave affects an object. When the object is close, the power of the wave reaching out to the object is strong. But at twice the distance, this power attenuates to only one-fourth of the previous strength. Furthermore, Einstein proved with his relativity theory (and experimenters have verified Einstein's relativity many times over) that influences can propagate in space and time only subject to a speed limit, the speed of light (300,000 km/sec). This is also part of the locality principle.

But for quantum objects, the locality principle does not hold. Ironically, Einstein, whose relativity theory was instrumental in establishing the locality principle, was the first, along with his two colleagues Nathan Rosen and Boris Podolsky, to see the viability of quantum nonlocality (Einstein, Podolsky, and Rosen 1935). If two quantum objects interact, they become so correlated that their mutual influence persists unabated even at a distance, even when they are not interacting via any local force or exchanging any local signals. Later the physicists John Bell and David Bohm developed ideas that made quantum nonlocality experimentally verifiable. As discussed in chapter 4, experimental verification of the idea came via the work of the physicist Alain Aspect and his collaborators. They watched two photons emitted with quantum correlation from the same calcium atom continue their correlated dance even after they were separated by distance, and without any signals exchanged between them.

As mentioned before, quantum nonlocality has now been directly verified even for human subjects (correlation between brains), leaving no doubt that quantum physics does apply to us, to the macroworld, under suitable subtle situations.

For millennia, nonlocal connections between humans have been known to exist in such phenomena as mental telepathy. What is special about the new experiments is that they are objective and the role of meditation and intention is so clearly seen in them (Grinberg-Zylberbaum et al. 1994).

Our consciousness ordinarily works with local stimuli, either from the physical environment or from memory; this is the ego mode. In nonlocal communication, we transcend the local ego mind and momentarily use quantum consciousness. Like creatives who (somewhat unconsciously) use momentary forays into quantum consciousness to process supramental intelligence in their professional field, psychics are people who have the access (again somewhat unconsciously) to quantum consciousness in the area of nonlocal communication. This access to quantum consciousness can be used to process supramental intelligence as well.

As I have stated before, quantum physics makes the idea of nonlocal communication of information scientifically feasible. Here are a couple of exercises for you to access quantum consciousness, God, through an experience of quantum nonlocality. This should open your door further for processing supramental intelligence.

One word of caution. Nonlocal communication is the easiest entry point to nonlocal consciousness. It can be used for accessing God, but it can and is often used in the pursuit of power. The sage Patanjali warned us all about this danger, and a quantum activist is well advised not to fall prey to this tendency.

Exercise 1: Distant Viewing Exercise

Sit with a friend who has in hand in a closed box an object about which you know nothing; your friend knows what it is. With the intention of direct communication, meditate together for about twenty minutes and maintain this meditative intention during the rest of the exercise, which is distant viewing. Try to "see" nonlocally without visual signals what's inside that box while your friend visualizes the thing inside the box. For best results, write down and draw pictures of what "pops" into your mind, distinct from stream-of-consciousness thinking. After the exercise, compare your drawing with the physical object. Then switch roles.

Exercise 2: Meditation with a Group of Other Meditators

To start with, get a reference point by meditating for about ten minutes by yourself. Then meditate for another ten minutes with a group of other meditators. Notice if the quality of meditation is deeper. Repeat daily for a few days. If group meditation is consistently better for you than individual meditation, you are getting the hang of quantum nonlocality. Your supramental intelligence is being enhanced. Incidentally, this nonlocal enhancement of meditative quality is what Jesus meant when he said, "When two or more gather in my name, there I am in the midst of them."

Exercise 3: Quantum Brainstorming or Dialoging

You may know about brainstorming or dialoging. The idea is to communicate freely with another, listening without judgment and with attention and respect. In quantum dialoging, you also include speaking from a silence to give nonlocality a chance to work its magic.

Take any topic, for example, transformation, and have a quantum dialog with a friend. Write down the result. If the dialoging begins to produce new insights of discontinuous thought, it is a telltale sign of growing supramental intelligence.

Exercise 4: Nonlocality in the Vital Arena

This practice should be done in two stages. At the first stage, find your local or nearest dowsing group and practice dowsing, which consists of using a divining rod to find water by virtue of water's vital energy signature.

At the second, more advanced stage, a group of you can try this experiment. Each of you writes his/her name on a card. One person collects all the cards and pins the cards to various objects in the room. Others are blindfolded and, in that condition, each tries to locate his/her own signature card.

Tangled Hierarchy

Self-referential collapse that gives us the subject-object split in an experience is tangled hierarchical as opposed to simple hierarchical. What does this mean? In a tangled hierarchy, the levels of the hierarchy are codependent, each has causal efficacy over the other, and yet, the causal efficacy is only an appearance, coming from an inviolate level. In the case of the subject-object split, the causal efficacy is neither in the subject nor in the object, but in the God consciousness beyond the subject-object split. When we learn to love tangled hierarchically, we have an opportunity to fall into the quantum self beyond the simple hierarchy of the ego. This gives another path to supramental intelligence. The spiritual tradition of Christianity mainly uses this tangled hierarchical path of love of God. "I am as needed by God," the mystic Meister Eckhart used to say, "as God is needed by me."

From Sex to Love: Sex and the New Physics

The subtitle of this section, I hope, does not give you the impression that I am talking about some exotic new quantum recipe for enhancing sexual pleasure, that I am trying to found a kind of new age tantra, quantum sex maybe? For ordinary people of the world who choose to remain householders, the path of love is best reached through intimate relationships involving sex. What does the new physics have to say about sex? A lot, but it is subtle.

You already know that quantum physics, when properly interpreted with the conceptual lens of primacy of consciousness, is all about nonlocality, quantum leaps, and tangled hierarchy. Can sex lead to relationships in which these quantum principles play a frequent role?

When we begin our sex lives, there is a definite tendency to use sex to explore power. This is especially true of men. But mysteriously, with some special partners, we hear a different drum, we feel a different vital energy, and we are in love. How does one take a quantum leap from the tendency to use sex to make power to a tendency to use sex always to make love, not power?

How does one transform the usual romantic relationships of linear causality to quantum relationships of circular causality, from simple hierarchy to tangled hierarchy? Face it, for all the hoopla surrounding it, romantic love is simple hierarchical: she (he) is mine. How do commitment and marriage fit into this discussion?

And finally, to the main subject: How does one utilize sexual relationships as springboards to practice unconditional love? How does one make a quantum leap to a transformed being for whom sex becomes a choice rather than a compulsion?

So these are the quantum questions of sex. The answers tell us about the three stages of sexual maturity in relationship, the three stages of sexual intelligence, if you will.

From Sex in the Service of Power to Sex to Make Love

Because of our instinctual brain circuits, our sexuality is aroused easily and often by a variety of stimuli. When we are teenagers and these feelings are unfamiliar, we become confused about our sexuality. Most societies have a taboo against educating the young about sexuality. In some spiritual societies, the idea of celibacy is introduced for the young. Unfortunately, this, too, is done without much guidance as to why or how. The original idea could have been good: remain celibate until you discover romantic love when you will no longer be confused about the real goal of your sexuality. But without any avenue for such education, how is the confusion going to go away?

If a teenager goes into sex without understanding the meaning and purpose of sex (and I am not talking here about "the birds and the bees" reproductive aspect of sex that is generally taught in schools as sex education), he or she will blindly respond to the brain circuits and look upon sexuality as a gratification, as a vehicle for a unique kind of intense pleasure. Since the fulfillment of sexual pleasure with a partner raises vital energy to the third chakra, associated with ego identity with the physical body, a sense of personal power enters the equation. Hence it is common to think of "sexual conquests" in connection with sex that is not associated with romantic love.

In the Western world, the pattern that has developed over the last few decades, at least for men, is this early conditioning of sex for power. Women, thanks to some protective ("conservative") parents, are somewhat exempt, although that is rapidly changing. What happens when we eventually discover a partner with whom our heart chakra resonates? We enter the romantic love relationship, but we tend not to give up the habit. So when the romance runs out, which it does sooner or later, the sex-for-power tendency returns. We then have a choice. We can look for another romantic partner, or go deep in the existing relationship.

Hence the social custom of the man being the one to ask his romantic partner to enter marriage. To enter marriage is to change the equation of sex: I will commit to changing my pattern of using sex for power to using sex always to make love. This means we always allow the energy to rise to the heart after a sexual encounter; we allow ourselves to become vulnerable. Marriage is a commitment to make love, not war (conquest).

Unfortunately, this vital body agreement has concurrently to find agreements between the mental bodies of the partners as well. There the ego conditionings are very deep and involve wide areas of overlap in which competitiveness can emerge and bring down the energy from the heart chakra. Competitiveness and other negative emotions will go away only when we begin to glimpse intuitively that it is possible to surrender the negative emotions within the positive energy of love.

Exercise: Practice of Love with an Intimate Partner in Three Parts

In the movie *The Wedding Date,* to my great satisfaction, the hero said to the heroine something to the effect, "I want to marry you, because I'd rather fight with you than make love with another person." To practice unconditional love, it is important to recognize your love partner shamelessly as "the intimate enemy." The behavioral advice is to use reason to settle the differences that cause fights ("renegotiating your contract"); but this amounts only to suppressing emotions. Or if emotions break out anyway, the behavioral advice is to leave the scene, not to let things "get out of hand," or to "kiss and make up," which is usually a pretension. This is perhaps good advice for people who are not ready, but for you, the quantum activist, your challenge is to love your partner in spite of your differences. And when these differences cause a fight, then so be it; remain in the fight explicitly or implicitly until a quantum leap takes place. The three parts of the practice here are suggestions for facilitating the quantum leap. For all three parts, wait for a situation when a fight has broken out between the two of you and has gone into a stage when no holds are barred, as the saying goes.

Caution: Don't engage in these exercises if you are not ready for it or if you don't feel secure in your relationship with your partner. Encouragement: Only a hero can try this path. Remember, even some of the world's most well-known spiritual teachers/mystics cannot easily pass the equanimity-in-intimate-relationship test.

Stage 1. Keep your awareness as much as you can during the fight. See yourself repeatedly losing awareness and becoming defensive, especially when the attacks are personal, "below the belt." Watch yourself helplessly reacting with jibes and insults below the belt.

Suddenly, forget all that and start laughing; allow the laughing to become uncontrollable belly laughs. Then may come a surprise: a quantum leap.

Stage 2. Wait for the same situation as in stage 1, with you becoming defensive and reacting helplessly. Suddenly make an about-turn and start hugging her (or him) intimately, laying her (or him) down on a sofa, or bed, or the floor, and hold her (or him) tightly with eyes closed until the defensiveness dissolves.

Stage 3. Wait for the same situation until helplessness descends. This time, go on fighting, occasionally focusing (internally) on an intention and a prayer for love energy to arise in the heart chakra. You may have to take mutually agreed upon breaks for this one. During the break, you try to bring energy to the heart through visualizing great masters of love, through remembering loving episodes with your partner, or just thinking about your favorite love story. When you feel energy in the heart, go back to the fight. Do this repeatedly, until . . . something new. A quantum leap?

A note in passing. These practices are preliminary and certainly not exclusive. You may have to look for more advanced practices, and the best way is to go to the traditions—Buddhist, Hindu, Sufi, Judaic, Taoist, Christian, or others, whatever appeals to you. Alternatively, you can seek out workshops by spiritual teachers, which can also be quite effective. Eventually, you will discover your own practice, what works for you.

Inviting God to Resolve your Conflicts:
The Practice of Unconditional Love

After it dawns on you that your intimate enemy can be your intimate friend as well, a truly respectful relationship begins to evolve between you and your partner. In this relationship, each of you are individuals, each of you can recognize the "otherness" of the other (to use sociologist Carol Gilligan's language). Now your relationship has taken a turn toward transforming from simple hierarchy to a tangled hierarchy.

Look again at the Escher picture *Drawing Hands* (see Figure 6 in chapter 1). In the picture the tangled hierarchy is created because the left hand is drawing the right, and the right hand is drawing the left, but you can see that this is an illusion. Behind the scene, Escher is drawing them both. When through your study of the quantum paradoxes (see chapter 4), you have truly taken the quantum leap of understanding that the reality of your manifest consciousness, the subject-hood of the subject-object partnership arises from the quantum choice and collapse from an undivided quantum consciousness, you have also identified the source of your real freedom. It is in the state of unmanifest quantum consciousness. But how do you shift your identity from the manifest to the unmanifest, even temporarily?

Now your intimate enemy-friend can become a huge boon. I spoke of creativity before. Creative insights are greatly helped if we can somehow produce a proliferation of the quantum possibilities from which our quantum consciousness chooses. Your partner is a boon in this regard because she or he introduces a second slit of a double slit arrangement through which the stimuli you process are sifted, allowing an enormous proliferation of possibilities. (Go back to the double slit experiment in chapter 4. When electrons pass through the double slit, the quantum possibilities available to them are much enhanced.)

You and your partner represent different slits, different points of view for sorting out stimuli, so conflicts are natural. Suppose you don't try to resolve these conflicts, but learn to live with unresolved conflicts, thus leaving it to your unmanifest quantum consciousness to process the possibilities and choose the resolution.

This practice, holding unresolved conflicts indefinitely until resolution comes from higher consciousness, is a difficult practice, but its rewards are enormous. The conditions that we impose on our love now can fall away, and love can blossom into unconditional, objective love. It is objective love because the love of quantum consciousness is objective.

And then we have choice. Once we can love unconditionally, sex is a choice. We do not need it to make love. We have a positive emotional love circuit in our brain now. We can still include sex in our love relationship if appropriate and if we so choose, of course, but sex is no longer compulsory. We don't have to engage in it helplessly.

This is the legendary love of Krishna and his gopis, celebrated in the Hindu Vaishnavite tradition. On special full moon nights, Krishna dances with his 10,000 gopis, all at once. Or so the legend goes. Can Krishna duplicate himself in 10,000 bodies? If you think of Krishna's love as love in space and time, you will be puzzled by this legend. It must be a metaphor! It is. The unconditional love of Krishna is always celebrated outside of space and time, nonlocally.

From Spiritual Materialism to Total Surrender

Some words of caution once more before we go further. In our materialist society, we have become corrupted by behavioral psychology and have moved toward a reward-punishment motivation for our spiritual accomplishments. Remember that this is spiritual materialism; it becomes a big barrier to your personal spiritual fulfillment, especially if you want to arrive at a permanent identity with God consciousness (called *nirvikalpa* or the "no boundaries" stage; see more on this in chapter 17 under the subsection "The Second-Person God and the Question of Gurus") and live mostly in your quantum self in this very human condition. Remember, gaining mastery in the form of the overmind is only a stopgap goal; the ultimate objective is to arrive at a station of consciousness wherein even ego-level memory-based responses conform to supramental intelligence as far as possible.

So one never loses sight of the ultimate goal—to give up ego supremacy in favor of the quantum self—God consciousness. The practice toward that end is to undermine the accomplisher within us, not to take ourselves too seriously. In other words, we dance, but always lightly, not caring what anyone thinks of us, not even what I think of me.

Karma Yoga

Karma yoga is the yoga of applying yogic practice right in the middle of real life. *Karma* means "action" and *yoga* means "union" or "integration," so karma yoga means the union of ego and spirit through the path of action. This is an important practice of service to others in many spiritual traditions, especially Hinduism, Christianity, and Soto Zen. In these traditions, however, this service is often not a part of one's livelihood. For a quantum activist, karma yoga as part of earning your living is encouraged.

If you are satisfied with your current livelihood, obviously you can practice karma yoga while earning your living. But if you have a mismatch, this is not practical. Part 3 takes you into real-life situations of our society and points you toward finding a suitable livelihood in which you can practice karma yoga for your quantum activism. As you read through it, look for the particular context for activism that turns you on. For example, if you are a healer at heart, clearly health and healing is your arena for quantum activism. Doesn't this require years of training and huge amounts of cash? Not necessarily. As the medical paradigm changes toward an integrative medicine, there will be many new ways to receive a healing education and one of these is bound to suit you.

CHAPTER 11

Can a Few People Make a Difference?

By now you must have figured out the problem with creativity and transformation en masse. Yes, anyone can be creative; yes, anyone can transform. But it is hard to be so motivated, especially today, in a materialist society in which there is hardly any support from your environment to encourage your creativity and transformation. Materialist societies have a vested interest in keeping people functioning within their conditioned behavior patterns so that they are predictable, subject to statistical projections. Economists want consumers to conform to a pattern by which they are manipulated via marketing techniques; if consumers are so conditioned and conform to the mathematical theory of consumer behavior, economics becomes predictable and can be used to make money risk free! In politics, politicians want you to register with a particular party; nobody likes you to be an independent. Even in schools, students who get good grades are often the ones who conform to the teacher's opinions.

And yet undoubtedly, some of us want to be creative, want to transform ourselves, want to transform the society. Where do we get our chutzpa? Some of us want to transform because we don't want to suffer anymore. Some of us are curious: what is it like to really love someone unconditionally? A large number of us become motivated because we are activists in our heart: the earth has crisis conditions right now that require urgent solutions; who but I will discover and deploy these solutions?

So here we are, quantum activists, with the audacity of hope that we can change our worldview, change ourselves, and change the world. "Never doubt that a small group of dedicated people can change the world," said anthropologist Margaret Mead. "It is the only thing that ever has." The latest theory of evolution is telling us how.

Evolving Positive Emotions as Instincts

Let's consider evolution once again. Usually, important evolution occurs through quantum leaps in the genetic makeup of organs. Long ago, however, even before Darwin, the biologist Lamarck suggested that there might be another way that the biological information about acquired characteristics can be transferred from one generation to the next. Rupert Sheldrake (1981) has theorized how: through the intermediary of nonlocal morphogenetic fields. Using quantum physics, I have taken Sheldrake's idea further (Goswami 2008b). With Darwinism and even with creative evolution, the phenomenon of instincts cannot be explained. But with Lamarckism Sheldrake style, we explain instincts (Goswami 2008b).

The vital body and its morphogenetic fields are of crucial importance here. I have spoken of the neuronal wiring that exists in the midbrain and the neocortex in an associative manner, which, when excited, gives us the experience of an instinctual negative emotion. Who does that wiring? Consciousness does, during the process of embryonic development, with the crucial help from the modifications of the vital morphogenetic fields correlated with the limbic brain and the neocortex of the entire human species.

Animals have instincts, too, but their instincts do not have a psychological, neocortical component. Early in the history of the evolution of the human species, humans learned to give meaning to their feelings, making correlated neocortical circuits associated with the limbic circuits that they inherited from their animal ancestors. The morphogenetic fields associated with the neocortex were modified accordingly. It is reasonable to assume that, in those early days of the human species, individual consciousness was secondary to group consciousness. In this way, individual modifications of the morphogenetic fields were available to an entire group for use via nonlocal transmigration, as in reincarnation. Eventually, the group inheritance of this particular acquired characteristic spread to the entire human species.

I really think that the wiring was completed for all the negative emotions that we experience today in that vital age of human evolution that I have discussed before. And more. I think those worthy ancestors of ours also completed a couple of positive emotional brain circuits as well. I have mentioned the recent neurophysiological discovery of the God spot in the midbrain. When you excite this spot, you experience spiritual awe. Another example of such wiring corresponds to the altruistic behavior that is also pretty much universal in humans.

But as I mentioned before, the vital age of human evolution was aborted prematurely due to the technological invention of heavy agricultural machinery, and so we never completed making the positive emotional brain circuits. Thus when negative emotions are aroused, clouding our reasoning power, we don't have the power to spontaneously balance these negative emotions with positive emotions.

Can we take up that aborted job of making positive emotional brain circuits in the brain of the human species once more? We can and we must. For millennia, we have been making such brain circuits individually; that does not much help the species in terms of inheritance. But suppose we make brain circuits in groups, as we did in those horticultural communities of long ago.

So far I have spoken of quantum activism as an individual endeavor. But suppose we take another step and practice quantum activism and make positive emotional brain circuits as a group activity. In principle, this should only prove easier since, in group consciousness, creativity is more potent than in individual consciousness.

This building of brain circuits of love, we do initially in two-way relationship, intimate relationships—lovers, therapist-client, parent-child, and so on. Then we work in families. And eventually, we learn to work even in big groups such as in a business setting or in an educational context. And always, we use the power of intention to propagate the effect: let my transformative experience be shared by all people; let the benefits of the quantum leaps accrue to all people.

Finally, we will use the Internet (the "global brain") as the local trigger needed to activate our quantum nonlocal connection, our interconnected consciousness, with really large groups all at once.

We start small with a lot of patience. Let those who can see the point of the new science, change their worldview pronto. Let those who can, take quantum leaps from negative to positive emotions with evolutionary intentions. Let those who can live increasingly with positive emotions, make brain circuits and make changes in the associated morphogenetic fields. Let those who can, spread positive emotions through relationships in bigger and bigger groups. To those who have the technical savvy to use the Internet and make a quantum connection with really large groups, let all power of our collective intention come to their aid.

How long will this take? Not too long. My guess is six to seven generations. Still, this is long term. Can we hold the energies of transformation that long? In the meantime, we must build institutions that facilitate this evolutionary journey for increasing numbers of people. This is the short-term goal of quantum activism. We change the worldview, we change our health-care system, we change economics, we revitalize democracy, liberal education, even religions. Can we do it? Why not? Remember that the evolutionary movement of consciousness is with us, events of synchronicity are helping us, and the archetypes that are living us are driving us.

The evolutionary movement of consciousness is clear: the worldview is already changed and our social systems will change accordingly in some future time. But we have to be the causal connection between now and then.

Ode to Love
I love you.
This is already true in possibility
The problem for me is one of representation
In the physical.

I love you
This is true in the supramental
The problem for me is representing it
In the physical.

I love you.
I am representing it
In the mental
In this poem.
And I promise to live my love
To make a brain circuit
That lasts as long as I shall live.

I love you.
I am representing my love

In the vital
In the energies of my heart throb
When I see you
When I think of you
When I dream you.

I love you.
When negative emotion grasps me
Sweeping you with it
I promise to stay with it
With you
Until that love
Our love
Becomes
Everybody's love
In the instructions
Of the morphic fields
To make a positive instinct
A new possibility in the limbic brain
Of some baby in the future.

PART 3

Right Livelihood for Everyone
Changing Our Social Systems

CHAPTER 12

You Want Real Change, Mr. President?

Here Is the Quantum Manifesto for Social Change

Dear Mr. President,

Your campaign slogan has always appealed to me: "Change we can believe in." But almost everyone talks about change at election time. Senator McCain sure did. At his convention acceptance speech, he downright tried to scare lobbyists with his change talk. But the lobbyists who try to influence the government on behalf of their clients are just a symptom that our democratic political system is not working. The government is not really doing what it should be doing.

Same situation everywhere. The economic meltdown is a symptom showing that there is something very wrong at the base: the economic models we are using aren't working. Health care in America is not even universal like in other advanced economies. But even so, health-care costs keep going up and up. This is not fundamentally the fault of the hospitals, the doctors, or even the insurance companies and the pharmaceutical firms. It's a symptom telling us that something is fundamentally wrong with our health science itself. There are a couple of other systems that need fixing, too: education and religion. But politics, economics, and health care are the biggies. For now let's stick to the biggies.

Let's take the case of the economy first. Financial institutions were frozen with their toxic assets; right or wrong, you bailed them out. When the house is burning, naturally you have to put the fire out first. But now that the fire seems to be out, where do we go from here? Some people are blaming the derivatives, some the deregulation that allowed investment banks to merge with commercial banks, some the institutionalized greed, some the availability of easy credit. Hell, all of those things contributed to the crisis; there is no doubt about that! But surely, the real cause is deeper.

Some economists did go deep and said, "Capitalism messed up." Echoing this, your treasury secretary said, "Capitalism will be different." But which capitalism is he talking about? The classical one that Adam Smith founded and that Keynes tinkered with a little bit? Or the capitalism that was co-opted by the followers of our most recent scientific worldview—scientific materialism—and modified over and over again? You must know, Mr. President, that Adam Smith was a moralist; he never mixed up need and greed. He believed that if we do things right—being guided by our individual self-interests, our needs—and produce and consume accordingly, and if we are free to do so, the "invisible hands" of the free market will allocate the resources properly, set the prices right, and the economy will be stable. This brand of capitalism was not perfect, so government intervention—Keynes style—was needed, but it did its job, which was to let many more people than a few feudal lords possess capital and explore meaning. Heck, the system was working so well that in the '70s, they said, a full 80 percent of America belonged to the middle class.

Of course, the materialists were playing with economics long before then. First they got rid of the individual and individual need and replaced them with behavior—worse, consumer behavior. To Adam Smith, it was to find expression for technological innovation that capitalism was needed. When recessions came, what but technological innovation could get us out? Not so under materialist economics. For these economists, it was consumerism, always consumerism that drove the expanding economy. Never mind that this was creating trouble because our resources were finite; never mind that consumerism feeds on greed, not need; never mind that consumerism pollutes the environment.

Greed unleashed does not restrict itself to satisfying needs; it wants to possess. Money was originally created to facilitate meaningful business transaction; it was a catalyst that you never hoard. But with the materialist greed in play, businesspeople and corporations began hoarding money for acquisition. Not acquisition of harmless toys to play with, no sirree. But acquisition of other businesses, even acquisition of political power. Now do you see why lobbies are needed?

So it is this materialist version of capitalism that you have to root out. And replace it with the original version. And while you are at it, do a little more tinkering. As Maslow said, we have a whole hierarchy of needs, not just the material need for survival. The recent paradigm shift of science to a consciousness- and quantum-based system is validating our subtle needs—the need for love, the need for the exploration of meaning, the need for justice, beauty, and goodness. They don't come from our brain or our genes; they come from nonmaterial subtle worlds and consciousness mediates their interaction with the material world. So please make them part of the production-consumption equation. Can we do it? Yes, we can. There is a fallout from it that you will like. The subtle economy in contrast to the gross material one is not a zero-sum game! So investing in it intelligently actually gets rid of those vicious business cycles without government intervention.

Let's tackle health care next. Mr. President, for some time we have known that in most situations, conventional allopathic medicine only gets rid of the symptoms and does not really heal because the disease is at the subtle level, produced by a mismanagement of vital feeling or mental meanings. In particular, allopathy does not work with chronic disease; in fact, the use of it to alleviate symptoms, because of side effects, may actually harm the body in the long run. When the disease is caused at the subtle level, doesn't it make sense that it is the subtle that we have to set right? There are already alternative medicine systems in place; they are legal and popular in this country, thanks to President Nixon's trip to China and thanks to President Clinton's creation of the office of alternative medicine.

Now here is my puzzlement with you. Are you so scared of the allopathic lobby, AMA and the like, that you are missing the simple fact that alternative medicine is much cheaper than conventional medicine? That its emphasis is on prevention, so insurance companies would not be pressed as hard with costly claims, the way they are now? Most importantly, intelligent use of alternative medicine really heals, so recurring expenses will be avoided.

Mr. President, there is now in place a paradigm of integrative medicine that establishes the perimeters of both conventional and alternative medicine and that is cost-effective. The best part of integrative medicine is striking: it empowers the patients to maintain health and even heal themselves. If one uses this integrative system, health-care management will become tractable.

Now to politics, and I will be brief. Under the influence of materialism, politicians, originally designed by Thomas Jefferson and the like to facilitate *the entry of more people into the arena of meaning processing, have become captivated in the pursuit of power—acquisition again. How can they change the lobbying system when they themselves have become dealers of power, not meaning? How can they bring change we can believe in, change that is meaningful to us?*

Mr. President, you wrote the excellent book The Audacity of Hope. *It gives me the audacity to hope that you will heed these new discoveries and if they seem right, you will give them a go. To get real changes through Congress is no joke, but one thing I know: your motive resonates with us, the change seekers, your heart is in the right place, and the "invisible hands" of downward causation will come to your aid.*

Sincerely,
Amit Goswami, Ph.D.

CHAPTER 13

Right Action, Right Livelihood

So finally, let's get down and dirty: what is the plan of action of the quantum activist? Using the oft-quoted term of the Hindus, what is the karma yoga of the quantum activist?

According to the Hindus, karma yoga is the yoga of applying the idea of spiritual practices right smack in the middle of real life. By doing selfless service, the strategy is to undermine the ego's control. This is an important practice of many spiritual traditions even outside Hinduism, especially of Christianity and Soto Zen. For a quantum activist, karma yoga is extended toward selflessly serving the society and the world with evolution in mind.

What's the difference? In conventional spirituality, the wisdom is that we can only change ourselves, not the world. So we try to change ourselves through selfless service to lessen ego's control. But in quantum activism, we try to become empowered to change the world also; because we have created the world, we can recreate it. If recreation is in synchrony with the evolution of consciousness, our job should be relatively effortless.

For the quantum activist, the ego needs to be strong and have an extensive repertoire of learned contexts in order to participate in the creative journey of recreating the world. (Of course, we still work on reducing the ego's control over unconscious processing. How else can God find an opportunity to encounter us?) This inspires us to do karma yoga right in the middle of our professional work, in our workplace. The workplace may not be conducive to your karma yoga, you say. Well, what is your activism for if not to bring change to wherever it is needed?

It is a fact that all our social institutions in which most people work today have lost their way from idealism to materialism. Aren't most workplaces by necessity places dedicated to earn a profit and make material gain? you say. Yes, but what is the material gain for? Is it not for the well-being of us and, eventually, our society? The problem is that, driven by materialist beliefs, we have limited the definition of our well-being to the material domain only. If well-being is extended to include the subtle, our institutions easily become places for karma yoga.

Doing our karma yoga practice at work has a great advantage in that it enables us to integrate the outer and the inner. In the industrial age, the necessity of mass production made the job of ordinary people repetitive and monotonous. Practicing karma yoga while working on the assembly line is easy to talk about, but not easy to carry out. But in advanced economies such as the United States, Europe, and Japan, we are just about ready to get out of the industrial age to a technological age that will relieve us from mass production (Friedman 2005). That and other factors such as ecological awareness are increasing the scope for creativity on the job like never before. With this, the future for karma yoga in the workplace is taking a quantum leap.

Your particular context for quantum activism then depends on how you choose to make your living. For example, if you are a businessperson, clearly business is your arena for quantum activism.

You have to choose your livelihood carefully. Ask, is this way of making a living a suitable vehicle for my creativity, my nonlocal needs of social consciousness, and my commitments to intimate relationship through which I work on my hierarchies? And most importantly, does this way of earning my livelihood bring me meaning, create avenues for me to learn and express my dharma, and give me satisfaction?

The cofounders of New Dimensions Radio, Michael and Justine Toms (1998) put it this way: "In the Thai language there is a word, *sanuk*, which means that whatever you do, you should enjoy it." Processing old meaning is computational, machine-like, at best joy-neutral, usually boring. How does joy enter meaning processing? When new meaning is processed, when our intuitive facility is engaged, because then the brow chakra and crown chakra vital energies (of clarity and satisfaction) are also engaged. When you process new meaning that you love, then additionally you engage the heart chakra, your consciousness becomes expansive, and you experience bliss or spiritual joy.

The next question we ask is this. Is the practice of our profession serving the purpose of evolution? If not, we attempt to change the ways of our profession. Theoretically, by understanding where the field of our profession went wrong and how to right the wrongness. Experientially, by putting our understanding in practice by activistic efforts. And this we do always in conjunction with our personal transformation on the job in mind. We try to leave egotism out of our activism, for example.

In our current materialist culture, material accomplishment is everything. When one acts for accomplishment of material orientation, any action, even those that are seemingly selfless, tends to strengthen the ego-centered narcissism. The accomplisher has to look after numero uno in a zero-sum game, has to compete and control. When we stop measuring our accomplishment in material terms and learn to enjoy our subtle accomplishments, we no longer have to be numero uno, we no longer have to seek power to dominate others. Only then can we seek meaning without violating our values and fulfill our dharma. No longer do we take ourselves too seriously. In other words, with such a shift in what we consider accomplishments, we dance, but always lightly, not caring what anyone thinks of us, not even what we think of ourselves.

In an issue of the comic strip *Mutts*, one of the canine characters says to another while looking at some birds flying, "How do birds fly?" "Because," the other canine responds, "They take themselves lightly."

Balancing the Qualities Called Gunas

Recall that there are three ways that we can process meaning. We can process meaning engaging fundamental creativity—creativity consisting of the discovery of new meaning in a new context. Engaging fundamental creativity is *sattva guna* (*guna* is Sanskrit for "quality"). We can also process meaning by engaging situational creativity in which we look to invent a new meaning but only within known contexts. This quality of the mind is *rajas* in Sanskrit. Finally, we can also process meaning within what we know, within our conditioned memory, without seeking new meaning. This is the guna of *tamas*, the propensity to act according to conditioning.

Fundamental creativity, being discovery of new meaning in a new context, is the hardest of the lot; its processing requires both being and doing.

In this way, people of sattva engage in a lot of tamas in the pursuit of being. So naturally, they are also accepting of people of tamas. However, rajas, the propensity for situational creativity (which consists of the horizontal movement of meaning—invention in already known contexts) requires doing, often for the sake of doing itself. Tamas is not as necessary and is often seen as a hindrance. Hence, people of rajas do not tolerate tamas in themselves and are often intolerant of people of tamas.

I have heard a joke about the degrees that our universities, mostly driven by the energy of rajas, bestow upon us. I am talking of BS; you can guess what it means. It takes four years of accumulation of the stuff to get the BS degree. Another two years of *more of the same* to get an MS. Finally, spend another five years accumulating it; now the stuff is *piled high and deep,* so you get a Ph.D.

Western people are dominated by rajas, and Eastern people by tamas. A modicum of people in the East, however, are people of sattva (which they use mostly for spiritual exploration). Only a little thought shows that historically this has primarily been due to the prevalent climate. Easterners have to relax because the very hot weather much of the time precludes too much activity. Westerners, on the other hand, have to be very active in order to survive the often-harsh weather conditions. A modicum of people in the West, however, are also people of sattva, but the rajas dominance of the culture restrains them to outer creativity—outer accomplishments.

But now due to modern technology, weather and climate need not have such an influence on our mental habits. Yet partly through the sheer force of inertia of social conditioning and partly due to the materialist malaise that continues to dominate us, we have not responded to this technological advance. As a quantum activist, however, it would behoove you to begin the practice of balancing your three gunas—sattva, rajas, and tamas—as soon as possible. It would behoove you to provide leadership in this area.

For Westerners, what it boils down to is to learn to relax, giving up the do-do-do lifestyle and make do-be-do-be-do your living mantra. Only then can fundamental creativity open to you, the door to love opens wide, and the beacon of conscious evolution becomes clearly visible. Giving up on outer accomplishments, however, is against the grain of the Western culture; this is why materialism has taken root here so fast. The only reason that the society can even entertain change now is because the zero-sum game is over, the limits of material growth have caught up with us, and the paradigm shift is upon us. Nevertheless, we quantum activists have to lead the rest of the culture in this respect; we have to change the social systems so subtle accomplishments are valued.

An important aspect of developing sattva is diet. As you know, the body proteins are our promoters of action. In this way, a protein-rich diet promotes rajas, the empire-building quality and the pursuit of power with the objective of dominating others. No wonder, several years back, that a protein-rich diet touched a popular nerve in America where most people covet rajas and actively cultivate it in the pursuit of power. For a quantum activist who is interested in fundamental creativity including spirituality, a diet with only moderate protein intake is helpful. In other words, not only keep away from fat (which grows tamas), but also keep away from excessive protein and develop a diet rich in complex carbohydrates, fruits, and vegetables. Moderate protein intake, by making room for sattva, allows you to channel your power to positive use, such as empowering not only yourself, but also other people to engage in meaning processing.

Quantum Activism in the Arena of Your Livelihood

In the Bhagavad Gita, Arjuna, the hero of the Indian epic story of Mahabharata, is given the teaching of karma yoga, the yoga of how to act appropriately. The mystery, said Krishna the teacher, is to exercise our right to act without implicitly believing that we have the right to the fruit of the action. You can see the relevance of this teaching to quantum activism. The problems, economic meltdowns, for example, that we purport to tackle with quantum activism are all not only short-term but also long-term problems. Solutions likewise require actions that will not necessarily bear any immediate fruit; thus the reluctance of today's politicians to attend to the solutions.

You may wonder if Krishna's advice is an easier way to partake in the activism required to tackle today's problems. Why develop sattva, the capacity for quantum creativity that does not come easily? Do we really need quantum activism—quantum creativity in activism—when such a simple recipe of giving up the right to the fruit of the action is available?

But we do need sattva. When we engage with problems with predominantly rajas, with its motivation of empire building, we cannot let go of short-term gains and the fruits of our action. Try it and see. But with spiritual purification, when rajas gives way in part to sattva, we can dedicate ourselves to long-term projects even though there is no immediate fruit of our actions in sight. It is no secret that this is how our greatest scientists and artists operate in the pursuit of their great science and great art. Einstein, for the last thirty years of his life, looked for a theory to unify all the material forces. He didn't care much that his work did not bear fruit during his lifetime (that is, his disappointments did not divert him). Indeed, the fruit came only after his death.

A thorough reading of the Bhagavad Gita shows us that Krishna was quite aware of this kind of consideration. The Bhagavad Gita begins with what sounds like a simple recipe: acting without the guarantee of the fruit of the action. But toward the end of the book, when we get the entire teaching, Krishna says that to accomplish that simple goal of fruitless action one has to cultivate sattva and balance all the gunas—sattva, rajas, and tamas. In other words, one has to combine simple activism with quantum creativity, with do-be-do-be-do, which is quantum activism.

In traditional societies, people who make their living in service jobs mostly engage the quality of conditioned tamas; their conditioned repertoire is all they need and all they are encouraged to use. They are predominantly tamas people. People who earn their living in business and trade are mostly driven by the conditioned instinctual emotion of greed for increasing their material possessions (in other words, love of money). They are also partly driven by rajas, the tendency to expand. So businesspeople are dominated by tamas mixed with a modicum of rajas. They serve, but they are also situationally creative in making money and building conglomerates. People of politics are people predominantly driven by the quality of rajas, and they use it to build their empires. But their rajas is tainted by tamas in the form of the emotion of desire for power to dominate, egotism. People of predominant sattva engage in the profession of teaching (worldly knowledge and the spiritual), the profession of healing (excluding cosmetic healing), and of course, in professions requiring fundamental creativity explicitly—arts, science, music, dance, and mathematics.

This fixity matching a person's guna and the profession in which he or she engages is very resistant to change. But as quantum activism becomes more prevalent in our societies, people will balance their gunas more and more, and people will engage in all professions with all three gunas. Only in this way shall we be able to get beyond the guna stereotypes of our livelihoods. Only then, winds of change can engulf the arenas of our livelihoods and workplaces, and mental evolution can proceed en masse.

How Capitalism, Democracy, and Liberal Education Must Change

Capitalism, democracy, and liberal education are the crowning achievements of the mental age of evolution in which the mind evolves so that more and more people engage the faculties of the mind—the various ways of meaning processing. There is something special about these three institutions that requires discussing them together. These three represent a quantum leap in ordinary people's access to what the mind does best: process deep questions of meaning—the meaning of the world, the meaning of their lives and feelings, the meaning of deep experiences of love and spirituality, and so forth.

The first thing you must notice is that all three institutions evolved to correct what went before, when the prevalent social institutions restricted meaning processing to a privileged few. For example, before capitalism, we had feudalism, in which the economy was owned and manipulated by the few people in power. Of course, before democracy, power belonged mostly to the monarchy—kings and their courtiers—shared to some extent by religious hierarchies in countries and cultures where spirituality was ruled by organized religion. And before liberal education, hardly any education in the service of meaning was available to common people except perhaps religious education.

From this background, capitalism evolved, and all of a sudden, a large number of people were controlling capital so that the discoveries and inventions of modern science and technology could produce fruit rapidly for the entire society. This gave rise to a quickly multiplying middle class, who became the centerpiece of meaning processing in modern societies.

Democracy, likewise, began with the idea of power sharing by the many instead of by the few, and it became workable when the idea of representative democracy took hold. So although power remained concentrated, periodic elections made sure that power changed hands often enough to stop its being the tool for domination, a practice of negative emotion that creates separateness. Instead, it was recognized that the objective of democracy is to spread the privilege of meaning processing to all. People who provided leadership toward the spreading of meaning were elected as leaders. Some American examples are Thomas Jefferson, Abraham Lincoln, Franklin Roosevelt, and John Kennedy. Their positive use of power helped evolve their respective societies to achieve eventually new heights of greatness.

Democracies use liberal education to spread meaning processing. On the other hand, the institution of capitalism depends on liberal education turning out people to serve as the labor force for business and industry. Notice that early ideas of liberal education emphasized meaning processing as primary and preparation for jobs as secondary. How different this is from today's job-centered education in which preparation for jobs has become the primary goal of education and meaning processing has been relegated to a secondary role.

In Thomas Jefferson's self-written epitaph, there is no mention of his being president of the United States, but it is mentioned that he established the University of Virginia. This seems surprising until you realize that Jefferson, one of the architects of modern democracy, understood perfectly the evolutionary reason for democracy: it is not for the sharing of power per se, but to bring power to the service of people, so that people in all spheres of life can, with the help of liberal education, engage in meaning processing.

In other words, the founding fathers of this country were very clear that the essence of education is to serve evolutionary enhancement of the processing of meaning and values.

Capitalism best serves the spreading of meaning processing in a democracy when a general (as opposed to specialized) system of education such as what traditional liberal education provides is in place to produce the labor force. Democracy thrives best when capitalism guides the economy and liberal education educates the electorate. And liberal education with an emphasis on meaning is possible only when there is a large middle class (for which capitalism is needed) and when the middle class is free to process meaning (for which democracy is needed).

In this way, capitalism, democracy, and liberal education are connected at base with the common goal of the spreading of meaning processing among people so that humankind can evolve their minds. Today, we have lost sight of this lofty evolutionary goal. Education has lost meaning and value as its driving force and instead has become job training in the various technologies that materialist science regularly produces. Democratic leaders increasingly opt for the negative use of power to dominate over its positive use in spreading the processing of meaning to more people. And capitalism once again is moving toward a concentration of capital in a few hands—capital sharing and the idea of a meaning-processing middle class forgotten. I think that many of the problems these institutions are facing today arose because of this.

The job of quantum activism is also now clear: to bring back meaning processing as the centerpiece of human societal and cultural institutions because evolution demands it. How do we do it for our economics? We do it by generalizing Adam Smith's capitalism, which recognizes only our material needs, to include our subtle and spiritual needs as well. I call this new economics "spiritual economics" (Goswami 2005; see also chapter 14).

The job of straightening out democracy is similar. The founders of democracy left spiritual principles implicit, at best. We must include the subtle and spiritual dimensions explicitly in the pursuit of democratic ideals. But even this is only a beginning.

Democracy is much degraded because of our unabashed tendency toward negative emotions and because we choose our leaders in a way that requires no recognition of the leaders' emotional intelligence. This has to change, but the job of the quantum activist is cut out for this one. We also need to bring people of sattva into the political arena, but the current domination of the political arena by media and money makes this very difficult (see chapter 16).

For liberal education, our primary challenge is to replace the very limiting ideas of materialist science and primacy of matter with the ideas of new science and the primacy of consciousness. Once this is done, liberal education can go back to its Jeffersonian roots (see chapter 19).

CHAPTER 14

Toward a Spiritual Economics

Many people think that capitalism and market economics grew out of materialist philosophy. But this is myopic thinking by people who have missed the evolution of consciousness in the affairs of the manifest world.

First notice that during the period that capitalism developed in the hands of such luminaries as Adam Smith, it was Cartesian dualism under the modernist umbrella that was the influential metaphysic, not scientific materialism. In modernism, both mind and meaning are valued.

Second, notice that capitalism replaced feudalism and the mercantile economy (Adam Smith's term for the economy prevalent in England in his time), in which the pursuit of meaning was highly limited and vast numbers of people were denied it. Compared to feudalism in which wealth or capital remained in the hands of a fortunate few, capitalism and a market economy have certainly brought capital into the hands of many more. This has given a large number of people the economic freedom and flexibility needed to pursue meaning in their lives.

Third, notice that the only serious challenge to capitalism since the demise of feudalism and the mercantile economy has been Marxist economics. And it has been a failure! Instead of Adam's Smith's "invisible hand" to drive the market and distribute capital, Marx envisioned that such a distribution can be done more effectively under a dictatorship of the proletariat in which the labor force takes over the distribution and equalizes wealth. But Marxist economics so far has been installed only under the politics of communism (in which the dictatorship of the proletariat became more like a dictatorship of bureaucracy), and it failed miserably. And the failure is primarily due to the fact that most people just cannot work hard or intelligently when it is not for the benefit of private property and private wealth (as Rabbi Hillel said, "If I am not for myself, who am I?").

Unfortunately, it does not take a genius to see that capitalist economics as it is practiced today with materialist philosophy at the helm—let's call it materialist economics—is also at a crisis point. First, materialist economics is based on continuous growth and expansion, which requires unlimited resources and unlimited expansion of consumption; this cannot be sustained on a finite planet. The finitude of resources may already have caught up with us. The finitude of the environment is an additional constraint on unlimited growth of consumerism.

Second, the free market does not seem to be free any more. Why? Much of this loss of freedom is due to the confusion about what to do with money. On one hand, we have quasi-governmental control of the money supply and government interventions in the economy at crisis times; on the other hand, we have market manipulations by financial institutions confused about what to do with excess money. And what is the remedy?

Third, capitalism and its continuing economic expansion produce higher and higher standards of living, and wages do not keep up with it without producing inflation. To meet the demands of the higher standard and its higher cost, people are forced to give up their higher needs such as the need of young children to have a nonworking mother or the need for leisure time to pursue meaning. Thus invariably, the basic promise of capitalism Adam Smith style is shortchanged by the nature of the materialist economics that has replaced it.

Fourth, no thanks to the development of multinational corporations, the management-labor equilibrium that feeds the equalization of the movement of meaning between the classes is stalled. What is the remedy for this?

Actually, market capitalism works better than Marxism because it recognizes one basic need for people: the survival and security of their physical bodies. This basic ego need requires private property, and any economics that ignores this basic need of people is bound to fail.

But as the psychologist Abraham Maslow pointed out, besides this basic need, we have an entire hierarchy of needs. One major shortcoming of Adam Smith's capitalist economics is the ignoring of people's higher needs. Following Maslow, but modifying his theory according to the insights of my general approach to spirituality, science within consciousness, we can easily see what these higher needs are.

Our Redefined Higher Needs and the Rudiments of a Spiritual Economics

It may help to recap the basic elements of the developing science within the primacy of consciousness as we begin to apply it to social systems:

☼ Consciousness is the ground of all being.

☼ The possibilities of consciousness are fourfold: material (which we sense); vital energy (which we feel, primarily through the chakras and secondarily through the brain); mental meaning (which we think); and supramental, discriminating contexts such as physical laws, ethics, love, justice, and aesthetics (which we intuit). The material is called gross and the other three make up the subtle domain of our experience.

☼ When consciousness chooses from the possibilities the actual event of its experience (with physical, vital, mental, and supramental components), the physical has the opportunity of making representations of the subtle. The physical is like computer hardware; the subtle is represented as software.

☼ Our capacity for making physical representation of the subtle evolves. First, the capacity for making representations of the vital developed through the evolution of life via more and more sophisticated organs to represent the living functions such as maintenance, reproduction, and sensing. Next the capacity of making more and more sophisticated representations of the mental evolved. This is the stage of evolution we are in right now.

☼ Our capacity to directly represent the supramental in the physical has not yet evolved. There is evolutionary pressure on us in this direction, however, which is the primary reason some of us are attracted to meaning, values, and spirituality.

☼ In times of cataclysmic crisis, survival needs bring many more people into creativity, in the search for solutions. Evolution takes place via the effect of this collective biological creativity.

Thus there must be the urge to satisfy not only physical needs, but also needs in all the other dimensions of our experience. In addition to the satisfaction of physical needs, a spiritual economics must address:

※ Our need to explore emotional needs, especially positive emotions such as love and satisfaction, both conditioned and unconditioned. Acknowledgment of this need will lead to a huge expansion of the economy involving the production and consumption of vital energy.

※ Our need for the pursuit of meaning, including the pursuit of new mental meaning that requires creativity.

※ Our need for the pursuit of spiritual and supramental (soul) needs such as altruism, unconditional love, and happiness.

In truth, this ladder of needs is not entirely simple hierarchical. If one satisfies higher needs, the urge to satisfy lower needs actually decreases. The opposite is also true. If a lower need is satisfied, the demand for satisfying a higher need increases. In this way, a strategy for a spiritual economics more suited for the human condition than materialist economics or even Adam Smith capitalism is to address all the needs simultaneously.

Whereas capitalism is an economics of physical well-being based on the satisfaction of our conditioned (physical) ego needs, idealist or spiritual economics must be an economics of holistic well-being based on the satisfaction of both our (physical) ego needs and higher needs (pertaining to the exploration of the vital, mental, soul, and spirit).

Microeconomics of the Subtle

Economics is about production-consumption, demand-supply, prices, and all that (never mind the fact that today the financial markets dominate the economy more than the production-consumption sector of the economy). How does that kind of stuff work for our subtle needs? Let's talk about these micro details.

Production of positive vital energy can be accomplished in many ways, including forestation (plants and trees have abundant vital energy) and cultivating positive health in society—just as people of positive mental health radiate enthusiasm, people of positive health radiate positive vital energy. But the best way to ensure production of vital energy is to encourage employers to install facilities in the workplace so that their employees can practice positive health through means such as yoga, tai chi, and meditation. You may think that this will reduce material profit for the company, but the opposite is more likely true because of reduced health-care costs. In any case, the government can easily offset the material cost of production via tax incentives. Instead of rewarding capital investment in consumer goods, reward capital investment in the subtle.

As for production of mental meaning, we already have some of the ways in place in the contexts of the arts and the entertainment industry. Both of these industries have the capacity of producing positive vital energy (positive emotions) as well. However, much of the arts and entertainment industry has bogged down in the negativity of a postmodern materialist culture. We have to shift the emphasis to meaningfulness and positivity.

Another big source of meaning production is higher education, universities, and research organizations. Right now these institutions do not compete directly in the market economy, but this is changing.

The production of supramental and spiritual energy requires more effort right now. In the olden days, spiritual organizations such as churches, temples, synagogues, mosques, and the like cultivated and produced supramental and spiritual intelligence in their leaders and practitioners. Nowadays, these organizations are more interested in influencing mundane politics than investing in the supramental. But make no mistake about it; investment in the supramental can be done, although we may have to develop new spiritual organizations to do it. In the olden days, perhaps the most effective means of production (and also dissemination) of supramental energy were traveling monks (called sadhus in India; in the West, troubadours are an example). This we can revive.

To some extent, the many New Age conferences on New Age ideas and spirituality are already serving this purpose. The idea of conferences originally came from science and business enterprises. A conference creates opportunities for research people in a given area to exchange ideas and make connections. But whereas research people in the sciences and technological areas are supported by government and private grants, the New

Age gurus usually do not enjoy that privilege. So from the get-go, driven by economic necessity, the New Age conferences have involved interested lay-people. This helps production of supramental energy and additionally helps consumption. Also effective are lectures and, especially, workshops by the New Age savants. This also is already happening; even business corpora-tions are taking part in it under the auspices of organizations such as the World Business Academy.

Also effective are group meditations through which, as some of para-psychologist Dean Radin's experiments show (Radin 2006), people can experience nonlocal consciousness and hence can take creative leaps to the supramental domain. This can be done even in workplaces.

Now let's turn to the question of consumption. Because the vital and mental are mappable in us, they can be consumed by both local and nonlo-cal means. For example, if we see good theater, it cultivates the processing of meaning in us, even new meaning. When we partake in good meaningful entertainment, we also feel positive emotions; we are consuming them. As we consume, we ourselves have the potential to become producers.

Supramental energy consumption is nonlocal, but it requires local triggers. There are scientists who subscribe to the so-called Maharishi effect, accord-ing to which the spiritual and supramental energy generated by a group medi-tation is consumed automatically in the local vicinity. Much data exist with claims of crime reduction in big cities where TM groups perform such medita-tion. The effect is temporary, however, and controversial; I am not advocating it. A purely quantum physical nonlocal consumption of your spiritual energy requires that I be correlated with you by some means or other. For example, experiments by Mexican neurophysiologist Jacobo Grinberg-Zylberbaum and colleagues suggest that if two people intend together, they become correlated in this way, but it should be simpler than that. There are many anecdotes of how people feel peace in the presence of a sage (I myself experienced this in the presence of Franklin Merrell-Wolff, an American sage now deceased; see Goswami 2000). So just being locally present can trigger consumption.

The best part of subtle energy products is that they are mostly free. The subtle dimensions have no limits. We can consume a sage's love all we wish; the supply is not going to diminish. There is no zero-sum game in the subtle. There may be a bit of material cost of production. So one may put a material price tag on subtle products to offset this, and that may not be such a bad idea because it enables people to be more serious about their intentions when they consume subtle products. Here is also an opportunity for the government to subsidize the subtle industry.

Redefining the GDP

In the view of most materialists, science has to deal only with the material world, because only the material can be quantified, can be measured reliably. We have to eradicate this prejudice.

We cannot measure vital energy, prana, or chi in the same sense that we can measure a quantity of rice, but it is not true that we cannot measure it at all. For example, when vital energy moves out of you, your feeling at the particular chakra will tell you the story, and the same is true of vital energy excesses. When vital energy moves out of the navel chakra, you feel insecurity, butterflies in the stomach. When vital energy moves into the same chakra, the feeling is quite different, that of self-confidence or pride. The feelings are clearly measurable and may pass the criterion of weak objectivity, that is, though subjective, they do not change much from one subject to another (see the following).

Actually, more objective measurements are becoming rapidly available. One method, Kirlian photography (see Goswami 2004), is so accurate that it is already accomplishing early diagnosis of breast cancer in women by looking for and finding vital energy blocks. An even more accurate method may be the biophoton imaging technique.

Similarly, meaning processing gives you a feeling of satisfaction in the crown chakra because vital energy moves in there. So we can quantify meaning by the "amount" of satisfaction we derive from processing it.

Even the supramental can be measured. If we perform a good deed for someone, an example of altruism, we are happy or blissful. Not because there is any particular influx of vitality in any of the chakras, but because our separateness is momentarily gone. With love, it is even easier. Because we not only feel the bliss of not being separate from the whole, but we also feel vital energy in the heart chakra. Both can be used as a measure.

Of course, this kind of measurement is not accurate; it is indeed subjective and always a little vague. But if we remove the prejudice that only accurate and objective measurements count, what then? Then we can certainly establish criteria to judge a nation's net gain or loss of currency (feeling, meaning, and godliness) in the subtle domain. We must note that quantum physics has already replaced complete (strong) objectivity with weak objectivity, in which subjectivity is permitted as long as we make sure that our conclusions do not depend on particular subjects.

For example, we can send questionnaires suitable for a statistical analysis to people to keep an ongoing tab on their feelings, meanings, and supramental experiences or lack thereof. When we tally all this for the entire year, we can easily calculate an index of vital, mental, and supramental well-being. This index then will complement the GDP, which is the index of our material well-being. This indexing of gross national well-being is already being practiced in at least one country, Bhutan.

In the same way, we can independently estimate the contribution to the production of vital, mental, and supramental energies by big production organizations with a view to providing tax incentives.

Some examples will show that well-being in the subtle dimensions really does count, and we are missing something in our economics because we do not include it. In Hindu India (before the 10th century), the country and culture were fundamentally spiritual. The economy was feudal, of course, but according to all accounts (not only indigenous but also by foreign visitors) people were satisfied and happy, despite the prevalence of the caste system. What gives? Hindu India certainly had wealth, but nothing compared to today's America. In a spiritual culture, lots of good vital energy, mental meaning, and spiritual wholeness are generated—that is the reason. The subtle wealth reduced the need for material wealth and more than made up for the lack of it. The same was true of Tibet (no doubt, this inspired the myth of Shangri-la, the place where there is no suffering including aging) until the takeover by communist China in 1950.

Of course, neither the Indian nor Tibetan cultures of old were perfect because they did limit meaning processing of the lower classes, so evolution of consciousness eventually caught up with them. But so much energy was generated in the subtle domains in the Indian culture that even today, when there is real poverty in the material domain, the Indian poor in the villages are quite happy because they continue to inherit and maintain their subtle wealth. If Karl Marx had seen that, it might have made him rethink his idea that the exploited classes are always unhappy!

Another example is the Native American culture before the advent of colonization. There was so much subtle wealth there that nobody even cared to own material wealth. They treated material wealth in the same way as subtle wealth, globally, collectively. And like their subtle wealth, their material wealth was also practically unlimited since they used renewable resources.

Can Spiritual Economics Solve Capitalism's Current Problems?

Can spiritual economics defined in this way solve the problems of capitalism and its current offshoot, materialist economics?

First, take the problem of limited resources. Materialistic growth economics depends crucially on keeping consumer demand going. This is often done by creating artificial physical needs. An example is new annual fashions for women's garments or male-ego-boosting new car models. It is very wasteful, very detrimental to finite resources.

In spiritual economics, as people's higher needs are met even partially, their physical needs reduce, reducing the demand for consumption, which, in turn, reduces the waste of limited material resources. The economy still expands, but in the higher subtle planes where the resources are unlimited (there is no limit on love and satisfaction).

There is a related problem with materialist expansion economics: environmental pollution. This is a tricky one. In the short term, production of pollution helps expand the economy by creating pollution cleanup sectors of the economy. Believe it or not, the *Exxon Valdez* oil-spill disaster actually produced an economic boom in Alaska. But in the long run, environmental pollution in a finite planetary environment is bound to end up with a doomsday of reckoning. Many environmentalists think that global warming has already reached doomsday criticality.

In spiritual economics, material consumption is reduced, thus automatically reducing environmental pollution.

Next, let us consider the free market. Why isn't it free in the way Adam Smith envisioned? The truth is, a truly free market has big ups and downs (the business cycles), but no democratic government can live without doing something about it (people, the voters, wouldn't allow it). So today, we allow government intervention either through the Keynesian approach (tax the rich and increase government programs to increase jobs and economic movement) or the supply-side approach (reduce taxes for the rich; the rich will invest and the investment will produce economic activity that will trickle down to the poor). If this requires deficit financing, so be it.

Now nothing is wrong with government intervention per se. Adam Smith himself was quite aware of this. He suggested government intervention to reduce unjust income distribution, to ensure that the entry to the free market is really free even for the small entrepreneur (regulation against monopoly, for example), and to provide liberal education to everyone participating in the market. Governments today tinker with the free market in a few ways besides those mentioned, of which Smith may not have approved. These include trying to control the money supply by adjusting interest rates via some central quasi-governmental organization (in the United States, this is the job of the Federal Reserve or Fed), making bureaucratic regulations, bailing out big companies from bankruptcy, and giving tax incentives to segments of the economy, counter to the spirit of capitalism. But who says Smith's is the final word on how the free market should operate? The world has changed. The real problem with this kind of tinkering is the indefinite growth economics in which we seem to have gotten stuck. I have already commented on how spiritual economics solves this problem (also see later).

Since the latter part of the 20th century, the freedom of the market has been affected by more than these traditional means. This is the result of the wounding that materialism has produced in our collective psyche. The wounding has confused the leaders among us to switch from the search for mental meaning to the slavery of instinctual greed, avarice, and competitiveness. One of the effects of this is the gross corruption of the practices that keep the market free. The current practice is to legalize corruption away, but this has very limited success. The other effect is subtle.

There is now an active counter-evolutionary movement for taking away meaning processing from large segments of people and monopolizing it for a few once again. Presently, this is more of an American phenomenon, but it may soon spread to other developed economies with strong currency.

Americans have been in a unique situation since the gold standard shifted to the dollar standard. Americans can borrow money to buy resources and goods from other countries almost indefinitely because those countries have little to no option but to reinvest their money in the American dollar and American economy. The American government has then the ability for large amounts of deficit financing, and it is using this deficit financing for cutting taxes for the rich (as for example, during the Bush II presidency). This is, of course, the previously mentioned supply-side economics. This is not immediately detrimental to the economy because the rich are the biggest consumers and they are also big investors, which should, in principle, trickle down. Unfortunately, presently, the rich seem to invest mainly in the financial market and not in the production-consumption sector of the economy that directly benefits ordinary people (for example, through job creation). So the practice has made the gap between rich and poor larger and recession-related unemployment greater. Even more detrimental to evolution, this tends to eliminate the middle class.

It's like the old good-news bad-news story. A surgeon is to amputate a patient's left arm, which is gangrenous. By carelessness, the surgeon takes off the right arm. So he tells the patient, "I have both good news and bad news for you. First the bad news. I cut off the wrong arm, I mean the right arm. But the good news is that the left arm is not as bad as I originally thought [which is a dubious message]." The government with its tax cut for the rich gives a similar message. "The bad news is that you (the poor and the middle class) are not getting any tax cut. But the good news is that the effect of cutting the tax for the rich will trickle down to you [again a dubious message]."

In this way, market share is becoming more and more concentrated in the hands of the rich, and a new class system is being created. Can the idealist goal of capitalism continue to function when the capital becomes concentrated again as in feudalism and its mercantile economy? I think not.

In spiritual economics, which would be part of a universal revival of idealist values, we do not deal with the symptoms of the materialist wound such as corruption, but heal the wound so the symptoms disappear.

For example, take the case of deficit financing. I commented that in America it has been used to increase the gap between the rich and the poor, contrary to the spirit of capitalism. Even worse, deficit financing removes the very important economic constraint against nations with aggressive ideas. George W. Bush's Iraq war would not have been possible if deficit financing was not permitted. So should we be against deficit financing in idealist economics? Not necessarily. How does spiritual economics deal with the government creating income disparity between rich and poor or aggressive war? In an idealist society, the root cause for the government actively creating income disparity or war—negative emotion—would be addressed and attempts would be made to eliminate them by creating an oversupply of positive emotions.

In spiritual economics, it is recognized from the beginning that money has no inherent value; it is a symbol that stands for something of value. The explicit recognition of this reveals the subversive nature of the financial markets, and suitable ways to regulate them (e.g., taxation) become acceptable.

Let's now take up the subject of the other counter-evolutionary tendency of a materialistic expansion economy—loss of the workers' leisure time. Spiritual economics has a built-in constraint on expansion, as already noted. So the standard of living does not have to move up and up at rates faster than wages increase. Even more importantly, spiritual economics values other needs and their satisfaction that require leisure time. So in this economics, standard of living is defined differently and increases not in the material dimension but in the higher dimensions and without compromising workers' leisure time.

Finally, let's take up the subject of multinational corporations. Multinational corporations have access to cheap labor in underdeveloped economies, and this they use by shifting manufacturing to underdeveloped countries, outsourcing, and other methods. Labor thus loses the leverage for wage increases through negotiations with management, since the labor laws are very different in underdeveloped countries due to economic necessities. The labor of developed countries lose leverage, too, because of increasing fear of outsourcing of jobs.

In order to subject multinationals to uniform management-labor practices, obviously we need to move from nation-state economies to more and more enlarged international economic unions. In other words, the tendency of spiritual economics would be to move toward one international economic union within which individual democracies function with political and cultural uniqueness and sovereignty but with increased cooperation.

How Spiritual Economics Solves the Problem of the Business Cycle

I mentioned the business cycle before which is commonly referred to as a boom and bust cycle. After some years of growth, in the 19th century capitalist economies seemed to fall into periodic recessions, and there was the possibility of an even deeper stagnation called depression. (In fact, such a depression actually happened in the United States in the 1930s.) It is to prevent this kind of fluctuation that the Keynesian and supply-side government intervention cures were proposed in the 20th century. With these cures, recessions still happen, but they are supposed to be milder. (They are not, necessarily, as the great recession beginning in 2007 sadly proves.) But these cures have created a perpetual expansion economy. Because recovery depends almost entirely on consumerism, a perpetual drain of the planetary resources has been created.

In a spiritual economy, since production of subtle products is cheap, in recession times we can soften the blow by increasing production in the subtle sector so that consumption in that sector will also increase. This would reduce demand in the material sector, giving businesses time to regroup and increase material productivity.

But most people can engage the subtle transformative practices only for a while. In a short period of a few months, they reach a plateau for the time being; the practice becomes conditioned and dries up, becomes routine. So by the end of a year or so, most ordinary people feel that they have had enough transformation for now and move on. In effect, they are ready to rejoin the labor force just when the businesses are ready to resume normal production, creativity and innovation being the movers of the new boom.

In the same way, in "boom" times, the production of material goods would increase, material consumerism would increase, and less subtle stuff would be produced and consumed. But as the economy recovers, people's material needs are satisfied again, and they once again become hungry for the satisfaction of their subtle needs, the production of which then increases. This has the effect of putting a damper on the inflationary tendencies of "boom" times in a capitalist economy. The important thing is that there is no subtle price for the subtle stuff; there is no inflationary pressure in the subtle dimensions. Paying attention to the subtle just enables the entire economy to soften the blow of recessions and boom-time inflationary pressure. In other words, cyclical variations of the economy would be much less severe, so mild that little to no government intervention could keep the economy in a steady state.

I am convinced that spiritualizing the economy is the way to accomplish the stable economy that many economists have wondered if it is even possible to achieve. It should be clear that if spiritual economics (with ethics built into it) were at the helm, the 2008 economic meltdown would never have taken place.

The million-dollar question is: how do we go about replacing capitalist economics with this spiritual economics?

Implementation: When and How?

How will spiritual economics replace capitalism and materialist economics? When? You might think that spiritual economics sounds good. It brings together spiritual values and what is best in capitalism. But how is it going to be implemented? By the government? By social revolution, as in the case of Marxist economics? By a paradigm shift in the academic practices of economics inspired by the paradigm shift in science and medicine?

How did capitalism come to replace feudalism and the mercantile economy? Yes, capitalism was the brainchild of Adam Smith. And indeed, it helped that academics welcomed Smith's research as it opened a new paradigm in academia: economics itself. But today's academic situation is quite different from the days of Smith. I mentioned before that, some time ago, academic economists chose to pursue not a real-world economics but an economics of certain ideal situations so that mathematical models could be used for economic prediction and control. For example, a recent economic theory was heralded as a breakthrough because it applied a new innovation of game theory mathematics to economics.

Previously, economists were handicapped in their application of game theory because they had to assume "perfect rationality," that is, that every economic player can figure out the best money-maximizing strategy combination used by the competition. But obviously, perfect rationality is impossible in practice because there are so many possibilities. What we have is "bounded rationality," that is, rational decisions made on the basis of incomplete information about the money-maximizing strategies of the competition. The new breakthrough is considered a breakthrough because it used information theory formulas to figure out the approximate description of a set of strategies even with the assumption of bounded rationality.

But this also is not the real world. Instead of increasing our pursuit of rationalism, materialism has, in fact, eroded it by taking away the religion-based constraints on our negative emotions. Today we are so subject to negative emotions in our decision making, that any theory that ignores the emotional component of the economic decisions of the competitor is not going to be much use.

Actually, the implementation of capitalism happened not because academics welcomed Adam Smith's idea, but because capitalism served the purpose of a modernist adventurous people. It was during a time that people were exploring new adventures of mind and meaning, which feudalism lacked the manpower to do; the exploration of meaning had to be opened up to more people as science broke free from religious authorities. As meaning exploration opened up, society had to be prepared for the implementation of the output of this exploration by making capital available to innovative people and keeping it available. Hence capitalism was inevitable. Similarly, as science breaks free of the stranglehold of scientific materialism, as subtle technologies grow, spiritual economics is inevitable.

With modernism having given way to postmodernism, the old-fashioned exploration and expansion in the material domain are practically over. The old frontier is gone. However many times you watch reruns of *Star Trek,* outer space is not going to emerge as mankind's final frontier to play out one final episode of defunct modernism.

Now the society has to deal with the shortcomings of materialist economics, with little opportunity to expand in the face of finite resources and challenges of environmental pollution. In addition, the society has to heal the wounds created by materialism. There *is* a new frontier; the new frontier belongs to the subtle dimensions of the human being and we need a subtler economics to ride in order to explore them.

So the implementation of spiritual economics is inevitable because our society needs it. As humanity collectively moves beyond our competitive ego needs, as we begin to explore the benefits of cooperation en masse, the old competition-only materialist economics has to give way to the new economics, in which competition exists simultaneously with cooperation, each in its own sphere of influence.

To understand this, we need to look at how any economics is really implemented. What are the elements that implement it? These elements are the businesses, of course. It is how business is done that provides the drive for the change in economics, and vice versa. The change in economics helps businesses along. Each is essential to the other.

So what will enable spiritual economics to replace materialist economics? Ultimately, it is the need of the workplace, the businesses. And there, if you look, you will find ample evidence that business is already changing its ways (Aburdene 2005).

Two recent trends in business are extremely noteworthy and are in consonance with the evolutionary movement of consciousness toward the implementation of a subtle sector of the economy. The first is the widespread recognition by a substantial segment of business and industry of the importance of creativity and innovation; the second is the recognition that converting to eco-friendly "green" ideas, even ideas of resource sustainability, may not be detrimental to profit making.

Yes, competition will continue to exist, without which there is no market economy. But in the workplace, inside how a business is run, there increasingly exists a different philosophy and a different aspect of the human being. In some of our business ventures, we have already discovered the value of creativity, leisure, love, cooperation, and happiness.

In 1988, the philosopher Willis Harman predicted: "The implications of research on consciousness ... suggest interconnection at a level that has yet to be fully recognized by Western science, and throw into doubt the pervasive conception of a world dominated by competition." Today's businesses are showing us how competition can coexist with cooperation.

Hints for a Quantum Activist

I have said that businesses are leading the way toward the implementation of spiritual economics. If you are a business-oriented person, the current situation gives you a wonderful opportunity to apply the principles of quantum activism in your existing business or in a new startup (see the next chapter). What a businessperson of a big company can do on a large scale, any quantum activist has an opportunity to do on a small scale. At the least, we can help the paradigm shift by a personal shift away from consumerism. We can help vanguards begin businesses based on spiritual economics.

Basically, the implementation of some form of spiritual economics is compulsory because evolution demands that we move away from the present materialist culture toward a multidimensional one with demand and supply in the subtle arena in addition to the material arena. Quantum activists will provide leadership in this movement. A quantum activist is one who has already satisfied his or her material cravings enough to heed the higher subtle needs and to hear the call of evolution. So a quantum activist, through creative exploration of meaning, through practicing emotional intelligence, through growing awareness of deep ecology, and through making brain circuits of supramental learning, starts contributing directly to both production and consumption in the subtle sector of a conscious spiritual economy that hasn't yet arrived.

I hope this is added motivation for quantum activism. By our intentions and practice, we are making room for a highly desirable shift of the economic paradigm from materialist economics to spiritual economics. Judging from the sociologist Paul Ray's study (Ray and Anderson 2000), a full one-fifth of Americans are ready to make this kind of shift.

CHAPTER 15

How Businesses Are Changing

Everything changes, in content at least, and businesses are no exception. In previous ages, business was about agriculture, then came industry, then technology, and, finally, the current high technology. This is one kind of change, and some authors, notably Alvin Toffler, make a big case for such changes. What I want to discuss is the question: are the changes in business practices over the years reflecting an evolution of consciousness? In slightly different words, can we see an evolution of consciousness, evolution of our capacity for meaning processing, in the ways business has changed over the past centuries? I think we can.

In olden-day India, businesspeople were placed in a separate caste called *Vaishya*. The Vaishya caste was allowed to pursue meaning, but there was a catch. A Vaishya person could only pursue meaning within the context dictated by the highest class, the Brahmins.

Other cultures, especially Western cultures, did not have an explicit class system, but the same practice was quite prevalent until Adam Smith's time, the 18th century. At that time in England, where Smith was born, the king (George III, for example, with whom every American is familiar) set the context, and landowners, merchants, and businesses carried out their quests for meaning within that context. In return for their loyalty to the king, they were allowed to hold very concentrated and corrupt power over England's economy. This was the "mercantile system" in Smith's terminology. One of the motivations for Smith's creativity came from the desire of breaking up this corruption. The result within a mere century was a transition from feudalism and the mercantile economy to capitalism. In capitalism, many more people are involved in the search for meaning; meaning processing expands. Consciousness evolves in the direction of increasing preoccupation with and processing of meaning.

Smith saw clearly that creative and innovative forces were developing that could revolutionize industry if only allowed to do so. The corruption of the mercantile system meant lost opportunities for creativity. The solution was to shift the power of setting context (of meaning processing) from a few selected people to the "invisible hands" of free-market competition. Any context would be okay in the new system; any idea could be explored for a new industry if it survived the competition of the free market.

Thus began the successful phase of capitalism. In the United States, the epitome of this success was innovative industrialists such as Henry Ford and Thomas Edison.

But something happened to the fulfillment of Smith's vision of a perfect capitalist society. His version of capitalism was replaced by a materialist version that gave rise to severe problems. I discussed these problems in the last chapter: unsustainable depletion of a finite resource base by a forever expanding consumer economy; environmental pollution arising from the finitude of the environment; loss of freedom of the free market; the closing down of the two openings that enabled the labor class to pursue meaning, namely, relative affluence and more leisure time; and finally, multinationals throwing the management-labor equilibrium into utter chaos.

So economics must have a paradigm shift from materialist economics to what I call spiritual economics. Whereas capitalism addresses the satisfaction of the most basic ego needs of people, spiritual economics addresses the holistic well-being of the people (which includes the vital energy, mental, soul, and spiritual needs in addition to the physical). Then the question is: what are the signs that the time for this new economics has come? For Smith, the sign of the need for capitalism was the innovative spirit that he saw already awakened in the society. What signs for change, if any, do we see now?

In this chapter, I want to make the point that businesses themselves are changing, a new wave is coming (to use Toffler's language), which is making room for an evolutionarily more appropriate spiritual economics.

I became aware of this in the 1990s when I was researching creativity and came across a book called *Creativity in Business* by Stanford professors

Michael Ray and Rochelle Myers (1986). Since then other books have appeared on the subject, and it is now well known that many companies and corporations, especially high-tech companies, are encouraging creativity, not only from their research teams, but also from their management.

Let's go back to the basics and look at the customary capitalist model of the beginning of a business venture. You get an innovative vision of a product or a service. You gather people who you think will be loyal to that vision, you find capital, and you start your business. But when we changed from an industrial to a technological society, this model had to give way because one person's creativity (or that of a few directors') was no longer enough to sustain the productivity of a business. So the burden of creative innovation shifted from the very top to middle management. In this new wave of capitalism, many more people are participating in the creative processing of meaning. Certainly, this suggests the evolution of consciousness. But more, it suggests that there is the budding of a new spiritual economics because the creative processing of meaning involves a quantum leap from the mind to the soul (supramental) level of our being. Creativity not only serves the ego, but also crucially involves the soul and serves the soul's purpose. It also increases the global output of mental meaning.

Another key development of businesses is the concept of the "green" business, which arose from the ecology movement. The green business has two components. The first is the realization that ecological considerations can be used for economic gains, for making profits. An example is recycling; the Xerox Corporation made a tenfold return on its investment in recycling toner cartridges. The second is the realization that, in the long run, ecological sustainability—harmonization of business activity with what the earth can support—is a good thing to aim for. Sooner or later it is going to be imposed by governments or by nature itself—whichever comes first.

But what is ecology based on? On the idea of the weblike relationship between life and its environment. To be sure, ecologists are talking about local connections alone. But from ecology, it is a small leap to realize that the connection of life and environment is much deeper. It is not only through material, local signals, but through vital energy, and, ultimately, through consciousness itself, through a quantum nonlocal connection.

So you see ecological businesses are also moving beyond the mere satisfaction of ego needs toward the satisfaction of more subtle needs of nonlocal consciousness. If shallow ecology is attended to, can deep ecology be far behind? Ecologically sustainable businesses are increasing our global vital energy output.

The board of directors of an old-wave capitalist corporation watches over its businesses to make sure of the selfish gain in the material profits of the corporation's shareholders. The board of directors of a new-wave capitalist corporation not only increases the material profit for its shareholders, but also contributes to the vital energy and meaning profits for everyone. This is already a good beginning of spiritual economics.

There are a couple of other trends that are also worth mentioning. One is that corporations have begun noticing that employees perform the best if their value structure is not in conflict with the corporation's value structure, as exemplified by its products and practices (Barrett 1998). This indicates that businesses are recognizing the value of values (the supramental dimension of humanity). The second one goes beyond this. In view of many recent market-related scandals, many business leaders are asking aloud if it is not more profitable in terms of public relations alone to follow ethical practices in business. And they don't mean the ethics of the greatest good for the greatest number, but the real McCoy, the way ethics is defined in spiritual traditions.

In this way, even the supramental dimension is gradually entering business.

What more does it take to make the transition complete from capitalism to spiritual economics? We still have some ways to go. And I think that businesses can and will lead the way to this transition.

The goal of spiritual economics is to maximize the profit, not only in the material output, but also in our vital energy output, mental meaning output, and supramental output. Even with creativity, ecology, and ethics included in the workplace in the ways mentioned here, we have only made a dent in the possibilities.

At the next stage, we can encourage creativity not only for the management or the research people, but also for everyone. True, only a professional can make quantum leaps of creativity that will produce a product in the outer arena, but everyone can be creative in their inner arena through the practice of inner creativity. If a corporation encourages inner creativity (a major component of which is transformation of negative emotions to positive ones) in all its employees, allows all employees to open to their souls, what happens? The entire environment of the corporation becomes an increasingly happy one, full of vitality and meaning. Is this valuable? Of course. It contributes directly to the production outputs in our subtle dimensions. And it is a fact that happy people produce better products. And more. Inner creativity can increase the outer creativity of already outerly creative people, the backbones of an innovative corporation. Ultimately, the practice will even improve material productivity and profits.

In addition to or instead of employing an ethics watcher, most likely an academic philosopher who preaches ethics but does not walk the talk, business can go one step further and start a subtle energy division with a few employees whose specific job is the production of subtle energy, including supramental energy. Obviously, such people would be practitioners of evolutionary ethics and would be much more effective watchdogs of ethics maintenance than mere academic philosophers.

From ecological sustainability, the next step is the awareness of the evolutionary movement of consciousness. Not only do we demand ecological sustainability, but we also ask: is my business contributing positively to the evolutionary movement of consciousness, or at least, not obstructing it? This is when we put explicit rather than implicit attention on tangible production in the vital energy, mental meaning, and supramental value sectors of the human economy.

Of course, much has to happen before businesses take these remaining steps. The paradigm shift from primacy of matter to primacy of consciousness has to take root in academe and in society. Our politics have to change from the politics of power to the politics of meaning. Our educational institutions have to stop their preoccupation with job training and revamp meaning and soul values in the classrooms. Our religions have to give up telling people how to vote and influence politicians, and return to the pursuit of godliness and teaching it to people. I believe all of this will happen soon, and some beginnings are already in sight.

Capitalism played a crucial role in where we are today, and as Adam Smith himself envisioned, small businesses are the backbones of capitalism and the free market. In the same way, the path to spiritual economics will also be paved by small businesses where everyone can be a quantum activist. So we should not lose heart that the big multinationals of today are corrupted and will take a while to begin practicing what I've discussed here. It is not unlike the corruption of the mercantile economy of Smith's day, but that corrupted mercantile economy disintegrated when a better way of doing business, one more conducive to people's needs, became clear. The same thing will now happen to capitalism and materialist economics. It will disintegrate before our eyes, making room for a spiritual economics. There are evolutionary pressures, the "new invisible hands," that are guiding this change. The forefront of economic expansion in the 21st century will involve subtle energy; there is no doubt about it.

New Tips for Aspiring Businesspeople

A time of rapid social change represents danger to some people and produces anxiety in them, but to quantum activists it represents a bonanza of opportunity. What kind of new opportunities are opening up for businesses? The following are a few tips. The businesses cited here may not necessarily produce huge material profit, but they will provide adequate material livelihood for a not necessarily small number of people, produce net profit in the subtle sector of the economy for the people involved and also for the society, and, most importantly, offer huge opportunities for transformation.

⸭ The worldview is changing anyway, but you can help accelerate the change and in the process make an adequate living for yourself and your resonating friends. The Message Company in Santa Fe, New Mexico, was one such company, successfully organizing consciousness-raising conferences until its founder, James Berry, died. But that is just one way of accelerating the paradigm shift. There must be many others. Explore, explore.

⸭ We are just beginning to become aware of our vital energy needs. This is one very promising area of new business enterprises involving food and nutrition, pain management, health and healing, and positive health.

☼ Another most promising area for new businesses for quantum activists is health-care management. The time for an integrative medicine that uses the best of conventional and alternative medicine, as appropriate, has come for economic reasons alone, but few are aware of it. This is an ideal situation for entrepreneurs. With integrative medicine, you can provide low-cost insurance with outcome-dependent coverage that includes prevention and health maintenance.

☼ This one is also a biggie—education. It will be a while before conventional education systems adapt to the new worldview. In the meantime, there is a vast scope for small businesses with new-paradigm education in mind. A big advantage is that such education can largely be done on the Internet.

There is another way to look at the new businesses I am proposing. In the conventional spiritual traditions, there is much talk about selfless service; there are also not many takers. In such traditions, the culture was such that rich people (with the expectation of heavenly rewards) supported the people giving selfless service. This is not the culture now. So "selfless" service will have to come at some cost, so the service givers can eke out a middle-class living from their service.

As I said before, if you go into such a subtle service sector business, the potential for transformation is huge. Behold what the poet Rabindranath Tagore wrote:

> I slept and dreamt that life was joy.
> I awoke and saw that life was service.
> I acted and behold, service was joy.

CHAPTER 16

From Power to Meaning

Can Quantum Thinking Rescue Democracy?

Democracy and capitalism (along with liberal education) are the crowning achievements so far of the mental era in the evolution of consciousness. For mind-dominated consciousness, the capacity for meaning processing is most important. And accordingly, the society progresses by spreading this capacity. Meaning processing by a group of humans is facilitated if the group settles down; hence the transition from nomadic to agricultural societies serves the purpose of evolution. But agricultural societies promote the class divisions of feudalism—landowners and serfs. The development of industrial societies changes the nature of the classes—capital-owners, management, and labor. In agricultural societies, there is a small middle-class service sector. In industrial societies, the middle class increases in population not only because a new management sector is created, but also because of a much larger service sector. This is crucial for the evolution of meaning processing.

Let's dwell on the concept of how people predominantly use their mental faculties according to the inherent qualities (*gunas*) that Easterners call *sattva, rajas,* and *tamas* (see chapter 6). The owners in both agricultural and industrial societies predominantly use rajas, the empire-building capacity. The labor force is dominated by conditioning, tamas. But in the middle class, there occasionally exist people of sattva, those interested in creativity and spirituality. It is these people and their embedding class—the middle class—that foster the evolutionary movement toward spreading meaning processing to all people. And it is this evolutionary movement that gave rise to democracy.

The fundamental creed of democracy is that all people are created (with) equal (potential). Justice demands that all people should have equal opportunity to manifest their potential, which at this stage of our evolution translates as equal opportunity for processing meaning—the meaning of life, liberty, and the pursuit of happiness. It does not matter if you are born poor, rich, or middle class. You should have equal opportunity for education, access to the primary centers where one learns meaning processing. Liberal education geared toward both know-how and know-why is a key ingredient of democracy. Another key ingredient is obviously ethics; one must give value to all people's right to meaning processing in the first place.

This view of the idealist nature of democracy may seem novel to you because, following Plato's ideas in *The Republic,* many people think that consciousness or idealist thinking leads to the political system of benevolent dictatorship, a society dominated by dictators who are also people of sattva. But this seldom worked. There was experimentation in India on a variation of this. Indians recognized that people of sattva would never be good at amassing or using power. So they retained the more pragmatic concept that people of power would always be people predominantly of rajas. But they tried to enforce the higher law that the people of sattva would be the ultimate arbiters of power. This worked for a time; eventually, however, the supposed arbiters of power began to usurp real power and the system became corrupted. Native Americans also used a variant of this system, which actually worked for their culture (although always on a small scale) for a time. The power rested in the chief, but only with the spiritual support of the shaman.

Ultimately, I think idealism favors democracy because democracy, at least in principle, affords equal opportunity for meaning processing to everyone.

Early Greeks and Romans also experimented with variations on democracy. Greeks tried the most idealist form of democracy: power shared by everyone. Unfortunately, this can work only for small communities. Romans tried a form that eventually succeeded after many centuries of dormancy: representative democracy. Of course, we have improved on the Roman version of democracy in many important ways, one of them being the political party system.

Incidentally, for the political party system truly to work in democracy, the party candidates for the elective representatives must themselves be elected. In many countries today (India is an example), democracy is much compromised because there is no election process for the selection of the candidates of the political parties for the eventual elective representation. If one is choosing between two undesirables, the existence of choice is largely meaningless.

I hope you see that the founding fathers of American democracy fit the model of middle-class idealists quite well. The greatest of them, Thomas Jefferson, was an aristocrat and landowner (and, as some people love to point out, a slave owner as well), but in his time, the British were the ruling class and so it is not wrong to see him as belonging to the middle-class service sector. The important point, of course, is that Jefferson was an idealist—one of the all-time truly great ones.

This brief history of the origin of democracy helps us identify why democracy is in great jeopardy in America and elsewhere. The five fundamental reasons are: 1) the marginalization of meaning; 2) consumerism and the rise of negative emotions in people and politics; 3) the erosion of ethics; 4) the compromise of the system of checks and balances; and, most important, 5) the polarization of politics. Let's examine these factors in some detail.

The Marginalization of Meaning

Public schools and colleges teach us about the arts, the humanities, social sciences, and the sciences. Science has traditionally dealt with the grossest questions of meaning—the meaning of the material world. The social sciences teach us the meaning of our social patterns. The humanities do the same but at a subtler level; also, these fields tend to get personal. The arts take the investigation of meaning to deep personal levels. The deepest questions about meaning, however, such as those of the soul and spirit, are left to the religions. Secularism excludes religious matters from public education, which consequently fails to include the deepest questions of meaning.

Even so, this division worked for democratic countries (of the West, mainly) until the 1950s. Tacitly, until then, the Cartesian split between body and mind was accepted. And so science kept more or less to its defined territory—the material world, the physical body. The mind and its activities were left to the social sciences, the humanities, the arts, and religion. But as I have mentioned previously, the discovery of molecular biology made scientists (most of them believers in scientific materialism) so ambitious that they sought a material explanation for whatever we are and whatever we do.

At the purely material level of physics, there is no scope for meaning, since consciousness remains dormant. In biology, materialists try to bring meaning through the back door (the front door is blocked by physics and the dogma that biology must be totally based on physics) by claiming that the ability for meaning processing evolves because it may have survival value. But in psychology, meaning is ignored altogether by materialists through the insistence that all behavior is conditioned behavior and that only behavior, not the inner processes of the psyche, is important.

With behavioral psychology as the guide for the social sciences, it is not surprising that the pursuit of meaning becomes of dubious value in human society—arts, humanities, and religions notwithstanding. At worst, these latter pursuits are seen as vehicles of entertainment alone. At best, in keeping with the existentialists, we assign "pretend meaning" to these pursuits.

When meaning is marginalized in this way, politics become primarily a pursuit of power for its own sake and is used to dominate others. And the pursuit of power apart from the pursuit of meaning corrupts representative democracy quite easily and undermines it.

In American presidential politics, when is the last time that you saw meaning given any importance? Before Obama, you have to go back as far as Lyndon Johnson to find meaningful pursuits in our government at the federal level. No wonder the most creative era in American life in recent times was the 1960s and '70s. This was a direct consequence of the idealist programs of John Kennedy that Johnson brought to fruition. Ever since then, it has been just one continuing backlash.

Why did the idealist purveyors of meaning—the artists, the humanists, and the religionists—lie low and not put up some resistance against this erosion of meaning in politics in America? Rock-and-rollers did protest, as did the humanists who went on to develop new forces of psychology—humanistic and transpersonal psychology—in an attempt to overthrow behaviorism. Some elements of religions protested, too. But the vast majority of the practitioners of the dominant religion in the United States, Christianity, perhaps because of their shallowness and cynicism, gave up on meaning as well and opted for the pursuit of power in order to dominate.

The net result of this is a collusion of religion and politics today that secularism is supposed to avoid. But if power precludes meaning, then what else can we expect?

The Republican Party has made great gains in the American South by siding with the fundamentalist Christians in the pursuit of power. People of the arts and the humanities, and of academe in general, have tended to shift toward the Democratic Party, but this shift has not had a major effect because of the ideological crisis in that party. Democrats are not as gung ho on using power for domination as the Republicans, but they have not remained committed to the pursuit of meaning either. More on this later.

With both politics and religion in America lost in the pursuit of power to dominate, education in America has become a mixed bag of confusion. The public schools and colleges in America remain "liberal," and yet, paradoxically, they are also bastions of materialism. Because materialist pursuits of science are big money projects, materialist science and its ideologies have had the maximum impact on university administrations, which have, as a result, become sold on materialism. This sellout then trickles down to the schools through the teachers and school administrators who are all educated in the institutions of higher education. As a consequence, meaning has become increasingly marginalized in our so-called liberal centers of learning.

It is wrong, however, to make materialist science the sole culprit in all this. Many religious leaders, for example, the ayatollahs in Iran, see materialist science and its stepchild, technology, as the "Great Satan" and the battle of science and religion as the battle between evil and good. Fundamentalist Christians in the United States fight the idea of evolution tooth and nail with the same good-versus-evil battle in mind, which blinds them against accepting data and simple reason. But this is too simplistic.

Actually, you must see that materialist science has also helped the evolution of consciousness. The materialist invasion of the territory of social sciences, arts and humanities, and religion led at first to much retreat on the part of the latter. But eventually, reactions to such an attack on meaning itself (since materialist ontology leaves no room for meaning except in the trivial sense of survival necessity) could not be ignored. Eventually, quantum physics, the pinnacle of materialist science, gave rise to meaning questions that are not only overthrowing the materialist approach altogether, but also showing promise in restoring the previous status quo, only better. We'll see how later in the chapter, but first, let's discuss the subjects of consumerism and ethics.

Consumerism

What do you think qualifies as a consumer good? Breakfast cereals, household appliances, and automobiles? In an earlier era, people would have answered differently. Consider the following conversation taken from a play by George Bernard Shaw:

> **Ellie:** A soul is a very expensive thing to keep; much more so than a motor car.
> **Shotover:** Is it? How much does your soul eat?
> **Ellie:** Oh, a lot. It eats music and pictures and books and mountains and lakes and beautiful things to wear and nice people to be with.

In those days, in addition to material goods, middle-class people consciously consumed soul food, food that gives aesthetic meaning to our lives. And the value accorded to soul food by these people pervaded the entire society.

It's not that we have stopped consuming soul food altogether. I am sure the New York Metropolitan Opera is as popular as ever. But soul food is not so readily available in middle America where the TV reigns supreme.

Undeniably there is a shift; the processing of meaning (of the new) is no longer considered important. Meaning is a consumer good today only so far as it is entertainment; as long as it sells, it has economic impact. Today, the bulk of the people live in anxiety: fear of losing their jobs, the pressure of the high standard of living, unease about coping with fast-moving technology, and on and on it goes. These anxieties crowd their crown chakras with streams of random anxious thoughts; lack of concentration leads to a random movement of vital energy in and out of the crown chakra and people feel ungrounded, disembodied. To embody themselves, what better way than to be manipulated by consumerism and watch TV entertainment that caters to the three lower chakras with fear, sex, and violence?

The main culprit behind this shift is, of course, misdirected capitalism—materialist economics (see chapter 14). But the cynicism of postmodernism—deconstructionism and existentialism—has also contributed. As an example, consider two good movies of the 1970s: *The Way We Were* and *Annie Hall*. In both, the heroines were pursuers of meaning compared to the heroes, and they ended up tragically (they didn't get their guys).

When meaning is marginalized in our education and in our consumer society in general, the result is a temporary suspension of the evolution of the mind. One urgent need of this evolution is the integration of our earlier evolutionary stage of the vital-body identity into our mental-ego identity. Instead of integrating meaning processing and the processing of feelings, giving up on meaning altogether leads to a sudden surge of unreasonable, irrational dominance of instinctual negative emotions in how we do things and how we treat others. Have you noticed how nasty politics have become? When was the last time you saw politicians, especially Republicans, act reasonably rather than pursue one-upmanship over the other party? Negative emotions have caused havoc not only in politics, but also in economics and business. Business and economics today are on a downslide because of rampant greed and competitiveness, as discussed earlier.

All three lower chakras are active now in our social institutions, not only the third chakra dominance that we see in the pursuit of power (to dominate) in politics and religion, but also second and first chakra dominance. How else can we explain the preoccupation with sex and violence in Hollywood and the media in general?

Have you noticed that recent movies have developed an affinity for displaying at least one toilet scene that would have been considered vulgar in an earlier time? This vulgarity is a sign of first chakra dominance.

The Erosion of Ethics: Post-Secularism

Materialist science cannot validate ethics and cannot prove the universality of ethical laws; you need quantum and reincarnational thinking for that (see chapter 9). But materialist philosophy does permit a myopic version of ethics. Following the sociobiologists and the idea of the selfish gene, it can purport to show that altruism is entirely due to genetic conditioning and has no universal value or necessity. Sociobiology also justifies our competitive nature. Thus the politician's pursuit of power for domination is what seems to follow from our materialist biology, not the pursuit of meaning within an ethical framework that the idealist proposes for politics.

The age of the mind, if anything, tends to be rational. When reason showed that one need only talk ethics, not walk them (live by them), politicians abandoned ethics.

Consider the 2004 presidential election in the United States. Many pundits saw it as a victory of the ethical side, the God-fearing side, over the unethical atheists. Alas, this only validates my point. The side that made the most cynical use of the value of maintaining a facade of belief in God and ethics won. But no one walked ethics in that election—neither the winning nor the losing party. It is this marginalization of ethics that is one of the most serious threats to democracy today.

Lack of ethics leads to corruption, first on a small scale and then on a large scale. First, surreptitiously, and then openly, like today. And corruption leads to concentration of power, maybe eventually to tyranny. This has already happened in post-communist Russia. And the United States has come pretty close.

Most democracies adapt some form of secularism. Secularism has two connotations: 1) the complete independence of the state from religion, all church; and 2) the state should maintain equidistance from all religions, that is, all religions should be treated equally.

Secularism in the second form is necessary because religions cannot agree with one another about the subtle questions of religiosity: the nature of God and the nature of the subtle bodies and how to go about investigating them. This disagreement, too, is to be expected. It is much harder to develop a monolithic approach about subtle things than about the gross material things.

Secularism in the first form, on the other hand, may have to do with the materialist suspicion that religion may be a deluded pursuit for humans (Dawkins 2006). If religion is marginalized in this fashion, so are religious ethics with it.

Science within consciousness is a science of spirituality and ethics. It is urgently needed that we move to an era of post-secularism in which spirituality is distinguished from religion and ethics are recognized as a fundamental prerogative for human beings.

Democracy and War and Peace

The act of aggression is one of the most unethical actions. Thus ethically speaking, aggressive war is immoral. If war is thrust upon you, however, war in self-defense is okay, but ethically speaking, one has to engage even in the war for self-defense without violence in one's heart, without demonizing ourselves. Only then is war part of one's moral prerogative.

When we humans discovered democracy back in the 18th century, one hope was that aggressive wars would become a thing of the past when all countries became democratic. The reason is obvious. If one person, a king or a dictator, decides war and peace, and the person is high in the quality of rajas, chances are also high for opting for an aggressive war that has more advantage over a defensive one. But to find more than 50 percent of an entire people favoring an unethical war of aggression is much less likely. Even mobilizing more than 50 percent of the elected representatives of a democracy toward supporting an unethical war of aggression should be quite difficult.

But something must be wrong with this picture! You are thinking of the war of the United States against Iraq. That war of unilateral aggression was supported by fully 96 percent of the elected representatives of the country! How is that possible in a democracy?

If you read newspaper columns and editorials, even the liberal-leaning ones, you will get the idea that the president of the country misled and bamboozled people and especially elected representatives to extract a mandate for unilateral aggression. But this does not jibe with the facts because there was plenty of information available even then to cast serious doubts on the necessity of that war. An ethical person never, never abandons ethical action if reasonable doubt exists.

Politicians and pundits aside, the war in Iraq is perhaps the most glaring example of how far ethics have eroded in the United States. Both political parties in this country are currently unethical; there is no doubt about it. And it is highly alarming to anyone who cares about ethics to find that a majority of the American people went along with this unethical war for so long, no doubt because of fear and other negative emotions that politicians were able to exploit. This is a glaring example of how deep the wound created by materialism is for Americans.

The political thinker Noam Chomsky has called the United States a "failed state" because of its blatant display of jingoism in the recent Iraq war and other events. Previously, the term was being applied only to rogue states that foster terrorism and such violent unethical things. But I agree with Chomsky. Unprovoked aggressive war is state-sponsored terrorism.

Once again: one cannot eradicate violence with violence. One cannot eliminate negative emotional energy by adding more negative vital energy to it. In the long run, there is only one way to deal with violence and terrorism: through transformation that requires abundant positive emotions—ethics and love.

How do we bring back meaning and ethics in our politics, now that we know that materialism is not the complete story, but only half of the apple of truth?

The Polarization of the Political Parties

If you are a Republican, you may already have concluded that the author is a Democrat and is using science for a veiled attack on Republican politics. But you would be wrong. Many Democrats are actually more likely to be skeptical of the contents of this book because they do not believe in spirituality, or God, period; they are unabashed materialists.

The situation looks so hopeless today because we cannot look at either party in this country to bring back the idealist values that are the foundation of democracy. Democrats miss these values because they look for values within the false philosophies of humanism or existentialism that are compatible with materialism. As mentioned earlier, we then get stuck with some sort of gene-based bioethics or, at best, an arbitrary humanistic ethics that is hard to define and has no scientific basis whatsoever.

Republicans seem to know that idealist values come from ideas of God and spirituality. But for all their pretend belief in God, they, too, have bought into scientific materialism and have become cynical. It is out of utter cynicism and hypocrisy that Republicans use the concept of God and moral values to further their pursuit of power, even at the cost of selling their souls to religious fundamentalism.

If both political parties in America have abandoned God and idealism, then why not found a third party based from the get-go on the scientific notions of God and the evolution of manifest spirituality that we are discussing here? Because two-party politics are most suited for an idealist society and government.

The Idealist Basis of the Two-Party System

Recall that there are three ways that we process mental meaning: fundamental creativity (sattva), situational creativity (rajas), and conditioning (tamas). Fundamental creativity is too rarefied to be of any practical day-to-day use by a political party for its dominant modus operandi. But situational creativity with an openness to fundamental creativity when available could be the basis, the modus operandi, of a political party. Following the Chinese way of thinking, we can call this the yang party—the party of change. It is the party of creativity or at least progressivity, advocating changes conducive to the advancement of meaning.

The other party would be based on the complementary yin—conditioned stasis. This party, ideally, is meant to balance the creative risk and adventurism of the other creative party by insisting on keeping to the basics, maintaining the status quo.

So in idealism, idealist government—democracy—is best run within a two-party system, with one party being creative and progressive in outlook and fostering change and the other party being conservative and maintaining the status quo.

This latter party, rightly, is called the conservative party in some parts of the world. In the United States, it is the Republican Party that fits the description.

But unfortunately, seldom in the world do we find a political party with the label of progressive or creative attached to it. Actually, an inappropriate label has done much damage to the image of the party of creativity in the United States and elsewhere—the label of "liberal."

The word *liberal* implies "openness," which is a prerequisite of creativity; that much is good. But the word can also mean permissionary (of undisciplined, even unethical conduct). And this is disastrous for the party's image and even more disastrous if the party decides to live up to its permissionary image. Indeed in this country, the Democrats have been identified as the party of fiscal irresponsibility, of sexual permissiveness, and of ethically ambiguous acts such as abortion, even as a party of "hippies," which has done much damage to its image. But ethics are compulsory for an idealist society, and liberalism in the sense of permissiveness is not the idea.

Liberalism also means, however, to be open to the ideals of liberal democracy, principal among which is social justice: to open up society so that everyone has access to meaning. It is this old meaning of the word "liberalism" that has to be brought back to politics.

In truth, in this country, the Democratic Party is neither a creative nor a progressive party because increasingly it just gives lip service to social justice, opting instead for looking after special interest groups. A good example is how it so readily abandons the ideals of a liberal education to please its interest group consisting of the teachers' unions. Indeed it is a lot like a liberal party in the pejorative sense of the word!

But nor is the Republican Party a conservative party today. The Republicans may have started as true conservatives and may have remained that way for a long time, aside from an occasional dalliance. But how can the Republican Party now be called the conservative party when it promotes unprecedented deficit financing and amasses huge national debt, when it pushes a clearly antievolutionary agenda of widening the wealth gap between the rich and the poor?

And more. American democracy is based on the separation of power—the existence of several independent estates. The three official estates are, of course, the executive, the legislature, and the judiciary. The fourth, unofficial but equally important, estate is the news media. And there is possibly even a fifth one, religion.

But look at what the Republican Party politicians have been trying to do (with some help from the Democrats)! They have blurred the secular separation of church and state; this we have already noted. Equally alarming is the fact that they are attempting and succeeding in blurring the separation of the executive branch from the news media. It is certainly not George Orwell's *1984* yet, but some authors have already noted the trend. Republicans are also trying to smudge the independence of the judiciary, but that is nothing new. Anyway, these tendencies are not kosher, and definitely not conservative.

No, both parties in America are parties of opportunism; both deviate from idealist principles and neither in its present form can be counted on to revitalize democracy, bringing back its idealist roots.

What's the solution then? Starting new parties would cause a proliferation of parties against idealist principles and would not work. So the only way out is to change the two existing parties, bring them back to the ideals on which they were founded. How do we do that? It has to be done from within.

Although the Republicans are not truly conservative any more, they not only have maintained their core support base (the coalition of military-industrial complex, multinationals, the traditional "less-government" conservatives), but also have added religious fundamentalists to their fold. Buoyed by this success, they have reverted to regressive old motifs (the neocon motif in a nutshell)—military adventurism reminiscent of the crusades and the creation of a huge gap between rich and poor reminiscent of feudal societies. This is truly going backward in time, truly against the evolution of consciousness, and success is unlikely. In fact, the Republican coalition is already showing signs of disagreement with the neocon adventurism. So except for the major issue of separation of the five estates of power in American politics, the restoration of the Republican Party is already under way.

Democrats, on the other hand, have not been able to maintain their core support. For example, the rank-and-file membership of labor unions is socially conservative and often votes against their pocketbooks because of a social issue. Democrats also have major confusion about the role of religion and morality in politics. And finally, the Democratic Party is the party of a progressive social agenda, of advancing social justice, and it is not keeping up with that task. So on the whole, the Democrats need much more of a redefinition. The Democratic Party is, in one word, clueless, and is a very fertile ground for quantum activism.

From Secularism to Post-Secularism

In the past, secularism worked for democracy. The state carried out the democratic ideal of bringing meaning to everyone in society. The church gave us the ethical canopy under which everyone pursued meaning. Unfortunately, the evolution of scientific materialism put a monkey wrench in this equilibrium.

In this country, the progressive Democrats, who are supposed to advance the pursuit of meaning, follow (correctly) the vehicle of creativity for that advancement. But science is supposed to be one of those creative activities of which Democrats utterly approve. When science advocates a godless materialism and meaningless existentialism, the Democrats get thoroughly confused. Many of these confused Democrats seem to be antireligion, even anti-ethics. How then can religious people trust them to be even-handed about religions and religious ethics?

Republicans have a different confusion. Being conservatives, they are not particularly tied to science and scientific advances. They can accept science's gifts to society—technology—and yet they don't have to accept, lock, stock, and barrel, science's ideology—materialism. Unfortunately, they did, starting with the presidency of Ronald Reagan (who was an out-and-out survival-of-the-fittest materialist who hated the poor and any idea of helping them to process meaning). Also unfortunately, Republicans, too, grow up in today's very materialist society and at heart become conditioned by materialist values enough to be confused as well, or even more so than Democrats. In this way, Republican politicians develop an unhealthy doubt about God and religious ethics, enough to make them into cynics, wishy-washy about religious ethics. It is from this ambiguity about religions and religious ethics that they can at once proclaim their belief in God and morality and yet partake in nonidealist conduct such as blocking the progress of spreading equal opportunity to the poor. They become an unholy alliance of the rich and the powerful, on one hand, and the fundamentalist Christians, on the other, but then the secularists—the ones that want to maintain the separation of church and state—lose confidence in them.

What is the way out of this conundrum, a near 50–50 split in the political attitudes in this country? (And don't forget that similar dynamics are operating elsewhere in the world, too.) We have to go back to the roots of secularism and ask: is secularism relevant today?

I have already mentioned one reason for secularism in democracy: freedom to pursue a minority religion. But this is not the only root reason.

You have to recognize that democracy evolved in Christian societies, and Christianity as a religion was antagonistic to affairs of the state from the very beginning. Didn't Jesus say to his disciples, "Render unto Caesar the things that are Caesar's and unto God the things that are God's?" So in Christianity, from the get-go, worldly pursuits are not considered spiritual; there is a split between state (the focus of this-worldly acts) and religion (the focus of otherworldly or transcendence-directed acts that take us to the kingdom of heaven; see also Zohar and Marshall 1995).

And Christianity is not the only religion with such a split. In Hinduism also, until Aurobindo, this worldliness was undermined as the pursuit of illusion, *maya.*

But this kind of thinking must give way to new evolutionary thinking, per Aurobindo. This worldliness is not meaningless as the materialists maintain, nor is it trivial, as Christians and Hindus think. Instead, worldly actions take place with a definite purpose, that of evolving the capacity for representing spiritual values in the manifest world. The pursuit of otherworldliness or transcendence is important. Without that pursuit, how would we have known firsthand (before the discovery of the new science) what God is, what spirituality is? But living what we discover in our pursuit of otherworldliness in this very world is equally important. How else would we ever evolve godliness in all humanity?

In the new science, this-worldliness and otherworldliness, immanence and transcendence, are both validated. Then what is the relevance of secularism except to avoid religious monopoly and to maintain the equidistance of state from all religions? We must move to an era of post-secularism in which spirituality is distinguished from religion.

To avoid the monopoly of one religion over others, all we need to do is distinguish between the concepts of spirituality and religion, with religion understood clearly as one's personal path to God. Spirituality should designate general ontological and epistemological considerations of God, godliness, ethics, and related matters.

Since spirituality in our new worldview is also the basis of our new science and science is already supported by the state and included in our education, all current conflicts and controversies in these matters should disappear like dew in the morning sun.

An example. Can creationism be taught in our schools? No, it clearly has a specific religious agenda, that of Christianity, and secularism demands that it stays out of our public schools. But can intelligent design theory be taught?

You bet, as one of the early theories of creation across cultures that, unfortunately, does not fully agree with data. Can neo-Darwinism be taught in our schools? You bet, also as a partial theory that explains intraspecies evolution and speciation in microevolution but not the giant evolutionary leaps of macroevolution. Can the biological creativity theory of evolution advocated in this book in which both upward and downward causation play roles be taught? You bet, as a better theory than both the previous ones, subject to further experimental and theoretical checks on it for details and fine-tuning.

Consider another example. Should community prayer be included in our schools? Yes, as long as it is generic and does not hurt the religious sensitivity of any particular individual or group. Can meditation? Yes, of course. Meditation is always generic since it is silent.

My vision is that the Democratic Party, once back on its journey to being the party of creativity and change, will be the first to accept the new scientific paradigm of science within consciousness. This would make the Democratic Party progressive again. Instead of being perceived as antireligion, Democrats would be perceived as the vanguards of spirituality. Republicans, initially, would have a lot of problems with the new paradigm because of the stranglehold of fundamentalist Christianity on them, but that too shall pass. Truth wins over everyone eventually. If the new ideas of God and spirituality are true, as they seem to be under quite rigorous experimental scrutiny, everyone will eventually accept their validity.

With science within consciousness—idealist science—to guide democracy and politics, there should never be the frontal attacks on meaning and ethics that undermine democracy today. Unfortunately, the shift from a power-for-meaning orientation to a power-for-dominance orientation that has taken place in politics today will take more than a paradigm shift of our science to reverse. It will require some degree of emotional intelligence (see later).

Balance of Power

The truth is, in this mental age of our evolution, we are far from transformed beings capable of harnessing the energies of love. In this age, which the Hindus call Kali Yuga, it is essential that we have someone watching over us to keep us honest in the pursuit of meaning and democratic ideals in general. Thus originated the idea of balance of power. Power in democracy should be shared among many separate institutions, each maintaining vigilance over the others.

But when power is pursued devoid of meaning and ethics hits the dust, collusion between the various sectors compromises the balance of power. This was the case in the first years of 21st-century America under President George W. Bush. Even a significant portion of the news media was bribed to forego its watchdog responsibility.

The news media now faces a huge credibility gap. The news media was founded upon the ideals of truth and justice. Economic pressure and competition led to an increase in the entertainment value of news, and newspeople began to compromise truth to make their commodity entertaining. Eventually, even the pursuit of justice came to be compromised. Now there is open discussion about establishing oversight of the news media—keeping a watch on the watcher. But then who will watch the watcher of the watcher?

The root cause of the erosion of credibility of the news media is its own ambivalence about the ideals of truth and justice. The materialist worldview has affected the objectivity and ethics of the news media itself.

When I was researching evolution for my book *Creative Evolution,* I could not help noticing how the news media has begun to use the words "evolutionism" and "Darwinism": as synonymous when obviously there is controversy. Similarly, "mind" has become synonymous with "brain" to many journalists, controversy notwithstanding.

The journey back to credibility of the news media has to begin with a healthy skepticism about the claims of materialist science and its worldview in which the place of idealist archetypes of truth, justice, and goodness (the basis of ethics) is already compromised. It is easy to find fault with Fox News or Rush Limbaugh because they exaggerate the distortion of truth. However, any journalist who has even unwittingly fallen prey to scientific materialism has already compromised his or her ideals, be it truth, justice, or ethics. Both behaviors originate from the same tendency to please the majority of one's perceived audience, and this is clearly neither objective nor ethical.

Emotional Intelligence

For the 1972 presidential primaries in the United States, the Democrats had a very promising candidate from New England, Ed Muskie. But Muskie's wife was maligned in some conservative newspapers. Muskie reacted to this emotionally; he cried in public. When this was reported in the media, Muskie's political career was over. The public perception guided by the media was that Muskie was emotionally immature.

I submit, as a few pundits commented even then, that the actual truth was perhaps the opposite: Muskie was emotionally more mature than most politicians. But he lost because he went against the American public perception of what emotional maturity means. Most Americans, maybe even today, mistake emotional maturity with emotion suppression.

It should then be obvious that bringing emotional intelligence—ascribing meaning to feeling with proper clarity of the archetypal context of both—to the political arena in this country is a daunting task. The entire culture needs to reevaluate its treatment of emotions, acknowledging the evils of suppression of emotions irrespective of the context and the desirability of achieving a balance. And then there is the difficult job of practicing what one conceptually accepts.

And yet this has to be done. The power to dominate is a negative emotion. Unless and until we balance it with the positivity of love, it won't let go. In the United States, during the Bush II administration, power became so entrenched in negativity that even the idea of torturing prisoners for information in violation of clear international rules could not be let go.

Only when we balance power with love can power be used in the service of meaning. Our political leaders must understand this and act accordingly, and we, the people, must insist that they do.

Democracy Must Accommodate Evolutionary Ethics

Science within consciousness gives a scientific basis for ethics—failure to be ethical produces proliferation of reincarnation (Goswami 2008a). Is the threat of reincarnation enough to keep people in line? Hardly. What if people defer the day of reckoning to future lives? What then?

Fortunately, fear of reincarnation is not the only incentive; there is also the evolutionary movement of consciousness that drives us toward ethics—evolutionary ethics. Synchronistically, this evolutionary pressure also expresses itself in creating crisis conditions if we do not heed its bidding. If we don't heed the needs of evolution, the social systems break down, as they did in the Soviet Union.

Democratic leaderships all over the world must recognize that the crisis conditions facing us today are largely because of the gross violation of evolutionary ethics. Our unethical antievolutionary actions have created the blockage in the progressive institutions of our society that have traditionally been the markers of the evolutionary movement of meaning such as democracy, capitalism, and liberal education. There is a block in the evolutionary movement of meaning. The call of evolutionary ethics for our democratic leaders is loud and clear. It is no longer merely "Be good, do good." It is to take actions that will unblock the evolutionary movement of consciousness. It is to restore idealism to democracy, capitalism, news enterprises, and liberal education.

One does not have to see a contradiction here. Indeed, the old ethics remain important, but their purpose has shifted. The purpose of the way of life signified by "Be good, do good" is no longer directed toward personal salvation or liberation alone, but also to the planetary movement of consciousness as a whole.

As long as the spiritual component of our culture is solely directed to personal "enlightenment," the block of democracy due to the shift of the search for meaning to the search of power-to-dominate is unmovable. Only when this unmovable block is confronted with the irresistible force of the evolutionary pressure of consciousness will there be unblocking. Only when we as a society recognize the evolutionary need for the transformation of the negative energies of domination into the positive energies of love, and act on it and demand that action from our elected representatives and leaders as well, can we make a quantum leap and make progress.

What does this mean in concrete terms? Right now, democracy is being practiced more and more in a way that leaves a lot of people out of the "loop." These people have no motivation to participate in democracy. This is in gross violation of evolutionary ethics to maximize people's participation in meaningful processes.

We must remember that in a democracy the elected representatives are but custodians of the people's power, our power. We must elect those leaders who can anticipate the evolutionary needs of the movement of consciousness and can lead people to that end. Gandhi was such a leader for India. Mikhail Gorbachev was such a leader for the Soviet Union. Nelson Mandela was such a leader for South Africa. Abraham Lincoln and John Kennedy were such leaders for the United States. What is the difference between these visionary leaders and ordinary leaders? These leaders correctly foresaw the way their country could respond to the evolutionary needs of consciousness. They personalized those needs and acted in synchrony with their persona. The rest is history.

In the political arena, it is also clear that so long as we bind ourselves to nation-states, negative emotions can always find a strong anchor in the concept of patriotism and rally around the nation's people, again temporarily thwarting evolution. This happened in the United States immediately after the disaster of 9/11 and continued until 2006. What is the remedy?

The short-term remedy is easy: get rid of the demagogue leadership in favor of those who will not use patriotism as the clarion call to block the evolutionary movement of consciousness.

But in the long term, only a movement toward internationalism, beginning with bigger units than a nation, will save us from myopic unethical leaders who use patriotism to their advantage. This movement toward internationalism is already taking place in Europe in the form of the European Union.

The Quantum Activist Plan for Rescuing Democracy: A Summary

The job is to steer politicians from the pursuit of power to dominate back to the pursuit of power to propagate meaning. How do we do it? Let's count the ways.

1. Democracy, an idealist system from the get-go, works best within a two-party system. The first and foremost task to rescue democracy is to direct the two major political parties of the country to conform to their idealist character. One party must be creativity and progressivity minded; the other must be conservative. We must change the focus of comparison between the two parties from the current conservative versus liberal to conservative versus progressive.

2. In this country, the Republican Party is the conservative party, and they still conform to their basic values except for a segment called the neocons. This segment is trying to bring back very old systems:

world domination through military means and the feudalistic huge gap between the haves and have-nots. The neocons are counter-evolutionary, and their power within the Republican Party must be contained.

3. Power likes company, and the Republicans have joined forces with the religious right, coming dangerously close to violating the separation of church and state, secularism. This also has to be contained. We must bring the message of post-secularism of the new science to the Republicans and work on their materialist cynicism as part of post-secularism's priority agenda.

4. The Democrats are the American equivalent of a progressive party, and their principal problem is the lack of a rudder. Their confusion is coming from accepting materialist science—lock, stock, and barrel. So here is an enormous opening for quantum activists. Bring the new science to Democrats. This will not only give them a rudder to wend their way out of their current cluelessness, but will also enable them to be on the right side of God and ethical values for a change. Democrats who want real change must realize that fundamental creativity is the force behind real change and it is a gift of God's downward causation.

5. Both parties must be persuaded to see the importance of maintaining the balance of power between the five independent estates—the presidency, the legislature, the judiciary, the news media, and (government-independent) religion.

6. The news media must be persuaded to give up its blind adherence to materialist beliefs in favor of idealism and to serve once again the cause of the archetypes of truth and justice without compromise.

7. The culture of a democratic country must pursue emotional intelligence and balance power with love. (Remember the saying "transform the love of power with the power of love.") Only then can its political parties and leaders be expected to find their way back from power to dominate others to power in the service of meaning.

8. The political parties of a country must follow ethical principles and, for best results, evolutionary ethics.

9. Political leaders will best serve democracy when they dedicate their power to the service of meaning, when they practice emotional intelligence before they preach it, and when they personalize evolutionary ethics before their actions. But we can only grow such political leaders through revamping meaning and ethics in our educational system.

10. Eventually, to help the evolution of consciousness, we must work toward internationalism and surrender the concept of sovereign nation-states as much as is practicable.

CHAPTER 17

Post-Secularism

Making Religions Work

Is there any need for religion once we develop a science of spirituality, as we have now reviewed in the foregoing pages? The answer is a resounding yes. This may require some explanation, however.

It may seem that since God is objective in our scientific approach, in agreement with the mystics, God is the same for all of us.

God is not *only* private. God is nonlocal consciousness; everyone's God is the same nonlocal cosmic quantum consciousness.

But we cannot readily see God outside of ourselves, so God is not public in the same way that the material world is public. It is more subtle than that. God is objective because we can experience with others the nonlocality of God consciousness; the company of God-loving others helps us experience more easily the public side of God consciousness.

I have previously referred to Dean Radin's experiments. Radin took random number generators to meditation halls and found that, indeed, their behavior deviated substantially from randomness. This substantiates what Buddha tried to do with his idea of *sangha* (meaning community), what Hindus do with *satsang* (meaning the company of people in search of reality), and what Jesus meant when he said:

> When two or more meditate in my name
> There I am in the midst of them.

Religions, communities of spiritually motivated people, grow out of the intuition of quantum nonlocality of God consciousness!

There is a second reason that religions are important when we look at spirituality, not in an old-fashioned mystical way but in a new-fashioned, scientific, Aurobindo-like way. There is a social dimension of spirituality. Spirituality is not only satisfying the personal goal of awakening to God consciousness, but also evolving the cream of God consciousness—the supramental archetypes that we call virtues or even godliness—right in the play of human consciousness.

So religion is needed to help us *religiere*, which means to reconnect—reconnect with our own divinity in our personhood, reconnect with the divine qualities in the evolution of our societies. The first requires creativity, the second love.

On both these scores, the Western religions have historically performed rather poorly. Judaism, the root of all Western religions, was a good beginning. It was, appropriately rooted in the Kabbala, based on a clear enunciation of nondual philosophy. But then came the Old Testament with its concept of a wrathful God, love became limited to God's chosen clan, and Judaism got bogged down in power politics. So Jesus appeared on the scene to reform Judaism; he himself was creative and a great lover (of all humanity), but look at the history of Christianity. The creatives are abundant—Saint Teresa of Avila, Meister Eckhart, Thomas Merton, just to name a few. As are the lovers—Saint Francis, Brother Lawrence, and Mother Teresa are glorious in their love! But most of these people were not treated well by the Christian hierarchy nor are their teachings emphasized in the way popular Christianity is presented. The same comment applies to Islam. They have the Sufis, the greatest of lovers—Rumi, Kabir, Monsoor—among them. They also have Ibn Arabi, one of the most creative sheiks that ever lived. But Sufism is not, and never has been, the popular trendsetter in Islam.

What dominated the history of Christianity and Islam are conversion, proselytizing, crusades, and the like.

It is the failure of organized religions, especially in the form of popular Christianity and Islam, that has maligned organized religion in modern eyes. Have you heard Krishnamurti's story? God and the Devil are taking a walk. God picks up a paper that reads, "Truth." Devil snatches it from God's hand. "Hey, I will organize it for you," exclaims he.

Religions of the East did better, at least until recently. There was dualism at the popular level, but nondual teachings were not exactly shunned. Most importantly, the God realizers—the creatives and the lovers—were revered in the East, not persecuted.

You can even see evolution in the way Hinduism and Buddhism have progressed. First, both of these religions were centered on inner journeys of self-realization and negated the world. But then some of the religious thinkers wondered aloud, "Does it make sense that one person is liberated when the rest of humanity is in darkness? After all, consciousness is one and only one!" So the *bodhisattva* idea grew that no one escapes the world until all of humanity is enlightened. And then, with Aurobindo, the idea of evolution of consciousness found at least some attention.

But in the West, who but a few New Agers are in the know about the great evolutionary insights of the Jesuit mystic-scientist Teilhard de Chardin?

The story of the second half of the 20th century is different. Here we find the East gradually succumbing to materialism, the Eastern mystics migrating to the West, and the West gradually waking up to consciousness, gradually being healed from the deep wound that materialism has created.

But we cannot afford for the East to go to sleep either or to suffer from the wound of materialism that the West has suffered. We need an integrated effort, East-West integration.

The Second-Person God and the Question of Gurus

Ken Wilber (2006), in his inimitable style, wrote about the 1 2 3 of God: the first-person God, the second-person God, and the third-person God. When we reconnect with God through creativity, first-person efforts, it is the first-person face of God, in Wilber's terminology. And when we are investigating God collectively, such as in religious organizations and in science, we are really addressing the third-person face of God. In addition to these two faces, God can be approached in the second person, says Wilber. And Wilber is right.

God in the second person, as you can easily guess, is approached in a second-person relationship with God. God in the intimate relationship of a lover, or as the philosopher Martin Buber put it, God in an I-Thou relationship. But how do we do it? How do we make a tangible intimate relationship with a concept? Not surprisingly, much confusion exists.

The Hindu tradition recognized the second-person God pretty early on (unfortunately without clarifying the concept much), recognized the difficulty in practicing it, and developed the guru tradition as the answer, creating more confusion. The idea sounds good. What you are trying to do is to surrender your ego so that God consciousness takes over your actions. Then all your actions are appropriate. Since surrendering to a nebulous idea is also going to be nebulous, surrender to a person in a simple hierarchical relationship, a guru, said the founders of Hinduism. And this guru system still runs strong in Indian spirituality. Only a guru can give you spiritual salvation, any Hindu will tell you.

Wilber, it seems, goes along with the guru tradition (Cohen and Wilber 2009). And since Wilber has earned, rightly, a great amount of respect as a spiritual philosopher, the guru idea is having a sort of revival after years of decline even in America, the land of the skeptics of authority.

So where does quantum activism stand in relation to this concept of a guru—the idea of surrendering to a guru? Previously, I admonished that quantum activists should not aspire to become gurus (see chapter 9). Why? These issues are subtle and controversial, but nevertheless need a discussion.

In the experience of a creative insight, outer or inner, in God consciousness we are choosing something new without the usual sifting through the reflections in the mirror of memory. In this way, there is an immediacy to any experience of insight. This immediacy becomes most obvious when we creatively look at the nature of awareness itself.

The creative process is the same as discussed before except now preparation consists of meditation on awareness itself. So we alternate between meditating on awareness and relaxing—relegating the processing to God consciousness. This do-be-do-be-do alternation of the ego and God consciousness has a lot of the intensity of Buber's I-Thou or *bhakti* (love) relationship. This is the stage when it helps to have a guru, not a simple-hierarchical but a tangled hierarchical relationship with a person in the flesh. At some point, we fall into the primary collapse state of subject-object split. As you recall, in this state, the subject in awareness is the quantum self. What is the object? Awareness, of course.

But who can be a guru? What one experiences in this culmination of the process of inner creativity is the oneness of everything, how the subject and object—the field of awareness—arise from an identity, consciousness. This "oneness" experience creates much confusion. Some people interpret this (wrongly) as the experience of the ultimate reality and declare themselves "enlightened," "transformed," qualified to be guru, and so forth.

In the yoga literature (Taimni 1961), however, there is clarity. Using quantum physics and science within consciousness helps to decipher a couple of highly esoteric yogic concepts. I have mentioned the concept of *samadhi* as the superconscious experience of the quantum self. But in Hinduism, when they talk about samadhi in the esoteric literature, they talk about two different kinds: *savikalpa* samadhi and *nirvikalpa* samadhi. What's the difference?

Samadhi means the equality of the two poles of subject and object. The superconscious experience is savikalpa samadhi. *Savikalpa* means "with separation." Buddhists clarify the situation further: in this experience, we become aware of the dependent co-arising of the universal quantum self and the world, albeit the self (subject) is already split from the world (object). Quantum physics makes it even clearer: we never *experience* consciousness undivided from its possibilities. Any experience, by definition, involves tangled hierarchical quantum measurement, self-reference, and the subject-object split. In other words, savikalpa samadhi is as deep (or high) as we can go in experience.

By contrast, *nirvikalpa* means "without (subject-object) separation." If there is no experience without subject-object split, what does this represent? How does one know? Very confusing.

To understand this, consider deep sleep. In deep sleep, there is no subject-object split and there is no experience, but no problem in accepting that we sleep either. We don't change because we sleep. We all do it without effort, and it is a universally accepted state of consciousness.

In ordinary deep sleep, the ego maintains such tight control on what we process unconsciously, that usually new possibilities are not entertained. But as we practice surrendering of the ego, the new is invited for unconscious processing even in deep sleep, and God is there to process it. This has to be understood as a deeper sleep, sometimes called *yoga nidra* (*nidra* is Sanskrit for "sleep") in the literature, in which some special unconscious processing takes place that is cognized at the moment of waking, resulting in spontaneous lucid dreams much like episodes of creative experiences. We change but still maintain the ego identity. This is not that rare an experience, and there are now neurophysiologists who have identified such deeper states of sleep.

Now imagine that the surrender of the ego is even deeper and such yoga nidra states occur in what would normally be waking hours. If you are not a connoisseur, you would misunderstand such states as "trance," and you would be wrong. The tradition recognizes these episodes as episodes of nirvikalpa samadhi—samadhi without separation—and of course, at this deep level of surrender, the world ceases to be important, and the creative outbursts upon waking up are ignored. There is now a transformation; there is no more ego in the old sense. At even deeper stage of surrender, these episodes become *sahaj,* a Sanskrit word meaning "easy, without effort."

There is still more subtlety here that quantum thinking helps us decipher, which I have discussed elsewhere (Goswami 2008a). I will only discuss some of it here.

Let's go back and ask: to what are we surrendering? Much confusion exists because the tendency is to think that this is like the I-Thou relationship, only that the relationship is with a "Thou" that is "the entire universe" and is "much bigger" than the "I" that is surrendering. The tendency is to imagine that this "Thou" is the "One on whom I'm dependent for every blessing and every grace, the One who knows me best . . . This One sees through all the games I might play" (Patten 2009). This kind of imagination is only marginally better than that of popular Christianity's in which God has a white beard, because God still has the omniscience, omnipotence, and benevolence of popular Christian vintage. Quantum thinking straightens us out: to what do we surrender? To the objective God, to the objective evolutionary movement of consciousness. And what do we surrender? We surrender the tendency to resolve our conflicts from the ego, the tendency to get what we (the ego) desire or intend. We surrender all accomplishment orientations.

When full surrender happens, it is called "nirvana," meaning a state of no desire. Traditions say that such a person is transformed, is a *sadguru* ("true guru"). And this little discussion should show you how rare a state this must be.

Surrendering to anybody who is less simply has the risks that usually come with simple hierarchical relationships. A sadguru is embodied God, a Son of God, because his or her identity has truly shifted to the quantum self and the ego is now relegated to mere trivial functions. Anybody less is a teacher and the teacher-student relationship for a transformational journey better be a tangled hierarchical one as much as is practicable, allowing that some simple hierarchy cannot be avoided in an organizational framework.

From Power to Meaning: The Politics of God

Actually, religions at the popular level, even in the East, have always supported the simple hierarchy that excludes love to a large extent. In India, the Brahmins were the top echelon of a caste hierarchy. In China, families became strictly patriarchal, following the teachings not of the idealist Lao Tzu, but of the more pragmatic Confucius. In the West, the church was at the head of a hierarchy, followed by the feudal monarch and aristocrats, all dominating the lowly serfs. In other words, religions have throughout our history played the power game and not always in conjunction with the play of meaning.

The politics of God are not seeking power to dominate others. The object of the politics of God are to bring power in the service of meaning and godliness to everyone. So historically, religions have not played the politics of God as they are supposed to.

Science grew out of the popular effort to end the Christian church's stranglehold on meaning processing, confining it to a select social elite. What science studied was the beauty and order of God's laws in the material world, laws that are part of the divine godliness of the supramental domain in the form of the archetype of truth. So, in truth, science and religions should never have been antagonistic to one another. The antagonism was initially the church's doing. Instead of enthusiasm for science's advancement of truth—the material laws—the church was defensive of its own scientific dogma. It took the Catholic Church 400 years to accept the validity of Galileo's 16th-century work! The antagonism has been much heightened with the creationism-evolutionism debate and by the philosophy of scientific materialism threatening to undermine all three of the church's essential fundamentals: downward causation, subtle bodies, and godly virtues.

But with quantum physics, as I have shown in the preceding pages, all the fundamentals not only of Christianity, but also of all religions have found their validation in a new formulation of science within the primacy of consciousness. Isn't it time for the Christian church, indeed all religions, to declare a truce with the new science and find their way back from the politics of power to the politics of God? It is time, and I joyfully note that some Christian thinkers agree with me (Teasdale 1999).

Religious Fundamentalism, Terrorism, and Democracy

One also has to recognize that fundamentalism in any form, materialist science or fundamentalist religion, is incompatible with democracy. When a democratic government is highly influenced by the (materialist) science-military-industrial complex as the United States is today, it tends to totalitarianism, characterized by hierarchy and intolerance. Can such a government impose democracy on another culture lost in religious hierarchy and intolerance? No indeed.

This is why America cannot impose democracy in the Middle East of religious fundamentalism any more than it could impose it on the Soviet Union, which was based on materialist fundamentalism. But the Soviet system broke down from eventual evolutionary pressure from inside. The same will happen in the Middle East, sooner or later.

Middle Easterners (correctly) look on the spread of democracy—American style—as the spread also of a materialism that would potentially destroy their ancient culture. This they try to contain. Of course, due to the evolutionary movement of consciousness, the social culture will eventually change, but it is prudent to let the change come from within.

In the meantime, rather than armed intervention, a better strategy for democratic countries is to clean up their own houses and develop a proper politics of God.

For America, it means a thorough examination of the materialist paradigm that currently continues to rule science, in spite of its many anomalies and inconsistencies. If the materialist paradigm is an inadequate description of reality, it must yield to the new paradigm of science within consciousness, which has the scope to provide a proper workable politics of God.

Terrorism is, to a large extent, a fundamentalist Islamic response to the evils of materialism. Let me elaborate. Confronted by the rapid spread of materialist science and consumer technology, people in religious societies are in dilemma. The ancient religions, especially Islam, need change no doubt, for example, in the treatment of women, which is socially unjust and inappropriate in today's world culture. The educated people of Islam, educated in modern ways, could help bring about these changes if not for the materialist bias they embrace while receiving modern education. This materialist bias tends them toward secularism and wishy-washiness about ethics. In reaction, the rest of the society would rather go back to the oppressive religion rather than embrace hedonism. The fight against secularism becomes a freedom movement that has always been what the opponents would call terrorism. Witness that the American secessionists were terrorists in the eyes of the British monarchy in the 18th century.

With a proper politics of God, terrorism becomes irrelevant. Perhaps from that high moral ground, a dialog between properly chastened non-fundamentalist science and fundamentalist religion may hasten the process of thawing the latter, relieving much suffering.

The truth is, the new paradigm of science within consciousness is able to distinguish between spirituality (which is scientific and therefore subject to consensus agreement) and religion (which does not need to be scientific and require consensus agreement), and it also embraces ethics as part of the scientific paradigm. So the society can move to post-secularism in which spirituality and ethics as per science can be embraced without the baggage of religion. And sooner or later terrorism becomes unnecessary.

Steps to the Politics of God

When people of power, be they in politics or religion, play the politics of God today, they ask incessantly, "Is God on our side?" They are always eager to proclaim that they have asked and have heard the answer from God. "Yes, God is on our side," they declare. "Since we are following moral values, of course God supports us against all those immoral people!"

Alas, the lesson of quantum physics is different. As the resolution of the paradox of Wigner's friend (see chapter 4) makes quite clear, God is objective. You can be on God's side when you are ready to take a creative quantum leap from your conditioned choices because they are conflicting and ambiguous, when your choice resonates with the evolutionary movement of consciousness. When both sides of an issue, the so-called moral side and the so-called immoral side, are just acting out their sociocultural conditioning without resolving the conflicts and ambiguities of the current time and space, then God does not play favorites. God goes along with the choices made by either side so each side can go on maintaining their ignorance. God remains objective and indifferent, quite neutral.

The right question to ask is not "Is God on my side?" but to inquire deeply, whenever there are conflicting choices, "Which choice will favor the evolutionary movement of consciousness—God's intention?" If the inquiry is rewarded with a response and an insight comes, one acts accordingly in resonation with it, which is truly Godspeak. If no insight comes, one must do one's best to use reason and feeling to come up with a choice that would serve God's evolutionary purpose.

And when there is no conflict and the choice that favors God's evolutionary agenda is obvious, religions must play the politics of God according to God's agenda, not their personal agenda of power. Only then will the pursuit of meaning return to our religions and the present pursuit of power to dominate give way.

Let's consider an example—the issue of poverty. The poor are, by and large, left out of the pursuit of meaning for a variety of reasons. Some people say that the reason is their own lack of initiative. But irrespective of the reasons, the purpose of evolution in meaning is to bring everybody under the tent where meaning is explored and not to leave anybody outside. There is no ambiguity here. We cannot say, oh, but the poor are so lazy. They may be lazy and, even when given the opportunity, may progress slowly, but so be it.

In the epic story of Mahabharata, there is a beautiful episode. The Mahabharata is the story of the Pandava brothers, and in this episode, they are in a forest and are thirsty. So the eldest brother, the crown prince, sits down to rest and sends the youngest to find water. The designate brother finds a beautiful lake soon enough. But as he prepares to drink from it and fetch some water, his path is obstructed by a mighty angelic being who demands, "Unless you answer my questions correctly, I won't let you have any water. If your answers are wrong, you die." Well, this brother could not give the right answers and died. The eldest brother sends his younger brothers, one by one, to fetch water, and none comes back. Then the prince himself searches for the water; he finds the lake and meets the angelic being. He sees the dead corpses of his brothers and confronts the questions upon being assured that if his answers are correct, not only will he have access to the water, but his brothers will also come alive and be able to quench their thirst. One by one, the prince gives satisfactory answers. Then comes the last question, "What is the path of religion, the path to God?" The prince replies, "The path to God is always the mystery. Fortunately, great people have charted some paths, so the prudent follows them." This answer satisfied the angelic being, and so the Pandava brothers were saved.

Great people who found their way to God and godliness founded great religions. So people of a religion have a charted path that they should always check for guidelines for action. Otherwise, what is the purpose of belonging to a religion? On any given issue, every Christian must ask, what would Jesus do? What did Jesus say about this? If Jesus has an answer and the answer is unambiguous, then the Christian prerogative is to follow Jesus.

So on the question of helping the poor, was Jesus ever unambiguous? Did he say, "Help the poor only if he or she shows some initiative?" No, indeed. In this way, when the religious right of the United States sides with the political party that unambiguously favors the rich and not the poor, they are clearly not doing the Christian thing.

In India, the Hindu fundamentalists also decided to play the politics of God left-handedly and found that there is more news media hoopla and financial support for helping the middle class and the rich rather than the poor. Fortunately, in India, the poor are the majority, who then voted for the opposition party who exploited the situation. So the Hindu fundamentalists could not get away with their antievolutionary agenda. But in America, the Christian fundamentalists get away with their antievolutionary agenda because they carefully manipulate issues of social morality as a decoy. We shall return to that subject a little later.

From Simple to Tangled Hierarchy

Religion is a lot like healing. People who actively come to religion (that is, attend a "church" regularly) come because they feel separateness in their lives. Even those people who regard "church" primarily as a social thing must feel a little lonely, otherwise what is the need for being social? Of course, with religions' shift from power for meaning toward power for domination, lots of people do come to foster power, but that is what we are trying to de-emphasize.

The job of the religious leader is to help heal the separateness. God, in this context, stands for wholeness. The religious God seeker is coming to the church to feel connected to a wholeness that he or she intuits. The rituals help because, as research is showing, the rituals help one connect to a brain center (the God spot) from which vantage point we feel expanded. But this expansion is only a beginning.

Ultimately, just as physical healing requires a quantum leap, so does spiritual healing. If the religious leader stays hierarchical, superior, and aloof, he or she cannot help the parishioner to quantum leap to wholeness. Like the quantum doctor, the spiritual leader must establish a tangled hierarchical relationship with the client, and they must approach spiritual healing together.

Notice how this automatically shifts the church from a power-for-domination emphasis to a power-for-meaning emphasis. Domination requires simple hierarchy. With simple hierarchy removed from the equation, the power game of the church disappears.

How did Jesus behave with people that came to him? It is well known that Jesus was prone to wash the feet of his disciples. This is not an empty gesture but a well-established ritual to arrive at tangled hierarchy!

One problem with modern organized religions is that there are too many followers and too few leaders. I really think that if tangled hierarchical relationships were encouraged, there would be more people ready for the leadership role. Ultimately, the discovery of the essence of spirituality, God and the oneness of everything, requires charting one's own path only to discover that there is no path to a quantum leap, only a process. As Jiddu Krishnamurti said, "Truth is a pathless land." After the discovery is complete, the discoverer may choose to remain within the religion that helped him or her initially. Then he or she would become a leader (not a guru).

But organized religions have too few of this kind of leader, one of the principal reasons for their decline.

Social Issues

Here is what the fundamentalists of this country say: we support the poor-opposed political party because of its stance in favor of morality in other issues. Surely those issues are important religious issues—abortion and homosexuality are two such major ones. These issues are good examples of morally ambiguous issues. So let's consider each in some detail.

The ambiguity of the issue of abortion arises from many factors. First, is the fetus a life? The old science, siding with Descartes, has more or less taken the view that a cell is a machine, and so a fetus is not alive. Abortion is then okay. But by the same token, in the materialist view, even the adult human is a machine. Is taking an adult human life also okay? Here the materialist physicians (the allopaths) do an about-turn and support tooth and nail the idea of keeping a person in a vegetative coma alive indefinitely with expensive life support systems (one reason for today's skyrocketing medical costs).

Actually, even popular Christianity has the view that any living thing short of a human is a machine. So strict logic would dictate that abortion is also in accordance with Christian belief. But what is pointed out is that a fetus is potential human life and is therefore not a machine. Good argument, but the argument is not unambiguous, is it?

The new science, on the other hand, declares unambiguously that even a living cell is alive; consciousness has identified with it, and vital blueprints are being represented in it. Here also, however, ambiguity cannot be avoided. It is a fact that until the twelfth week or so, the brain of the fetus does not develop and therefore, no mapping of the mind is possible. This means that until the twelfth week (many would say until the sixteenth week), the fetus has the potency of only a lower animal, not that of a human being with a mind. And so abortion can be allowed until the brain develops, which is more or less now the law of the land in the United States. One can argue that we kill lower animals all the time for food, how can we be hypocrites and do otherwise for a fetus? But the big ambiguity is still there; the fetus is a potential human, at conception as at the twelfth week.

As I have stated, the Christian right's argument is well taken. But suppose we legally forbid abortion, what happens then? Our laws cannot control people's instinctual sexuality (the brain circuits) and teenage hormones. Self-discipline is easier to preach than practice. Witness all the sexual scandals of the Catholic Church in recent history. So some young girls and boys will always make mistakes, girls will become pregnant and will seek abortion. If legal abortion is not available, they would go to the back alleys and take a huge risk of death. Is that something we as a society should push them to by making a law forbidding abortion?

What would Jesus do? This is the Christian question. And most would agree, I hope, that Jesus would ask for our compassion, not only for the life of the fetus, but also for the life of the girl.

For the new science aficionado, the question is: what would favor evolution? Taking the life of a teenage girl in preference of the life of an unborn fetus? We cannot be sure of that! And we cannot be sure of the opposite either!

So the ambiguity of this kind of issue won't quit; it is that complicated. Actually, this is why the present solution, leaving the matter to the pregnant woman's personal choice based on the issue of privacy, is the only solution that makes sense. At least we are guaranteeing that no young girl will die in the back alley trying to abort her unwanted pregnancy, putting not one life, but two in jeopardy!

As our new science progresses, we can contemplate doing better. As we bring creativity to our schools, a young pregnant girl may be able to handle the question of abortion as a creative, spiritual question of evolutionary ethics and seek a quantum leap of an unambiguously ethical choice for herself. But it still will be *her* choice! Because only if she is free to choose, can she be creative, which true ethics demands from her.

Let's discuss the issue of homosexuality. Homosexuality was very poorly understood in the olden days, so it is not surprising that most religions take an adverse stand on the issue. We may still not be correctly understanding homosexuality. Materialists think it may be wired into the genes or the brain. I think it may be a reincarnationally inherited gender confusion. But about one thing both the old science and the new science agree: hardly any heterosexual becomes a homosexual by choice. There is some sort of deep conditioning, resembling instinct that is behind it. If it is not choice, then should we discriminate against homosexuality? Science, new or old, would vote against any kind of discrimination.

What would Jesus say or do? One thing we all can be sure, Jesus would always be compassionate and never discriminate against another human being.

Notice neither science nor Jesus endorses homosexuality on the part of people who are heterosexual. Such an endorsement is neither necessary nor implicit in order to oppose discrimination. The new science is very clear on this. To discriminate against any human being is to deny him or her meaning processing—a truly antievolutionary and ungodly act.

Infallibility

The problem of religious bigotry, and most religions have it, arises primarily from the doctrine of infallibility of the religious scriptures. It's like the scientists' dogma of exclusive upward causation.

But evidence is coming down hard on the scientist to allow downward causation. Similarly, scientific evidence is telling us that the Genesis of the Old Testament cannot be literally true, although it can still be metaphorically and mythically true.

If we look at the problem of scriptural infallibility from a scientific point of view, what then? A great burden can be lifted. No doubt, religious scriptures came from the supramental intuitions and insights of great mystics as a result of direct creative encounters with God. Indeed, what we now understand about creativity is that God dictates and ego makes mental representations, making the revelations really revelations. But there is, undeniably, the question of the accuracy of mental representations. The truth is, a mental representation of the supramental can never be completely accurate, can never be infallible. Every religion has to come to terms with this, the sooner the better.

And once we see only metaphorical and mythical truth in our scriptures, we also see that all research, scientific or otherwise, is geared to make our metaphors better. In this way, freeing ourselves from the tyranny of infallibility also frees us to support creative exploration, research about the nature of reality. Then religions can easily come to terms with science.

Dialog

Different people, even great mystics, then, would see supramental truth a little differently, and it is this different seeing and mental representing that creates the differences between religions, about which human beings still fight.

We have to heed what cultural anthropologists have been saying for some time. For things subtle, we need a plurality of viewpoints. For a time, science seemed to be exempt from this, but that was because we restricted science to the gross material domain. Now that we are dealing with the subtle dimensions of consciousness, it is clear that the cultural anthropologists are right, and biology, medicine, psychology, and religion—all human fields of endeavor that involve our subtle dimensions—must favor a pluralistic approach in preference to a monolithic one.

The truth is, intuitively, we have always known this, and in this way, we have many religions—a very good thing. We should be proud of it; we should learn to take advantage of it.

The fable of the blind people studying an elephant comes to mind. One blind person thought that the elephant is like a wall. Another thought that it is hard and sharp. Still another thought it soft and highly flexible. We are no different when we are studying the subtle. Can blind people study the elephant and find out its nature? Sure, if they can integrate all that they can learn separately, if the separate pieces they collect are exhaustive enough, and if they skillfully use intuition to fill in the gaps. The same goes for religions. We can only improve our understanding of God and the subtle if we integrate what we learn separately and use intuition. And now it can be even better, because science has joined the adventure. Science is very good in the investigation of those aspects of God and the subtle that can be subjected to laboratory verification.

So we can look forward to an era in which our understanding of God and the subtle takes a quantum leap. But only if religions learn to cooperate with one another and with the new science and begin dialoging.

The good news is that such dialogs have already begun under the leadership of such people as Jiddu Krishnamurti and David Bohm and the current Dalai Lama and his scientist disciples.

I will end this section with a story I heard. A clergyman goes to heaven and Saint Peter keeps him waiting at the pearly gates. "Look, a very important fellow is coming, let him be received first, then we will take care of you," says Saint Peter to console the fellow.

Soon the other guy arrives, most ordinary looking. But a big hoopla is made to receive him. Afterward, Saint Peter looks at our waiting clergy and says kindly, "Now it's your turn." The clergyman is most curious. He says, "Thanks. But can you tell me who that guy is? Why so much hoopla about him?"

"Oh, he is a New York City taxi driver," says Saint Peter.

The clergyman is dumbfounded and angry, too. "What! You kept me waiting for a mere cabdriver? Here I have devoted my entire life to the service of the Lord!" he accosts Saint Peter.

Saint Peter chuckles. "Oh, but people only fell asleep when you preached. When people rode in his taxicab, they prayed."

I can never make up my mind if this is a joke about how dangerous it is to ride in a New York City cab or how boring it is to attend a Christian church sermon. But one thing I know: The winds of change will do the Christian church, nay churches in every religion, good.

In Summary

Let us summarize the activist plan that we need to activate to change the practices of our religions:

- Religions must value the people within their fold who engage in creatively discovering God in their lives and living their discovery through the exploration of the energies of love. They must hold those people up as examples to follow. They must allow them to be leaders instead of persecuting them.

- Religions must acknowledge the importance of quantum nonlocality and provide the people in their denominations with opportunities for nonlocal exploration of God consciousness.

- Religions must stop their dabbling in power and must begin the urgent step back to the exploration of meaning. The politics of God, the only sort of politics God approves (that is, politics that are consistent with the evolution of consciousness), are politics in the service of making meaning available to all people. Religions must shift from practicing the politics of power to practicing the politics of God.

- Religious organizations must recognize a tangled hierarchy of relationship between "leaders" and "followers." In particular, they need to seriously revise their simple hierarchical organizations as far as is practicable.

❖ Complex social issues require a creative approach suited to the times. Religions have to recognize this and take appropriate steps. As a starter, they should always ask, what would our creative exemplars do to resolve this issue?

❖ Religions must reexamine the issue of infallibility of their scriptures in view of what we now know about the nature of revelation (namely, that revelations are creative insights that the ego translates into mental meaning and language).

❖ Religions must begin dialogs with other religions and with scientists of the new God-based science. I have happily noticed that conferences with this agenda are on the increase.

CHAPTER 18

Quantum Activism

For Better Health and Healing

Materialist medicine practitioners, like all other scientists of materialist ilk, do not like accepting responsibility for their actions. Thus without thinking through the consequences of their actions, in the past decades, driven by avarice and opportunities, they sold their souls en masse to pharmaceutical companies and makers of expensive diagnostic tools. This liberated them from using intuition and creativity in the diagnosis and treatment of their patients. This was quite in accordance with the materialist belief that medicine should be machine medicine, consisting of mechanical stuff (drugs, surgery, and radiation), designed for machines (the patients), and administered by machines (the pharmaceuticals, the toolmakers, and the physicians). This is expensive, however, and health-care costs skyrocketed.

The greed of a few patients in cooperation with their greedy lawyers raised the specter of malpractice suits and sealed the machine nature of modern allopathic medicine. This ensured that medical expenses skyrocketed even higher.

Meanwhile, an opposite current was flowing. Along with Eastern spirituality had come Indian medicine (Ayurveda) and Tibetan medicine. Along with the political and economic exchange between China and the United States came traditional Chinese medicine and acupuncture. When allopathic medicine became too costly for people, in a vain search for a cure for their chronic diseases, which allopathy cannot do much for anyway, they began to look elsewhere and discovered the cost-effective Eastern medicine, which provided them at least disease control for their chronic conditions, if not outright healing. Soon, the West's own alternative medicine, homeopathy and naturopathy, made a much-deserved comeback.

Medicine of course, had its own brand of paradigm shifters, notable among them Ken Pelletier, Larry Dossey, Herbert Benson, Dean Ornish, Andrew Weil, and Deepak Chopra (the list is far from being inclusive). These and many other mavericks developed the new field of mind-body medicine, a new thorn in the side of allopathic supremacy. And once again, people started to partake of the techniques of this new medicine in preference to conventional allopathy.

Eventually, quantum thinking also entered the field of alternative medicine and provided a much-needed integration, defining clearly the domains of each of the various forms of alternative medicine (Goswami 2004).

A crucial role in this scenario was played by the establishment of federal government funding for the research of alternative medicine as part of the National Institutes of Health.

Toward an Integrative Medicine

Health and healing all over the world are in a crisis situation because of sky-rocketing costs. I submit that the rising costs are primarily due to the exclusive use of costly allopathic medicine even when allopathic medicine has harmful side effects and even when this line of medicine brings only temporary relief of symptoms (especially for chronic disease), does not really heal, and the disease returns. The costs rise also because there is no real understanding of what healing or even health consists. This non-understanding leads to little use for the idea of disease prevention. Not knowing what health is also prevents people from attempting to achieve and maintain positive health.

Allopathic medicine is based on scientific materialism, the idea that all things including our body are made of matter and its interactions. By contrast, the alternative medicine practices hold that we have not only our material bodies but also subtle bodies. Until recently, allopathic medicine practitioners have been able to deny scientific validity to alternative medicine because of the paradox of dualism: how can these nonmaterial subtle bodies interact with the material body without the mediation of energy-carrying signals? But if such signals were really there, how could the energy of the physical world alone remain constant? This is a logical contradiction, a paradox.

A breakthrough toward an integrative medicine combining allopathic and alternative medicine under one paradigmatic umbrella has arrived with the application of quantum physics to the situation. In quantum physics, all objects—physical, vital, mental, and supramental—are waves of possibilities for consciousness to choose from. Conscious choice converts or "collapses" the possibility waves into unique manifest actualities (Goswami 2000). Consciousness undivided from its quantum possibilities is the bliss body, one nonlocal interconnectedness that we call quantum consciousness. The idea of nonlocal communication without signals eliminates the paradox of dualism.

Recall that the organs of our physical body are physical representations of the morphogenetic fields of the vital body that consciousness uses as blueprints of biological functions to represent the latter in the physical. Similarly, consciousness makes representations of mental meaning in the brain.

With the paradox of dualism resolved and the relation of the physical and the subtle bodies clarified, the door is open for a theory of integrative medicine that combines conventional and alternative medicine practices under one paradigm. The details can be found elsewhere (Goswami 2004). Here, I summarize the major aspects of the theory important for the practitioners of quantum activism for both personal transformation (to positive health) and social transformation (to universal low-cost health care).

Quantum Activism and Integrative Medicine

To repeat for the umpteenth time, quantum activism is the idea of using quantum principles such as quantum nonlocality (signal-less communication between correlated partners) and the quantum leap (discontinuous movement) to transform self and society. It is a new integration of age-old ideas of spiritual transformation for personal growth with ideas of social activism.

Quantum activism in the field of health and healing begins with an appreciation of what health is. What is health? In integrative medicine, we are able to define health in an inclusive manner. Health is when not only the physical organs function properly, but also when all our other bodies function properly in synchrony with their physical representations. In particular, even physical health is defined not only by the proper functioning of the physical organs, but also by the proper functioning of their correlated morphogenetic fields and the correlated mental body that gives meaning to the physical and vital experiences, all in synchrony.

A quantum activist must realize that disease occurs not only because of genetic factors (such as genetic defects) and environmental factors (such as climate change, bacteria, and viruses), but also due to internal experiences and the internal environment that the memory of these experiences creates. Memory of past experiences also creates patterns of conditioning (Mitchell and Goswami 1992) through which we tend to lose our freedom to choose healthy possibilities. In this way, disease may occur at the vital body level (vital body disease), at the level of the mind (mind-body disease), and even at the level of the supramental and bliss bodies. Consequently, there are five levels of disease corresponding to the five bodies in consciousness. Disease at a higher level percolates down to lower levels. In this way, a wrong mental meaning can cause vital energy blocks that can then affect physical body functioning. It makes sense then that the true healing of a disease must involve the level at which the disease starts. That is, there are five levels of healing corresponding to each of the five levels of disease.

The quantum activist recognizes from the get-go that integrative medicine based on quantum physics is fundamentally optimistic. If the world consists of possibilities, not determined events, then we can hope to choose health over disease. Neither disease nor healing need be entirely objective. Subjective experiences and our attitudes toward them have a role to play. By using creativity, the quantum activist learns to change his or her attitude, which takes the individual from illness to health and from ordinary health to positive health.

A shortcoming of materialist biology and allopathic medicine is that they are unable to properly incorporate an important aspect of biological organisms: heterogeneity. In conventional biology based on genetic determinism, all individual differences are of genetic origin. In vital body and mind-body medicine, individual differences also arise from the differences in the individualization of the vital and the mental body.

I mentioned before that our physical organs are representations of vital morphogenetic field blueprints of biological functions. How we use the morphogenetic fields in the formative developmental years give us our body types.

In traditional Chinese medicine, two body types are recognized. The yin type occurs when conditioning is the operating principle for the use of the morphogenetic fields; and the yang type when the morphogenetic fields are used creatively to meet the challenges of the environmental changes during development. Ayurveda distinguishes between two types of creativity: situational, in which creativity is used but only as a combination and permutation of what is already known in known contexts; and fundamental, in which creativity is used with a discontinuous quantum leap to explore a brand-new way in the new context that is the case. In this way, Ayurveda has threefold body types (*doshas*): *kapha,* corresponding to conditioning mode; *vata,* corresponding to situational creativity; and *pitta,* corresponding to fundamental creativity. This typology also characterizes how mental meaning is mapped into the brain in our formative years; in other words, we have threefold mind-brain doshas—intellectualism, hyperactivity, and mental sleuth (Goswami 2004).

In truth, we usually have a mixture of all the vital/physical doshas and mind-brain doshas. The mixture for a particular person is known in Ayurveda as this person's *prokriti* (a Sanskrit word that literally means "nature").

Health maintenance at the personal level for a quantum activist begins with the knowledge of one's body type, prokriti. This may require the help of trained physicians. The details of how to use this knowledge for maintaining one's health can be found in books on Ayurveda and traditional Chinese medicine (see also Goswami 2004). I encourage you to get this information.

The Chakras

Next in the line of important dos for quantum activism for health and healing is an investigation of the major chakra points, the places in our body where we feel the movement of vital energies in a major way. The chakras are the focus of the rapidly developing fields of energy medicine and energy psychology (Page 1992, Eden 1998).

As discussed before, there are seven such major chakra points (see Figure 14). The new science says that chakras are points where consciousness collapses the physical representations, the organs, along with their associated morphogenetic fields. It is the movement of the latter that we feel; our particular feeling at a chakra depends crucially on the biological functioning of the physical organs at that chakra.

As a quantum activist, your first task is to explore your chakras and directly verify the feelings associated with each chakra.

To go deeper, try this exercise, which will quickly tell you how to discern and explore the movement of vital energy. Rub your palms together and then move them apart by about half an inch, holding them in the style of the East Indian gesture of "namaste." You will feel tingles. Convince yourself that they are not due to blood flow or the movement of nerve impulses.

Next find a friend and have him or her sit comfortably in front of you. Now activate your palms as before by rubbing them and then bring your palms close to your friend's heart chakra. Close your eyes and try to feel any change in your tingles. Not much change, you say. Now tell your friend to think of, or better yet, visualize a beloved person for a few minutes. Activate your palms once again and bring them close to your friend's heart chakra. This time you will notice significant change. What happened? Your friend's visualization activated his or her heart chakra.

Vital energy blockage at a chakra can lead to malfunctioning of one or more organs at that chakra. If we pay systematic attention to each chakra, these energy blockages may be avoided. To have a healthy vital body is to keep the energy movement balanced at each of the chakras.

You can practice chakra balancing easily with the aid of a friend who shares your enthusiasm about applying quantum activism to health and healing. Tell your friend to energize his or her palms and bring the energized palms close to each of your chakras for a few seconds, as if massaging your chakras without touching your physical body. It is best for you to lie down during this exercise and maintain a relaxed receptive and aware mind. Your friend should start with "massaging" your crown chakra and end with your root chakra. After your friend has finished, it is only fair that you reciprocate.

The Management of Chronic Disease

It is estimated that fully 70 percent of the annual medical expenditure in the United States is due to the high cost of the treatment of chronic disease. There is no healing of chronic disease in allopathic medicine. Doctors prescribe the very costly drugs that pharmaceutical firms routinely dole out. These drugs do relieve symptoms such as pain in the short run. But you have to keep taking them, and eventually their side effects will catch up with you.

Many chronic diseases are part of our aging process; they happen due to the wear and tear of our organs. In some cases we have the technology of organ replacement, which is also costly and is not always available. Is there an alternative to these costly procedures? There is. Vital body medicine.

Organs are physical representations of the vital body morphogenetic fields that are the blueprints of the organs. For health and vitality, the organ and its correlated morphogenetic blueprint must function in synchrony. When the organs go awry due to wear and tear, the vital energies can no longer maintain synchrony with their corresponding organs. This lack of synchrony is a part of what we experience as chronic disease.

Short of replacement, it is not feasible to repair the affected organ and bring it back into synchrony with its vital counterpart, but it is possible to manipulate the vital energy movements to bring them into synchrony with the worn-out organ. You can call it situational creativity if you like. This is what acupuncture, massage therapy, homeopathy, and herbal medicine (of both Chinese and Indian vintage) try to do. This is inexpensive and has no side effects.

Ultimately, this is also temporary because the wear and tear of the organ will continue with aging and the vital medicinal treatments have also to be repeated, but not nearly as frequently as allopathic drugs.

In principle, even a permanent healing of a chronic condition is not out of the question in the form of applying fundamental creativity to the problem, effecting what is called quantum healing. This aspect requires further research.

In any case, even from this short exposition, it should be clear that integrative medicine—using allopathic drugs for immediate relief, using established vital body medicine practices for intermediate relief, and quantum healing for permanent relief—is the way to go in the management of chronic disease.

Mind-Body Healing

It is now well established that the mind, in giving wrong meaning to an experience, can produce disease (Dossey 1992). A teenager is jilted by his girlfriend and suffers pain. Hence he decides that falling in love is bad and henceforth shuns all opportunities for romantic love. Prolonged inattention to the heart chakra (the chakra where romance is experienced) blocks the movement of heart energy and produces disease of the correlated heart chakra organ called the thymus gland. The thymus gland is an important part of the immune system. When the immune system goes awry, the body loses its ability to distinguish potentially cancerous cells and kill them off. This then can lead to malignant growth or cancer.

How do you keep your mind from giving wrong meaning to a situation? There are many practices of health maintenance for the mind, but a main one is meditation. The purpose of meditation is to slow down the mind. This slowing down helps precisely where it hurts. It enables us not to jump into a wrong meaning; instead we learn to deliberate before giving meaning to an experience.

Once having contracted a mind-body disease, how do we go about healing it? Treatment at the physical or even the vital level will only get rid of the symptoms, not the root cause. However, once wrong meaning is established, producing vital energy blockage at a chakra and a physical organ malfunction, we cannot heal the disease at the mind level.

The physician Deepak Chopra (1990) first discovered how spontaneous healing (healing without the intervention of medical procedures) takes place. Via quantum healing, he said. Quantum healing consists of a discontinuous leap from the mind to the supramental—the realm of the archetypal contexts of mental meaning.

Go back to our assumed young man whose wrong thinking about love produced vital energy blockage at his heart chakra, leading to cancer. To heal the cancer, he has to take a quantum leap from his mind and its known mental representations of love to the supramental, directly encounter the archetype of love once again, and rediscover the value of love. Only then can quantum healing occur!

Creativity researchers have shown that such quantum leaps of thought are much facilitated by following the steps of a creative process: doing (preparation), being (relaxation), alternative doing and being (do-be-do-be-do), insight (quantum leap), and manifestation (integrating the insight in one's lifestyle).

When confronted with mind-body disease, a quantum activist, while undergoing treatment of the physical and the vital from allopathic and alternative medicine practitioners, respectively, must also partake in the creative process with the intention of quantum healing. And when healed, he or she must manifest the insight gained in his or her lifestyle.

Nutrition for All Five Bodies

A quantum activist must become aware of the importance of nutrition, not only for the physical body, but also for all the bodies: physical, vital, mental, supramental, and the whole. This is holistic nutrition, and it is this that can take us to positive health.

Much of the success of modern medicine is due to our understanding of hygiene, avoiding harmful physical stimuli in the environment. Similarly, we must avoid harmful mental and vital stimuli.

The yoga psychologist Uma Krishnamurthy (2010) says, "Emotions are as contagious as bacteria and viruses." So a good strategy for positive health is to avoid negative emotional stimuli and negative thoughts as far as is practicable.

Back to nutrition. Most of our food has both a physical and a correlated vital component. When we take food, we must remember the vital component, which is why fresh food is better than stale food, even refrigerated food. The way meat is manufactured in current cultures speaks against eating that meat. Cattle raised in confinement will be angry and fearful (Robins 1996), emotions that remain correlated with the physical meat. When we eat that, we literally eat "angry" beef!

I am also, in general, against genetically engineered food because I am not sure that such food preserves the original, needed vital ingredient of the food. More research is needed.

Other than physical food, nutrition of the vital is obtained through positive emotional relationship. Food for the mind is, of course, good literature, good music, evocative art, stimulating discussions, and so forth.

We can also engage in various practices of exercise for the various bodies. Besides physical exercise for keeping the physical body in shape, a quantum activist engages in hatha yoga, breathing exercises, tai chi, and martial arts to exercise the vital body. For the mental body, the main exercise vehicle is meditation.

The objective of vital and mental exercise is to slow down the vital energies and thoughts so that there are more "unconscious" moments between conscious thoughts. Thoughts are quantum objects—waves of possibilities of meaning. In between thoughts or collapse events, the meaning waves proliferate in possibility, making room for creative choice. Creative choices are tantamount to quantum leaps to the supramental, which is how we "feed" the supramental.

To feed the wholeness within us, deep sleep is built into our manifest existence. If we can learn to sleep creatively (Goswami 2008b; see also chapter 17), we can nourish our whole self ever more effectively.

Social Impact

The social impact of these personal changes cannot be overstated. Integrative medicine opens an opportunity to transform from a negative and suffering-oriented society to a positive and happiness-oriented society. We don't wait for suffering to hit us before we become concerned about our health. Instead, we work on our health in an ongoing way because health is an essential aspect of being happy and ultimately holy.

As the paradigm changes and the society transforms in this way, our medical costs will go down drastically. On the way to that future, we have to work hard for health-care organizations to accept integrative medicine.

CHAPTER 19

Our Path Back to Liberal Education

In all this talk about change, education reform is a priority because education has shifted in this country from its liberal meaning-oriented roots to a materialist job-oriented program that emphasizes quantity over quality, measurables over intangibles, and information over meaning and transformation.

In particular, the materialist dogma—everything is matter, all traits are genetic, everything experienced internally is brain product, evolution is synonymous with Darwinism, there is nothing to the self other than genetic and psychosocial conditioning, and consciousness itself is an operational appendage without any causal power or efficacy—is taught early on in our schools, some of it directly and some of it indirectly. As a result, today's young people contract permanent cognitive dissonance—a permanent lack of synchrony between their experience and the belief system through which they sift their experience. It can be worse than the training that a child of a religious fundamentalist family receives. For the latter child, the public schools bring a different viewpoint; so at least that student gets the benefit of two points of view.

Fortunately, here again some movement of consciousness is taking place. And of all things, unexpected help is coming from Christian fundamentalists, from the struggle between creationism–intelligent design scientists and the Darwinists. In many states, the boards of education and the legislatures are no longer buying that a multicultural exposure to science is harmful to the student.

The quantum activist should follow up this breakthrough in the case of the teaching of evolution theory to the teaching of all scientific theory wherever there are controversies, wherever there are alternatives. Before students pick up the dogma that consciousness is a brain phenomenon, let them get a balance between the facts (for example, conditioning) that overtly support the materialist view and the facts (for example, creativity) that overtly oppose that view. Let them get equal exposure to mechanistic and consciousness-based theories of both conditioning and creativity. Let creativity be emphasized in the classroom as much as conditioned rote learning and let the students make up their own minds as to where creativity comes from—downward or upward causation. We owe our children this much courtesy.

Right now it is imperative that we begin to distinguish spirituality from religion, an attitude that is increasingly being identified as post-secularism. As demonstrated in this book, spirituality is scientific, objective, and universal. By contrast, religion is scripture bound, subjective, and parochial. It is religion, not spirituality, that must rightly be forbidden from our classrooms.

But by the same token, scientific materialism that excludes other paradox-free metaphysics such as the one being presented here should also be recognized for what it is, namely, a fundamentalist dogma in the same vein as Christian or other religious fundamentalism. A post-secular attitude should be welcome in the practice and teaching of science as well. In other words, a multiculturalist post-secular attitude should prevail in science whenever living beings are involved.

A case in point is health education. Right now, most students learn only the allopathic view; the sole emphasis is on the material body. We must insist that the alternative medicine views of the importance of the nonmaterial vital body and the nonmaterial mind get equal emphasis. This will also open the door to paying attention to the feeling aspects of our being. Right now, education is very head-centered, which shortchanges the potential artists and humanists. We need an equal emphasis on reason and emotion, head and heart, so to speak, to do justice to the feeling sensitive part of the student population (who actually may be a majority).

By the same token, sex educators in school must complement their materialist and mechanical orientation with teaching about what is subtle—that sex is also making love. Maybe this would open the door to parental education; maybe girls would learn about their maternal instinct and boys could learn about fatherly sensitivities.

From Machine to Mind: From Information to Meaning

A 2005 survey found that meaning comprehension is going down rapidly among our teens who cannot follow even a simple table of various data. The researchers on this survey could not explain why this was so. I suspect it is because, in today's culture, what is suffering the most is the student's ability to maintain attention. Not everyone suffers from attention deficit disorder, which is a pathological condition. But it is true that most students of today suffer from an attention deficit to a great extent. And the main culprit for this is their addiction to machines such as the computer, the cell phone, and the television. On the computer and the TV, everything is fast-moving; the cell phone can be kept perpetually active. Who has the time for something that takes a little patience like processing meaning?

In the comic strip *Zits,* the teen hero complains to his father about his homework, reading Dickens' *Great Expectations.* "I am saying that if you can't say what you want to say in 100 pages, maybe it is not worth saying," he grumbles. This is the typical attitude of schoolchildren today.

The truth is, following Professor Alan Bloom, today we teach children great literature more as information than as a conveyance of great meaning to ponder. So schoolchildren are assigned huge amounts of reading and hardly any time to read them, let alone assimilate their meaning and ponder over that.

Both creativity and meaning processing suffer because of the speed of today's educational life. This has got to change. In Italy, I have noticed the beginning of a slow food movement to balance our propensity for fast food. Similarly, we need a grassroots movement toward slowness in education. If it does not prepare our children with adequate job training for our fast-moving workplace, so be it. The change will make them intelligent, intelligent enough to change the workplace, which will be urgently needed as the economy shifts from the current consumer-driven one to a more spiritual and balanced economy.

A return to the emphasis on meaning processing also demands that the focus of education changes from the current emphasis on job training for business, science (including social science), and technology to the olden-day emphasis on liberal arts, in which arts and humanities were treated as equal to science and business. In other words, we must complement the education of know-how with know-why. We can do this without de-emphasizing our need for know-how, which is important for dealing with the machine-dominated world we have created. But we must balance the know-how education with know-why, with metaphysics, mythology, and meaning, for us to be aware of who we really are and why we do things.

Teaching Emotional Intelligence

A young man is playing with his computer. His mother enters his room. He sees his mother and remembers something that was discussed in one of his classes that day. Impetuously, he says, "Mother, if it so happens that I become dependent on a machine to keep functioning, pull the plug. I don't want to be sustained that way." The mother calmly goes and pulls the plug from the teenager's computer.

But in real life today, how many mothers are aware of the perils of children growing up with the computer and machines in general? Today we see young men walking with young women, talking animatedly, not to each other but to their cell phones. Talking to a machine or writing on a machine (as in email) is comfortable and safe to our young people. They are avoiding encountering real people, people with feelings.

Need I say that we badly need awareness in this area and to begin some active teaching of emotional intelligence, although this will require some major thinking about how to do it. One possibility is to do it through health education, extending the concept of health to include emotional and mental health.

Teaching Values and Ethics

And finally, let's discuss the question of teaching values and ethics. In the olden days, we could count on religions to teach values and ethics to our children. So secular education demanded that values and ethics not be taught in our public schools because they are part of "religion." But now religious education is no longer part of the life experience of many children. So where do they learn values? On top of this, there is a continuous barrage of materialist dogma that they pick up from the media, which points them to the meaningless existential nature of everything. From television and computer games, they pick up a cynicism toward violence. From parents, they pick up a do-do-do busy life that has no time for leisure, meaning, and spirituality.

No wonder then that in the 2004 presidential election in the United States, many voters sided with one political party over the other on the basis of at least an "appearance" of value-emphasis from that party.

So what is fair? How do we make education on values accessible to everyone, not just the religious population? By recognizing and teaching in our public schools the idea that there is a new science based on the primacy of consciousness that reestablishes the value of meaning and gives a solid scientific foundation to ethics. Turnabout is fair play. If materialists want to teach their version of why there is no meaning in the world and why we need not follow any ethics, let them have equal time.

To summarize, here is our plan for quantum activism toward changes in our education system:

- Keep a vigil against the sneaky introduction of any materialist dogma in public school textbooks (similar to the vigil we keep against the teaching of religious dogma). Whenever such dogma is found, insist on balancing it with appropriate alternatives including the spiritual (but not the religious).

- We must go back to a liberal arts emphasis from the current emphasis on outer-directed science and business. This is essential for inner-outer integration in education.

- We must supplement the current "fast" education of information training with the "slow" education that meaning processing requires. We must also supplement the educational emphasis of know-how with know-why.

- Education must achieve a balance between teaching conditioning and teaching creativity. Along with the conventional three R's (reading, writing, and 'rithmetic), we must also emphasize the three I's (imagination, intuition, and insight) for education in public schools.

- We must bring the energies of feeling to education and balance the excessive thinking orientation, balance head with heart. This can probably best be done through health education suitably expanded in scope. This will begin early the process of male-female integration that is so important for our evolution.

✧ Education on spiritual values and ethics must be recognized as part and parcel of public schools. In this way, the integration of the transcendent and the immanent can begin early.

CHAPTER 20

2012 and Beyond

There is some excitement connected to the idea that one of the known Mayan calendars seems to suddenly end with the year 2012. Is this a forecast for a doomsday?

As human beings, we love doomsday scenarios. All our major spiritual traditions thrive on it. Christians have their Second Coming, Judaism has the coming of the Messiah, Hindus have the concept of the change of yugas with the coming of Kalki Avatar, Buddhists have their coming of the Bodhisattva Maitreya, and the followers of Zarathustra top all such doomsday scenarios with the idea of a big farewell and ushering-in party. Is 2012 the culmination of all these predictions, in which case is it not only a doomsday end of the world as we know it, but also the beginning of a new age?

We have seen such excitement before; as I said, we seem to love doomsday scenarios. We were quite agitated when the new millennium began in 2000, with the prediction of a worldwide computer meltdown. Speaking realistically as a scientist of evolution, what can I add to the growing speculations about the significance of 2012?

If you look at the fossil data, it is striking that our greatest eras of macroevolutionary progress have come in association with geological catastrophes. But they are all about the evolution of the vital-physical duo. Human evolution has been an evolution of the meaning processing capacity of the mind (see chapter 6). The steps of such an evolution are not associated with any change of species; no creativity other than mental creativity has been necessary for the evolutionary steps already taken, and there is no record of any geological or even historical catastrophe in connection with any of them. Why should the next step of the evolution of the mind from the rational mind to the intuitive mind be any different?

In chapter 11, I shared with you my futuristic scenario of how the next step of evolution will occur. Through Lamarckian evolution, the morphogenetic fields of positive emotional brain circuits that we develop now will be universally shared by all humans in a period of roughly six to seven generations, at which time more or less all humans will be born with love circuits in their brains. As we begin harnessing the energies of love, the center of the mass of our meaning processing will shift to the supramental archetypes, and the last and final stage of the mental age will begin.

So is 2012 a metaphor for such an evolutionary shift? It could be. But I can't help thinking, could something happen in 2012 that could significantly help the evolution scenario I just described? If not a big bang, at least a big whimper? Remember that the key phrase is "the world as we know it" will end in 2012. Didn't Richard Bach write, "What the caterpillar calls the end of the world the master calls a butterfly?"

Suppose that, encouraged by our success in mounting quantum activism as a viable agent of change, on a fine morning of 2012 (which will be an election year in the United States), President Obama makes a declaration that henceforth government agencies will be directed to issue substantial grants for research on science within consciousness. Research grants on subjects such as causal authenticity of downward causation, the relation of science and religion in a post-secular world, integrative medicine, quantum healing, spiritual economics, creativity in education, and so forth.

I submit that this produces a chain reaction:

- Overnight, universities in the United States initiate departments of consciousness research; they banish mathematical economists from their economics departments, replacing them with spiritual economists. They also insist that their cognitive researchers begin studying superconscious states. The universities of the rest of world follow suit shortly thereafter.

- Businesses, including big business, begin a division of subtle energy production.

- The CEOs of all financial institutions resign en masse.

☼ The pope acknowledges the authenticity of the concept of creative evolution within four years of the publication of the concept, instead of waiting for the 150 years it took for the Vatican to acknowledge Darwin.

☼ The U.S. Congress passes a comprehensive health-care bill, putting alternative medicine as the go-to system for all chronic conditions. And the world rejoices. The containment of health-care costs is finally at hand.

☼ The politicians of all denominations in the Middle East sit down at a conference table and begin brainstorming, determined to invoke quantum consciousness for the resolution of their conflicts.

☼ The story of the scientific discovery of God spreads in the media like wildfire.

☼ Global warming . . .

I must be dreaming. Or am I?

Bibliography

Aburdene, P. (2005). *Megatrends 2010.* Charlottesville, VA: Hampton Roads.

Ager, D. (1981). "The nature of fossil record." *Proceedings of the Geological Association,* vol. 87, pp. 131–59.

Amabile, T. (1990). "Within you, without you: The social psychology of creativity and beyond." In Runco, M. A., and Albert, R. S. (eds.). *Theories of Creativity.* Newbury Park, CA: Sage.

Aspect, A., Dalibar, J., and Roger, G. (1982). "Experimental test of Bell's inequalities with time varying analyzers." *Physical Review Letters,* vol. 49, pp. 1804–6.

Aurobindo, S. (1996). *The Life Divine.* Pondicherry, India: Sri Aurobindo Ashram.

Bache, C. (2000). *Dark Night, Early Dawn.* Albany, NY: SUNY Press.

Barrett, R. (1998). *Liberating the Corporate Soul.* Boston: Butterworth-Heinemann.

Bass, L. (1971). "The mind of Wigner's friend." *Hermathena,* no. CXII, pp. 52–68.

Bateson, G. (1980). *Mind and Nature.* New York: Bantam.

Behe, M. J. (1996). *Darwin's Black Box.* New York: Simon & Schuster.

Bell, J. S. (1965). "On the Einstein, Podolsky, Rosen paradox." *Physics,* vol. 1, pp. 195–200.

Blood, C. (1993). "On the Relation of the mathematics of quantum mechanics to the perceived physical universe and free will." Preprint. Camden, NJ: Rutgers University.

————. (2001). *Science, Sense, and Soul*. Los Angeles: Renaissance Books.

Bloom, A. (1988). *The Closing of the American Mind*. New York: Touchstone.

Bohm, D. (1980). *Wholeness and Implicate Order*. London: Rutledge & Kegan Paul.

Bolen, J.S. (1984). *Goddesses in Everywoman*. San Francisco: Harper & Row.

————. (1989). *Gods in Everyman*. San Francisco: Harper & Row.

Briggs, J. (1990). *Fire in the Crucible*. Los Angeles: J. P. Tarcher.

Byrd, C. (1988). "Positive and therapeutic effects of intercessor prayer in a coronary care unit population." *Southern Medical Journal,* vol. 81, pp. 826–29.

Capra, F. (1975). *The Tao of Physics*. New York: Bantam.

Chalmers, D. (1995). *Toward a Theory of Consciousness*. Cambridge, MA: MIT Press.

Chopra, D. (1990). *Quantum Healing*. New York: Bantam-Doubleday.

Cohen, A., and Wilber, K. (2009). "The second face of God." *EnlightenNext,* issue 45, pp. 44–53.

Csikszentmihalyi, M. (1990). *Flow: The Psychology of Optimal Experience*. New York: Harper & Row.

Darwin, C. (1859). *On the Origin of Species by Means of Natural Selection or the Preservation of Favored Races in the Struggle for Life*. London: Murray.

Dawkins, R. (1976). *The Selfish Gene*. New York: Oxford University Press.

D'Espagnat, B. (1983). *In Search of Reality*. New York: Springer-Verlag.

Devall, B., and Sessions, G. (1985). *Deep Ecology*. Salt Lake City, UT: G. M. Smith.

Dossey, L. (1982). *Space, Time, and Medicine*. Boulder, CO: Shambhala.

————. (1992). *Meaning and Medicine*. New York: Bantam.

Eden, D. (1998). *Energy Medicine*. New York: J. P. Tarcher/Putnam.

————. (1999). *Energy Psychology*. Putnam: J. P. Tarcher.

Einstein, A., Podolsky, B., and Rosen, N. (1935). "Can quantum mechanical description of physical reality be considered complete?" *Physical Review Letters,* vol. 47, pp. 777–80.

Eldredge, N., and Gould, S. J. (1972). "Punctuated equilibria: An alternative to phyletic gradualism." In Schopf, T. J. M. (ed.). *Models in Paleobiology.* San Francisco: Freeman, Cooper.

Eliot, T. S. (1943). *Four Quartets.* New York: Harcourt, Brace, and Jovanovich.

Ferguson, M. (1980). *The Aquarian Conspiracy.* Los Angeles: J. P. Tarcher.

Feynman, R. P. (1981). "Simulating physics with computers." *International Journal of Theoretical Physics,* vol. 21, pp. 467–88.

Friedman, T. L. (2005). *The World Is Flat.* New York: Farrar, Straus & Giroux.

Goleman, D. (1995). *Emotional Intelligence.* New York: Bantam.

Goodwin, B. (1994). *How the Leopard Changed Its Spots: The Evolution of Complexity.* New York: C. Scribner's Sons.

———. (2009). "Resilient economics." Totnes, UK: Schumacher College.

Goswami, A. (1988). "Creativity and the quantum theory." *Journal of Creative Behavior,* vol. 22, pp. 9–31.

———. (1989). "The idealist interpretation of quantum mechanics." *Physics Essays,* vol. 2, pp. 385–400.

———. (1993). *The Self-Aware Universe: How Consciousness Creates the Material World.* New York: Tarcher/Putnam.

———. (1999). *Quantum Creativity.* Cresskill, NJ: Hampton Press.

———. (2000). *The Visionary Window: A Quantum Physicist's Guide to Enlightenment.* Wheaton, IL: Quest Books.

———. (2001). *Physics of the Soul.* Charlottesville, VA: Hampton Roads.

———. (2004). *The Quantum Doctor.* Charlottesville, VA: Hampton Roads.

———. (2005). "Toward a spiritual economics." *Transformation* (World Business Academy), issues 2, 3, and 4.

———. (2008a). *God Is Not Dead.* Charlottesville, VA: Hampton Roads.

———. (2008b). *Creative Evolution.* Wheaton, IL: Theosophical Publishing House.

Green, E. E., and Green, A. M. (1977). *Beyond Biofeedback.* New York: Delacorte.

Grinberg-Zylberbaum, J., Delaflor, M., Attie, L., and Goswami, A. (1994). "Einstein Podolsky Rosen paradox in the human brain: The transferred potential." *Physics Essays,* vol. 7, pp. 422–28.

Grof, S. (1992). *The Holotropic Mind.* San Francisco: HarperSanFrancisco.

———. (1998). *The Cosmic Game.* Albany, NY: SUNY Press.

Harman, W. (1988). *Global Mind Change.* Indianapolis: Knowledge Systems.

Harman, W., and Rheingold, H. (1984). *Higher Creativity.* Los Angeles: J. P. Tarcher.

Ho, M. W., and Saunders, P. T. (eds.). (1984). *Beyond Neo-Darwinism: An Introduction to the New Evolutionary Paradigm.* London: Academic Press.

Hofstadter, D. R. (1980). *Gödel, Escher, Bach: The Eternal Golden Braid.* New York: Basic Books.

Jahn, R. (1982). "The persistent paradox of psychic phenomena: An engineering perspective." *Proceedings of the IEEE,* vol. 70, pp. 135–70.

Jahn, R. and Dunn, B. (1986). "On the quantum mechanics of consciousness, with application to anomalous phenomena." *Foundations of Physics,* vol. 16, no. 8, pp. 721–72.

Jung, C. G. (1971). *The Portable Jung.* Ed. J. Campbell. New York: Viking.

Keynes, J. M. (1977). *The Collected Writings of John Maynard Keynes.* London: Palgrave Macmillan.

Krishnamurthy, U. (2010). *Living with the Sacred.* Unpublished manuscript.

Kumar, S. (2008). "Economics of place." Totnes, UK: Schumacher College.

Laszlo, E. (2004). *Science and the Akashic Field.* Rochester, VT: Inner Traditions.

Libet, B. (1985). "Unconscious cerebral initiative and the role of conscious will in voluntary action." *Behavioral and Brain Sciences,* vol. 8, pp. 529–66.

Libet, B., Wright, E., Feinstein, B., and Pearl, D. (1979). "Subjective referral of the timing for a cognitive sensory experience." *Brain,* vol. 102, p. 193.

Liem, I. (2005). *Interdependent Economy.* Holland: iUniverse.

Lovelock, J. E. (1982). *Gaia: A New Look at Life on Earth.* Oxford: Oxford University Press.

Maslow, A. H. (1971). *The Further Reaches of Human Nature.* New York: Viking.

Mitchell, M., and Goswami, A. (1992). "Quantum mechanics for observer systems." *Physics Essays,* vol. 5, pp. 526–29.

Page, C. (1992). *Frontiers of Health.* Saffron Walden, UK: C. W. Daniel.

Patten, T. (2009). "Cross training for the soul." *EnlightenNext,* issue 45, pp. 83–94.

Penrose, R. (1991). *The Emperor's New Mind.* New York: Penguin.

Peres, A., and Zurek, W. H. (1982). *American Journal of Physics,* vol. 50, p. 807.

Radin, D. (1997). *The Conscious Universe.* New York: HarperEdge.

————. (2006). *Entangled Minds.* New York: Paraview Pocket Books.

Ray, M., and Myers, R. (1986). *Creativity in Business.* Garden City, NY: Doubleday.

Ray, P., and Anderson, S. (2000). *The Cultural Creatives.* New York: Harmony Books.

Reps, P. (1957). *Zen Flesh, Zen Bones.* Rutland, VT: C. E. Tuttle.

Ring, K. (1984). *Heading Toward Omega.* New York: William Morrow.

Robins, J. (1996). *Reclaiming Our Health.* Tiburon, CA: H. J. Kramer.

Robinson, H. J. (1984). "A theorist's philosophy of science." *Physics Today,* vol. 37, pp. 24–32.

Sabel, A., Clarke, C., and Fenwick, P. (2001). "Intersubject EEG correlations at a distance—the transferred potential." In Alvarado, C. S. (ed.). *Proceedings of the 46th Annual Convention of the Parapsychological Association,* New York, pp. 419–22.

Sabom, M. (1982). *Recollections of Death: A Medical Investigation*. New York: Harper & Row.

Samuelson, P. A., and Nordhaus, W. D. (1998). *Economics*. Boston: Irwin/ McGraw-Hill.

Schmidt, H. (1993). "Observation of a psychokinetic effect under highly controlled conditions." *Journal of Parapsychology*, vol. 57, pp. 351–72.

Schumacher, E. F. (1973). *Small Is Beautiful*. London: Blond and Briggs.

———. (1977). *A Guide for the Perplexed*. New York: Harper & Row.

Searle, J. (1987). "Minds and Brains without programs." In Blackmore, C., and Greenfield, S. (eds.). *Mind Waves*. Oxford: Basil Blackwell.

———. (1994). *The Rediscovery of the Mind*. Cambridge, MA: MIT Press.

Sen, A. (1999). *Development as Freedom*. New York: Knopf.

Sheldrake, R. (1981). *A New Science of Life*. Los Angeles: J. P. Tarcher.

Smith, A. (1994). *The Wealth of Nations*. New York: Modern Library.

Smythies, J. R. (1994). *The Walls of Plato's Cave: the Science and Philosophy of Brain, Consciousness, and Perception*. Aldershot, UK: Avebury.

Standish, L. J., Kozak, L., Clark Johnson, L., and Richards, T. (2004). "Electroencephalographic evidence of correlated event-related signals between the brains of spatially and sensory isolated human subjects." *Journal of Alternative and Complementary Medicine*, vol. 10. pp. 307–14.

Stapp, H. P. (1993). *Mind, Matter, and Quantum Mechanics*. New York: Springer-Verlag.

Stevenson, I. (1974). *Twenty Cases Suggestive of Reincarnation*. Charlottesville, VA: University Press of Virginia.

———. (1977). "Research into the evidence of man's survival after death." *Journal of Nervous and Mental Disease*, vol. 165, pp. 153–83.

———. (1987). *Children Who Remember Previous Lives: A Question of Reincarnation*. Charlottesville, VA: University Press of Virginia.

Taimni, I. K. (1961). *The Science of Yoga*. Wheaton, IL: Theosophical Publishing House.

Teasdale, W. (1999). *The Mystic Heart.* Novato, CA: New World Library.

Teilhard de Chardin, P. (1961). *The Phenomenon of Man.* New York: Harper & Row.

Tiller, W. A. Dibble, W. E. and Kohane, M. J. (2001). *Conscious Acts of Creation.* Walnut Creek, CA: Pavior Publishing.

Toms, M. and Toms, J. W. (1998). *True Work: The Sacred Dimension of Earning a Living.* New York: Harmony Books.

Von Neumann, J. (1955). *Mathematical Foundations of Quantum Mechanics.* Princeton, NJ: Princeton University Press.

Wackermann, J., Seiter, C., and Holger, K. (2003). "Correlation between brain electrical activities of two spatially separated human subjects." *Neuroscience Letters,* vol. 336, pp. 60–64.

Wallas, G. (1926). *The Art of Thought.* New York: Harcourt, Brace, and World.

Wilber, K. (1977). *The Spectrum of Consciousness.* Wheaton, IL: Theosophical Publishing House.

———. (1981). *Up from Eden.* Garden City, NY: Anchor/Doubleday.

———. (2000). *Integral Psychology.* Boston: Shambhala.

———. (2006). *Integral Spirituality.* Boston: Integral Books.

Wyller, A. (1999). *The Creating Consciousness.* Denver, CO: Divina.

Zohar, D. and Marshall, I. (1995). *The Quantum Society.* New York: Harper Perennial.

Index

About the Author

 AMIT GOSWAMI, PH.D. is a professor of physics (retired) at the University of Oregon, Eugene. He is a pioneer of the new paradigm of science called Science within Consciousness, an idea he explicated in his seminal book *The Self-Aware Universe*, where he also solved the quantum measurement problem elucidating the famous observer effect.

Goswami has written six other popular books based on his research on quantum physics and consciousness including *The Quantum Doctor, God is not Dead*, and *Creative Evolution*. His work has been translated into fifteen languages. He has been featured in the following films: *What the Bleep Do We Know, Down the Rabbit Hole, The Dalai Lama Renaissance*, and the award-winning biographic documentary, *The Quantum Activist*.

Hampton Roads Publishing Company
. . . for the evolving human spirit

Hampton Roads Publishing Company
publishes books on a variety of subjects,
including spirituality, health, and other
related topics.

For a copy of our latest trade catalog,
call 978–465–0504 or visit our website at *www.hrpub.com.*